# AIR FORCE ADVISING AND ASSISTANCE

*Modern Military History*

**Series Editors**

ALARIC SEARLE, Professor of Modern European History, University of Salford, UK

DONALD STOKER, Professor of Strategy and Policy, US Naval War College, Naval Postgraduate School, Monterey, CA, USA, 1999-2017

This series is dedicated to making available, at a reasonable price, quality academic military history, based on innovative and thorough scholarly research. While the main emphasis is on the publication of single-authored monographs, there will be scope for edited collections which focus primarily on new perspectives and evidence, as well as occasional translations of important foreign-language studies. *Modern Military History* will be framed in an 'inclusive' fashion, so that it encompasses armies, navies and air forces. While the traditional core concerns of military history—such as tactics, combat experience, technology, strategy and officer education—remain important fields of consideration, the encouragement of new angles and original approaches, whether methodologically, geographically or thematically, form a significant part of the editors' agenda.

**Titles**

No 1 *Genesis, Employment, Aftermath: First World War Tanks and the New Warfare, 1900–1945* edited by Alaric Searle (ISBN 978-1-909982-22-2)

No 2 *Naval Advising and Assistance: History, Challenges, and Analysis* edited by Donald Stoker and Michael T. McMaster (ISBN 978-1-911512-82-0)

No 3 *Expeditionary Police Advising and Militarization: Building Security in A Fractured World* edited by Donald Stoker and Edward B. Westermann (ISBN 978-1-911512-86-8)

No 4 *Kursk 1943: The Greatest Battle of the Second World War* by Roman Töppel (ISBN 978-1-912390-03-8)

No 5 *Air Force Advising and Assistance* edited by Edward B. Westermann and Donald Stoker (ISBN 978-1-912390-60-1)

# Air Force Advising and Assistance

Modern Military History No.5

Edited by
Edward B. Westermann and Donald Stoker

Helion & Company Limited

To the American and coalition personnel who served as air advisors in Afghanistan and Iraq

Helion & Company Limited
Unit 8 Amherst Business Centre
Budbrooke Road
Warwick
CV34 5WE
England
Tel. 01926 499 619
Fax 0121 711 4075
Email: info@helion.co.uk
Website: www.helion.co.uk
Twitter: @helionbooks
Visit our blog http://blog.helion.co.uk/

Published by Helion & Company 2018
Designed and typeset by Mary Woolley, Battlefield Design (www.battlefield-design.co.uk)
Cover designed by Paul Hewitt, Battlefield Design (www.battlefield-design.co.uk)
Printed by Lightning Source Ltd, Milton Keynes, Buckinghamshire



ISBN 978-1-912390-60-1

British Library Cataloguing-in-Publication Data.

A catalogue record for this book is available from the British Library.



For details of other military history titles published by Helion & Company Limited contact the above address, or visit our website: http://www.helion.co.uk.

We always welcome receiving book proposals from prospective authors.

## Contents

## About the Contributors

LORENZO DELGADO GÓMEZ-ESCALONILLA is a Senior Researcher at the National Research Council of Spain (CSIC). A specialist in the history of international affairs, he has extensively published on several dimensions of Spanish foreign relations, including propaganda and public diplomacy, cultural, educational and scientific transfers, and military assistance. He is the author and editor of numerous publications including *US Public Diplomacy and Democratization in Spain: Selling Democracy?* (Palgrave MacMillan, 2015) and *La apertura internacional de España. Entre el franquismo y la democracia (1953-1986)* (Sílex, 2016). He has been a visiting professor at several European universities and has participated in the US International Visitors Program.

PATRICK FACON (1949-2016), was a French historian and director of research for the historical service of the French Air Force. He also led the Center for Strategic Aerospace Studies. Born in Algeria, he received his doctorate from the University of Paris X Nanterre in 1977. A prolific author, Dr. Facon published 18 books and numerous shorter works, most on the history of French military aviation.

NIKOLAS GARDNER is the Class of 1965 Professor in Leadership and the Chair of the War Studies graduate program at the Royal Military College of Canada, in Kingston, Ontario. From 2006-2011 he taught at the USAF Air War College in Montgomery AL, where he served as the first Academic Director of the Air War College Grand Strategy Program. Dr. Gardner is the author of *Trial by Fire: Command and the British Expeditionary Force in 1914* (Praeger, 2003), and *The Siege of Kut-al-Amara: At War in Mesopotamia, 1915-1916* (Indiana University Press, 2014). He has published on a broad range of topics, including the First World War and military and strategic thought. His current research examines the role of mercenaries or "contractors" in British foreign policy in the Middle East during the 1970s.

JAMES HORNCASTLE is a PhD Candidate at Simon Fraser University. His dissertation examines the role of ethnic minorities in the Greek Civil War. James' current research focuses on civil conflict and ethnic relations in Twentieth Century Southeast European history. He has most recently published "Reaping the Whirlwind:

Total National Defense's Role in Slovenia's Bid for Secession" in the *Journal of Slavic Military Studies*. He is currently a researcher at the Stavros Niarchos Foundation Centre for Hellenic Studies, and previously received his MA in history from the University of New Brunswick, Canada.

PABLO LEÓN-AGUINAGA is a Lecturer of History and International Relations at the Centro Universitario de la Defensa (CUD) in Zaragoza, Spain. He was Prince of Asturias Visiting Researcher at Georgetown University, where he also taught on Spanish-American relations. A specialist in modern international history and US foreign relations, his work has been published in journals such as the *International History Review* and *Ayer*. He is a coauthor of the forthcoming *Los Estados Unidos y el Mundo*, Volume I, *El ascenso de la superpotencia, 1898-1953* (Síntesis).

XIAOBING LI is Professor and Chair of the Department of History and Geography and Director of the Western Pacific Institute at the University of Central Oklahoma. He is also the Executive Editor of the *Journal of American Review of China Studies* and *Journal of the Western Pacific*. He served in the Chinese People's Liberation Army (PLA) in the 1970s. Among his recent books are *Ethnic China* (first co-editor, Lexington, 2015), *Modern China* (ABC-CLIO, 2015), *China's Battle for Korea* (Indiana University Press, 2014), *Oil: A Cultural and Geographic Encyclopedia* (first co-editor, ABC-CLIO, 2014), *Evolution of Power* (first co-editor, Lexington, 2014), *Modern Chinese Legal Reforms* (first co-editor; University Press of Kentucky, 2013), *China at War* (ABC-CLIO, 2012), *Voices from the Vietnam War* (University Press of Kentucky, 2011), *Civil Liberties in China* (ABC-CLIO, 2010), *A History of the Modern Chinese Army* (University Press of Kentucky, 2009), *New Historiography in the Contemporary West* (in Chinese; first co-editor; Shanghai: Lexicographical Press, 2008), *Taiwan in the 21st Century* (first co-editor; University Press of America, 2005), *Voices from the Korean War* (co-author; University Press of Kentucky, 2004), and *Mao's Generals Remember Korea* (first co-editor with Allan Millett, University Press of Kansas, 2002).

FABIO DE NINNO is a PhD candidate at the University of Turin where he is doing research on the Italian Navy in the interwar period. He is visiting reader in military history and contemporary history at the interfaculty School of Strategic Studies of Turin, and editorial secretary for the Italian section of the 1914-1918 online encyclopedia of the First World War. In 2014 he won the Italian Navy historical branch prize for the best MA thesis on the history of the Italian Navy. He is the author of *I sommergibili del fascismo* and the co-editor of the *Dizionario storico della Prima guerra mondiale*, both published in 2014.

JACOPO PILI received his Master's degree in International Relations in 2015 at Roma Tre University where he wrote his thesis on Italian military attachés. He began a PhD in History under the supervision of Professor Christopher Duggan at the University of Reading, and is now studying for a PhD at the School of History of the

University of Leeds. His research concentrates on the representation of Great Britain in Fascist Italy.

CHRISTIAN POLAK received his PhD in International Law (with honors) from Hitotsubashi University in Tokyo in 1980. He is the Founder and President of SERIC, and has been living in Japan for the past 45 years. He has developed an extensive network of personal contacts with the Japanese administration as well as with industrial and economic leaders in Asia and Europe. His expertise is in the field of Europe-Japan relations, and his thorough understanding of the respective business environments and cultures has led to his appointment as advisor to several Japanese government bodies. He is also the author or coauthor of a number of works on Japanese history and business.

ERIC ROEHRKASSE is a Major in the United States Air Force and former Assistant Professor of History at the Air Force Academy in Colorado Springs, CO. Major Roehrkasse graduated from the Air Force Academy in 2002 where he received a Bachelor of Science in Military History. Upon graduation, he served as an Airfield Operations Officer in South Dakota and New Jersey, and was responsible for leading Airmen conducting air traffic control, airfield management, and airspace management functions. He has deployed twice, first to Kabul, Afghanistan as the Airfield Operations Advisor to the Afghan Army Air Corps and then to the US Embassy, Islamabad, Pakistan, as Airspace Liaison to the Pakistani Air Force. Shortly after returning from Pakistan, Major Roehrkasse began full-time graduate studies in the History of US Foreign Relations at Temple University under the Air Force Institute of Technology Civilian Institutions program. He completed his MA at Temple in December 2011 and taught world, military, and diplomatic history courses at the Air Force Academy from January 2012 to February 2015. He is currently on a 2-year assignment as the Director of Operations for the Operations Support Squadron at Al Udeid Air Base, Qatar.

DONALD STOKER was Professor of Strategy and Policy for the US Naval War College's Monterey Program at the Naval Postgraduate School in Monterey, California, from 1999-2018. The author or editor of ten books, his, *Carl von Clausewitz: His Life and Work* (Oxford University Press, 2014), is on the British Army professional reading list. His *The Grand Design: Strategy and the US Civil War, 1861-1865* (Oxford University Press, 2010), won the prestigious Fletcher Pratt award for the best non-fiction Civil War book of 2010, was a Main Selection of the History Book Club, is on the US Army Chief of Staff's reading list, and is commonly used as a text in history graduate seminars and strategic studies courses. His other works include an edited volume on strategy in the War for American Independence, and works on military advising, conscription, and the arms trade. He has written for numerous magazines such as *MHQ* (*Military History Quarterly*), *North & South*, and *Naval History*. In 2016, he was a Fellow of the Changing Character of War Programme at the University of Oxford's Pembroke College, and Fulbright Scholar in Austria in 2018. He is currently completing a book on limited war for Cambridge University Press and writing a history of American grand strategy for Basic Books.

EDWARD B. WESTERMANN is a professor of history at Texas A&M University–San Antonio. He teaches courses on European History, the Holocaust, and War and Society. He has been a Fulbright Fellow, a German Academic Exchange Service Fellow, and a Fellow at the US Holocaust Memorial Museum. He is the author of numerous publications including *Hitler's Police Battalions: Enforcing Racial War in the East* and *Flak: German Anti-Aircraft Defenses, 1914–1945*. His latest book, *Hitler's Ostkrieg and the Indian Wars: Comparing Conquest and Genocide*, was published in 2016. He is a former helicopter pilot with the US Air Force and retired at the rank of Colonel.

# Introduction

*Edward B. Westermann and Donald Stoker*

The increased focus on counterinsurgency warfare and US nation building efforts since the attacks of 11 September 2001 reignited interest in the area of military advising within the US military community, and among a range of government organizations, private think tanks, and defense related contractors. With respect to military advising, the overwhelming number of studies on this subject, based on the chronological scope and numerical preponderance of ground advising missions, has quite naturally focused on these past efforts. In contrast, less attention has been given to air or naval advisory missions.[1] This work seeks in part to redress this current imbalance by examining a number of historical case studies dealing with air advisory efforts. While advisory missions in all domains (i.e., air, land, and sea) share some similar issues and concerns such as cultural awareness, language fluency, length of mission, and type of training, air advisory efforts have a number of unique elements based on the fundamental role of advanced technology and the extensive resource requirements associated with aviation operations. For example, air advisory efforts are profoundly influenced by the type of aircraft involved (e.g., jet, propeller, rotary-wing), the nature of flight (e.g., manned versus remotely piloted aircraft), and the types of mission flown (e.g., transport, ground attack, reconnaissance, etc.). Likewise, the issues of maintenance support for aerial platforms and the infrastructure needed for these missions plays a key role in determining capabilities available to the host nation. In the case of infrastructure, airfields, fueling depots, maintenance and repair facilities, and radar and communications equipment offer a few of the most obvious requirements to support flight operations.

By examining a number of historical case studies, this volume analyzes the challenges and opportunities inherent in aerial advisory efforts and offers insights into the methods by which such missions succeed or fail. Air advisory missions date

1 For an evaluation of naval advising efforts see Donald Stoker and Michael T. McMaster (eds), *Naval Advising and Assistance: History, Challenges, and Analysis* (Solihull, UK: Helion, 2017).

almost to the first days of powered flight as demonstrated by British and French air advisory missions in Imperial Japan after World War I (1914-1918). As the historian Mark Peattie notes, 'The postwar decade in Japanese aviation was therefore marked by two related and intensive efforts: the infusion of considerable amounts of Western technological and training assistance and, at the same time, an effort by Japan to establish its own fledgling aircraft industry'.[2] This early advisory effort reveals a number of issues that would continue to remain relevant throughout the twentieth century and even to the present day, including questions related to the nature of aerial technology to be shared, the type of training to be provided, and the potential economic benefits that might accrue to the donor nation as a result of the sale of aviation technology to the host country. In many respects, air advisory efforts raise a number of profound strategic questions for the donor nation. Among others, these questions relate to the type of technology to be shared, the nature of training to be given, the role of foreign advisors in operations, the issue of infrastructure development and auxiliary training programs, the preparation of foreign advisors for their duties, and perhaps most significantly the development of the type of capabilities required to address the host nation's security environment.

## Technology: Gold-plated or the Right Fit?

Perhaps one of the most critical issues related to air advising involves the type of aircraft and the level of aviation technology that will be provided to the host country. This is a critical issue for several reasons. First and foremost, the type of aircraft supplied should be those which most closely correspond with the security interests of the host nation. For example, the latest and most advanced fighter or bomber aircraft may serve as symbols of prestige for the host nation; however, if these aircraft are incapable or less adept at executing the specific operational missions required, then they may in fact be detrimental to the strategic goals of the advisory effort. As Martin van Creveld observes in the case of South Vietnam, 'the Vietnamese never received the most advanced jet combat aircraft such as fighters and bombers . . . those would have been useless in counterinsurgency warfare anyhow'.[3] Likewise, if the host nation does not have the requisite infrastructure from parts and maintenance to airfields and sufficiently trained personnel to support these aircraft, they threaten to become expensive and essentially useless white elephants.[4] Similarly, decisions associated with supplying advanced technology whether in the form of specific platforms or avionics

2 Mark R. Peattie, *Sunburst: The Rise of Japanese Naval Air Power, 1909-1941* (Annapolis, MD: Naval Institute Press, 2001), p. 18.

3 Martin van Creveld, *The Age of Airpower* (New York: Public Affairs, 2011), p. 381.

4 For a study of this concept see Sidharth Kaushal, 'Adoption Capacity Theory and Naval Doctrine: A Theory of Success and Failure in Naval Advise and Assist Missions to Modernizing States—China, the Ottoman Empire, and Japan', in Stoker and McMaster (eds), *Naval Advising and Assistance*, pp. 41-67.

entails a certain risk to the donor nation of such technologies being transferred or stolen by adversaries. In this case, the acquisition of such technology by an adversary may allow them to improve their own capabilities or to design countermeasures against one's own capabilities. In fact, the US Air Force development of the Aggressor Program and Red Flag in the early 1970s was not only designed to provide US pilots dissimilar air combat training based on Soviet Air Force tactics and doctrine, but also included a classified program for acquiring advanced Soviet aircraft from friendly states or former Soviet client states in order to test the capabilities of these aircraft.[5] In the case of Imperial Japan, the Japanese naval air force used aircraft provided under the auspices of the British Sempill Mission in 1921 to experience a 'quantum jump in aviation training and technology' in part by using existing British aircraft designs to advance their own aviation program, an effort that would have profound effects with the Japanese naval air arm's success against British and US forces in the Pacific in 1941.[6]

## The Question of Training

Based on the technological sophistication of modern aircraft, the issue of flight training is a critical element in any advisory effort. This issue encompasses a number of areas ranging from initial academic instruction related to the principles of flight on to advanced lessons dealing with navigation and communication procedures and weapons systems employment. Likewise, any flight training program must be aimed at the right level for developing or enhancing the existing host nation's aviation program. In the case of an air force with a small cadre of pilots and support personnel, the initial effort must be focused on expanding the entry level flight program in order to provide academic and flight instruction to qualified candidates. This issue alone raises questions concerning the language of instruction, the types of aircraft used for initial training, the locations of the instruction sites, and the question of whether to use host nation or foreign instructors during the course of training. Similarly, these same issues need to be addressed in the case of advanced or specialized aviation training programs in which the training regimen for a fighter pilot may be substantially different from that of a transport pilot with the former having to achieve proficiency in advanced aerial acrobatics or weapons system use with the latter focused on navigation procedures or specialized take-off and landing requirements.

5 Benjamin S. Lambeth, *The Transformation of American Air Power* (Ithaca, NY: Cornell University Press, 2000), pp. 60-64, and Steve Davies, *Red Eagles: America's Secret MiGs* (Oxford, UK: Osprey Publishing, 2012).

6 Peattie, *Sunburst*, pp. 19-20.

## The Right Capabilities for the Right Missions

In addition to the issue of the level of training programs and the content of the curriculum, the question of the types of aircraft to be supplied is fundamentally tied to the issue of the specific operational and mission requirements of the host nation. The Prussian military theorist Carl von Clausewitz remarked, 'The first, the supreme, the most far-reaching act of judgement that the statesman and commander have to make is to establish by that test the kind of war on which they are embarking; neither mistaking it for, nor trying to turn it into, something that is alien to its nature'.[7] Despite being written in the early nineteenth century in an age before manned flight, Clausewitz' admonition is especially apt for airmen today. Any advisory efforts must first seek to determine the appropriate capabilities required by the host nation in addressing their specific security environment. For example, the Afghan Air Force in conjunction with US advisors identified a critical need for a ground attack capability in the war against the Taliban, a mission that requires close coordination between air and ground forces and considerable skill at identifying and striking targets from the air. In this case, aircraft capable of long loiter times and operations at lower altitudes offer some of the most effective platforms for these operations. In turn, the acquisition of the A-29 Super Tucano, an aircraft designed for counterinsurgency operations and low operating costs, versus other strike aircraft such as the more capable and significantly more expensive F-16 Fighting Falcon, provide the most suitable option.[8]

## If You Fly Them, You Have to Fix Them

One of the primary challenges related to operating an aviation system involves the high cost of initial acquisition and continuing costs related to maintenance and support. These costs increase substantially based on the increased sophistication of the air frame, the propulsion system, and the avionics systems. For example, the estimated per flight hour cost of operating the US Air Force's most modern fighter aircraft, the F-35A Lightning II and the F-22 Raptor, is $67,550 and $58,059 respectively. In contrast, the cost per flight hour of the aging but still capable A-10 Warthog is a relatively modest $11,500, and that of the Predator drone a mere $1,500.[9] As this comparison indicates, lower technology aviation systems may offer substantial cost

7 Carl von Clausewitz, *On War*, Michael Howard and Peter Paret (trans. and eds), (Princeton, NJ: Princeton University Press, 1976), p. 88.

8 Franz-Stefan Gady, 'Afghan Air Force Receives 4 Light Attack Aircraft', *The Diplomat*, 24 March 2017, http://thediplomat.com/2017/03/afghan-air-force-receives-4-light-attack-aircraft/.

9 Jeremy Bender and Mike Nudelman, 'The Chart Shows the Incredible Cost of Operating the US Air Force's most Expensive Planes', *Business Insider*, 3 March 2016, http://www.businessinsider.com/air-force-plane-cost-per-flight-hour-chart-2016-3. For a discussion of the calculation of these costs, see Michael Boito, Edward G. Keating, John Wallace,

savings, a key point that allows for increased numbers of training sorties to improve aircrew proficiency, and increased numbers of operational flight hours per air frame. This comparison also underlines the hidden costs of flight operations related to maintenance and support requirements. For donor nations embarking on air advisory efforts, these hidden costs need to be included during the initial planning phase and must extend beyond the training of aircrew to encompass the training of maintenance and support personnel from those capable of servicing the propulsion and navigation systems to those qualified in refueling operations. In the end, such investment is not only prudent but necessary since 'broken' or unserviceable aircraft are little more than expensive static displays.

## Who Flies and Who Fights?

Another key concern related to air advising cuts across all domains of advising and relates to who will ultimately be in charge of such efforts and who will be actively engaged in operations. By definition, advising efforts should be restricted to providing training and advice to host nation personnel in support of their operational activities. In reality, however, this distinction is often blurred or non-existent with donor nation advisors either taking an active and lead role in directing operations, or, as in the case of the Farm Gate air advisory mission to South Vietnam, US instructors only 'grudgingly' embraced the role of providing flight training to their South Vietnamese counterparts and repeatedly sought to take the lead in operational missions.[10] This issue was not unique to the US air advisory effort, but also extended to the British air advisory mission to Oman during the Dhofar insurgency in the 1970s that included Loan Service Personnel seconded from the Royal Air Force (RAF), retired RAF personnel, and civilian contractors.[11] This issue also extended to the Russian air advisory effort to the Chinese Air Force (PLAAF) during the Korean War (1950-1953) in which the Russians took a heavy hand in dictating Chinese operations and air strategy while assuming a major, if ostensibly covert, role in aerial combat.[12] Similarly, Soviet air advisors in China in the early 1920s flew combat and support missions in several campaigns.[13] North Koreans have often advised the Syrian Air

Bradley DeBlois, and Ilana Blum, *Metrics to Compare Aircraft Operating and Support Costs in the Department of Defense* (Santa Monica, CA: RAND Corporation, 2015).

10 Robert Futrell, *The Advisory Years to 1965* (Washington, DC: Office of Air Force History, 1981), p. 127.

11 Ian Gardiner, *In the Service of the Sultan: A First Hand Account of the Dhofar Insurgency* (Barnsley, UK: Pen & Sword Military, 2006), p. 85.

12 See Xiaobing Li, *China's Battle for Korea: The 1951 Spring Offensive* (Bloomington: Indiana University Press, 2014), pp. 70-71, 229-230.

13 C. Martin Wilbur, 'A Different Kind of Missionary: Soviet Advisors in China in the 1920s', *Chinese Studies in History*, 21:4 (1988), pp. 21-22; Julie Lien-ying How, 'Introduction: Soviet Advisors with the Kuominchun, 1925-1926: A Documentary Study', *Chinese Studies in History*, 19:1 (1985), p. 57.

Force. Twenty-five North Korean aviators served in Syria during the 1967 Arab-Israeli War and another 30 in Syria and Egypt during the 1973 Arab-Israeli conflict. In addition to training their Syrian peers, some of the North Koreans flew combat missions. North Korea sent 75 instructors and 40 pilots to serve the Assad regime in 1975-1976.[14] The question of who flies and who fights is especially relevant to air advising since the execution of flight operations requires a highly trained and skilled cadre of pilots and maintenance and support personnel, the absence of which creates a great deal of pressure for substituting the donor nation's forces in these roles, leading to a dependency relationship and often causing resentment within the host nation's air force.

## For Want of a Nail...

The story about the battle lost for want of a nail to shoe the horse offers an apt reminder of the importance of support, logistics, and infrastructure for aviation operations. Such support is not merely limited to parts, ammunition, and fuel for aircraft but extends to a number of other areas including airfield upkeep and maintenance, communications infrastructure, navigational aids, etc. In certain circumstances, some of these requirements can be lessened, such as in the case of rotary wing aircraft with the capability of operating from unimproved areas or from so-called bare bases. However, even then aircraft need to be refueled and rearmed and require communication and navigation support. In other words, air advising missions depending on the existing human resources and physical infrastructure need to be viewed in a holistic perspective and planning needs to include an evaluation of the ability of the host nation to support the forecast requirements of aviation operations.

## Lost in Translation?

In addition to the technical and material requirements associated with flight activities, all advisory efforts are similar with respect to the importance of understanding the cultural context of the host nation and the specific political, social, and cultural factors that determine their security environment and their own needs. While widely recognized as a key element of successful advising, cultural competency is a fundamental building block for creating trust and cooperation between the donor and the host nation. Unfortunately, as the psychologist George Guthrie noted in a 1966 study, 'Training efforts for advisors vary from limited attempts to teach customs and danger spots to intensive study of the language and culture'. He then concludes, 'Time

14 Franz-Stefan Gady, 'Is North Korea Fighting for Assad in Syria?', *The Diplomat*, 24 March 2016, http://thediplomat.com/2016/03/is-north-korea-fighting-for-assad-in-syria/.

does not usually permit more than a cursory preparation'.[15] In most cases, profound cultural competency can only be achieved with fluency in the host country's language, a process that requires a significant investment in both resources and time, and, as a result, remains one of the most widely neglected issues across all advisory efforts.[16] In the case of US armed forces, this deficiency is normally addressed through the extensive use of contract translators or by the ethnocentric expectation of host nation personnel speaking English. In South Vietnam for example, air advisors had little understanding of the culture or the history of their Vietnamese hosts and this lack of cultural awareness significantly handicapped the advising effort. Similarly, the inability of advisors to speak Vietnamese, or even French, created a major impediment to the success of the advisory and training mission. Furthermore, this deficiency extended across all aspects of the advising mission as Stuart Herrington, an army advisor, observed that during the war 'thousands of Vietnamese learned English . . . but only a handful of the many thousands of Americans who received language training ever learned to really speak Vietnamese'.[17] In fact, one senior Vietnamese general could not recall a single instance 'in which a US advisor effectively discussed professional matters with his counterpart in Vietnamese'.[18] This was not an isolated issue but also extended to the military advising mission in Thailand in the late 1960s in which advisors received a two-week training course on language and customs prior to their deployment.[19] The importance of cultural competency and the frustrations and frictions associated with a lack of linguistic ability and cultural blind spots continued to affect US and coalition operations in Afghanistan and Iraq in the twenty-first century.[20]

One significant barrier to cultural competency often found in US advising efforts involves the length of tour associated with such missions. During the war in Vietnam, some advisory efforts lasted a mere 179-days, too short a period of time to sharpen language skills, build relationships, and integrate efforts. While some senior USAF

15 George M. Guthrie, *Conflicts of Culture and the Military Advisor* (n.p: Institute for Defense Analysis, 1966), p. iv.
16 Betty Barton Christiansen, *The United States Air Force in Southeast Asia: Military Civic Action* (Washington, DC: Air Force History and Museums Program, 1998), p. 189, https://media.defense.gov/2010/Dec/21/2001330160/-1/-1/0/AFD-101221-013.pdf.
17 Stuart A Herrington, *Stalking the Vietcong: Inside Operation Phoenix: A Personal Account* (New York: Ballantine Books, 1982), p. 253.
18 Ronald Spector, *Advice and Support: The Early Years* (Washington, DC: Center of Military History, 1983), p. 286.
19 Christiansen, *Military Civic Action*, p. 189.
20 Jonathan Byrom, 'Training the New Afghan Tank Force: A Multi-National Advisory Mission, 2 June 2003 to 3 December 2003', in Donald Stoker (ed.), *Military Advising and Assistance: From Mercenaries to Privatization, 1815-2007* (London: Routledge, 2008), pp. 205-208, and William H. Grube, 'The Evolution of Combined USMC/Iraqi Army Operations: A Company Commander's Perspective, Fallujah, Iraq, September 2005 to April 2006', in Stoker (ed.), *Military Advising and Assistance*, p. 220.

leaders recognized this deficiency and advocated for tour lengths as long as two years, the longest tour length for Farm Gate personnel was one year.[21] In contrast, the British use of Loan Service Personnel seconded to the Omani armed forces and contractors during the Dhofar Insurgency allowed for continuity in personnel and strategic planning, but these extended tours resulted in concerns that 'their [the British officers'] loyalties could become distorted over time by friendships and financial incentives' and in part retarded the emergence of an independent Omani Air Force capability.[22]

## Some Concluding Thoughts

There is a growing body of literature on the history and practice of advising and assistance to other nations, but the study of air advising offers the broadest opening for future research. The following chapters provide a range of case studies that examine air advising missions beginning immediately after the First World War. The authors examine the efforts of French, British, Italian, US, and Soviet advisory missions over a period of seven decades. The reader will find that each of these entries offers insights into the questions and issues raised in this introduction concerning the challenges and opportunities related to air advisory missions. The editors hope that these historical case studies may illuminate issues related to current advisory efforts and serve as a useful resource for both students of history as well as contemporary military practitioners involved in these missions.

21 Edward B. Westermann, 'Relegated to the Backseat: Farm Gate and the Failure of the US Air Advisory Effort in South Vietnam, 1961-1963', in Stoker (ed.), *Military Advising and Assistance*, p. 132.

22 See Nikolas Gardner's contribution to this volume.

# 1

# The French Military Aviation Mission in Japan, 1919-1921

*Christian Polak*

*Translated and Adapted by Nabih Kanbar*

## Introduction

From the very beginning of relations between France and Japan in the 1860s, military relations played a preponderant role. France brought to Japan its technologies and know-how, provided locally by its engineers, and supplied the most recent equipment and technology to the Japanese government. Specific initiatives included the construction of the naval base of Yokosuka from 1865 to 1876. Likewise, French involvement can be divided into three periods: from 1867 to 1868, the first French military mission in Japan; from 1872 to 1880, the second military mission; from 1884 to 1889, the third military mission; from 1886 to 1890, the modernization of the Imperial Navy by the engineer Émile Bertin, who designed its new ships, some of which were ordered in France, Great Britain, and in Yokosuka. Starting in 1910, France supplied Japan with fighter planes and aviation equipment. In 1918, Japan requested France send an aviation military mission. In recognition of Japan's participation in the First World War, Prime Minister Georges Clemenceau sent more than 50 French engineers and pilots at the expense of the French Republic, which from 1919 to 1922, laid the foundations of the military and civil aviation industry of Japan. This mission, like the construction project at Yokosuka naval base, was another example of a transfer of French knowledge and technology to Japan to support the country's development of a modern aviation industry.

## The Franco-Japanese Relationship

In 1918, the relations between France and Japan were governed by the Franco-Japanese agreement of 1907 and were based on the friendship between two great personalities, Georges Clemenceau and Saionji Kinmochi 西園寺公望 (1849-1940). The 1907 agreement guaranteed the respect of the status quo in the Far East and the integrity of China. It detailed the mutual respect for the possessions of France and Japan in Asia via the 'maintenance of the respective situation and the territorial rights of the two countries on the Asian Continent'. For France this included Indochina and the Chinese lease territory of Guangzhouwan, and their zone of influence over the provinces of Yunnan, Guangxi, and Guangdong. For Japan this included Formosa, Liadong, and a zone of influence in southern Manchuria, part of Mongolia, and Fujian. Korea, considered a protectorate, was included under the territorial rights, France thus accepting its colonization by Japan.

Japan was interested in aviation, beginning with hot air balloons at the end of the Edo period (1603-1868). It was a Frenchman, Yves Paul Gaston Le Prieur (1885-1963), the naval attaché at the French embassy in Tokyo, who, with his friend Captain Aibara Shirō 相原四郎 (1879-1911), flew the first glider in Japan, one they built by hand from bamboo and towed to Ikenohata in Ueno on 26 December 1909. It flew for 130 meters at a height of 10 meters.

The first Japanese pilot received his flight education in France: it was Tokugawa Yoshitoshi 徳川好敏 (1884-1963). He brought back from France a Henri-Farman aircraft with which he made the first flight of a motorized plane in Japan on 19 December 1910, on the Yoyogi maneuvering field in Tokyo. The Henri-Farman aircraft, becoming famous, would appear in many illustrations.[1]

The year 1911 proved to be a pivotal year for Japan: political and military leaders became aware of the importance of aviation, which was strategically attractive because of the guarantee it offered regarding the defense of the country and the protection of its colonies in Formosa and Korea. To form an air force, Japan turned to France, which was at the forefront in this field both in terms of equipment and practice. A mission of the Imperial Navy visited France in 1911, led by Vice-Admiral Shimamura Hayao 島村速雄 (1858-1923), who visited the Mauritius Farman (1877-1964) pilot school in Buc and had his aerial baptism with the famous manufacturer as the pilot. By deciding to support Japan's request for aviation technology, France was thinking of its interests in Asia, particularly in Indochina. This cooperation also fit perfectly within the framework of the 1907 arrangement. A close relationship was being built in this new field of aviation in which France would transfer its know-how and technologies to Japan for more than 20 years. The result was that we have beginning in 1912 the

1 For example, for the 50th anniversary of this first flight of a plane in Japan, the Japanese postal service issued a commemorative stamp with a Henri-Farman in the sky alongside a modern airliner.

training of new Japanese pilots in France, and the supplying of Maurice Farman, Nieuport, Spad, and Morane-Saulnier aircraft. The army established its first air base in Tokorozawa in the Saitama Prefecture just north of Tokyo, and the navy built its first air base near Yokosuka in Oihama (later Oppama) using Maurice Farman seaplanes and afterwards several Nieuport aircraft ordered in France in 1913.

Through the interplay of alliances, including the 1907 arrangement, Japan declared war on Germany on 23 August 1914. The next day, an army squadron consisting of four Maurice-Farman aircraft and one Nieuport flew from Tokorozawa to China, followed by a navy squadron composed of four seaplanes recently acquired in France. Following numerous aerial bombardments, the German concession of Tsingtao (Qingdao) fell on 7 November.

In 1917, despite its war effort, France agreed to deliver new fighters to Japan to be deployed on the new Kagamigahara base near Gifu. In early 1918, Japan requested the delivery of 16 new fighters. In May of the same year, France agreed to the delivery of six Spad fighter planes, but bound this purchase to Japan's decision to enter combat alongside the Allies, proposing to create an eastern front, a military intervention in Siberia, of which Japan became the main actor by deploying 73,000 soldiers in three Russian provinces of the Far East by August. On 15 July 1918, the French War Committee decided not to deliver six Spad planes, but to send 30 Salmson aircraft. In exchange, Japan agreed that the aeronautic organization of its army should be reserved

Admiral Hideki Tōgō with Colonel Faure in front of a Salmson, Gifu, 1919. (via the Author)

for a French military mission proposed by the French government on 21 August 1918. Negotiations were held in Paris. Georges Clemenceau considered this matter of the utmost importance for French interests in Japan and Asia, and oversaw the negotiations with Japan's military attaché, Colonel Nagai Kitaru 永井来 (1877-1934). A note from Clemenceau, dated 26 August 1918, addressed to the Undersecretary of State for Aeronautics, gives us the following particulars:

> The Military Attaché of Japan has made known that it accepts our proposals... The Mission will be led by Colonel Faure who will choose his collaborators ... The Government of Japan has also expressed the desire to include in this Mission alongside the Military staff, some engineers or specialists in aeronautics....

Later in the note—and to the great surprise of Japan—Clemenceau explained that to thank Japan for its actions in the war, 'The French Government will bear all the costs of pay, maintenance, and transport of the Mission's personnel'. The choice of the person responsible for the mission was decided by Clemenceau himself. By sending this mission at its own expense, France eliminated the Italians, the British, and the Americans. It hoped in return that Japan would pass many orders to French industry.

On 25 August 1918, Colonel Jacques-Paul Faure (1869-1924) was officially appointed 'Head of the French Military Aircraft Mission in Japan'. He took care of the composition of the mission by choosing experienced collaborators with the best qualifications. He took as deputy commander Louis Ragon (1878-1919), and finally chose 21 officers and non-commissioned officers in artillery, engineering, cavalry, infantry, and aeronautics, and 27 enlisted men, in particular engineers and technicians, and of course pilots, including several aces of the First World War. Covering all sectors of aeronautics, the mission initially comprised 50 members. A long list of material to be taken was also prepared: Salmson 2A2 planes, various types of Nieuport, Spad, and Bréguet aircraft, as well as Caquot balloons. Faure foresaw a departure from Marseille on 20 November 1918, and a return to France on 1 October 1919, envisioning, however, that the personnel directing the manufacturing would stay longer, until 1920 at least. A dozen new French instructors joined the mission over the next weeks and months. Number 10 on this list was artillery Lieutenant Roger Poidatz (1894-1976), a graduate of the École *Polytechnique* and a reconnaissance pilot. During his stay he wrote the famous book *L'Honorable Partie de Campagne* (*The Honorable Picnic*), published in 1924 under the pseudonym Thomas Raucat.

The mission embarked in Marseille on 24 November 1918, 13 days after the signing of the Armistice which consecrated the victory of the Allies in the First World War. The mission members were transshipped via the Japanese steamer *Yamashiro-maru*, which was sent to Shanghai by the Japanese government. They arrived in Nagasaki on 12 January 1919, where they received a triumphant reception. They arrived in Kobe and took the train to Tokyo, reaching there on 15 January. At each stop at stations along the way, there was the singing of *La Marseillaise*, speeches, and gifts.

The highest authorities reserved for the mission a triumphant welcoming in Tokyo: the Director of Aeronautics, Inoue Ikutarō 井上幾太郎 (1872-1965), and the Minister of the Army, Tanaka Giichi 義一中義一 (1864-1929). The latter amplified the responsibilities of the head of the mission by opening to him all military establishments without reservation. On 27 January, the mission was received in audience by the Emperor Taishō.

After all these festivities, the mission began its work. Faure and his deputy Ragon moved to the premises of the Ministry of the Army and worked directly with Minister Tanaka, who set up the 'Provisional Commission for Training in Aviation Techniques' chaired by General Inoue Ikutarō. An agreement signed on 18 January with Faure specified the areas of training: piloting, gunnery, bombing, telegraphy, photography, and using factory equipment for production and maintenance.

After visiting the existing facilities in February, new land was proposed for future developments, and the mission was divided into eight training sections at eight sites:

- Piloting (air combat), at the Kagamigahara base near Gifu;
- Aerial gunnery, at the Arai-machi base in the Shizuoka Prefecture;
- Bombing, at the Mikatagahara base in the Shizuoka Prefecture;
- Observation, at Yotsukaido in the Chiba Prefecture;
- Construction of aircraft, at the Tokorozawa base, Prefecture of Saitama;
- Manufacturing of engines, at the Atsuta arsenal in Nagoya;
- Inspection, at the Tokyo arsenal;
- Air base, the base at Tokorozawa.

The mission received from France the delivery of several Salmson planes in boxes that were assembled with the Japanese teams. Delivered also were Nieuport, Bréguet, Spad, Sopwith, and Caudron aircraft, one FBA seaplane, and one Hanriot.

At the end of August 1919, the Japanese government requested the extension of the mission until 31 March 1920, an extension which France accepted at its own expense. The French military aviation mission in Japan thus returned to the policy of transferring know-how and technology to Japan, 30 years after the departure for Japan of the navy engineer, Émile Bertin (1840-1924). The mission had brought to Japan and sold a total of 40 Nieuport aircraft, reconnaissance, photography, radio, gunnery, and bombardment equipment, and two Bréguet 400 aircraft. In the wake of the mission, Japan bought 80 Salmsom 2A2, and 100 Spad 13 fighter planes. The Nieuports, Salmsons, and Spads would become the benchmark fighters of the Japanese Army, which organized its units on the French model. The Japanese bought the licenses to manufacture Salmson 2A2 and Nieuport 24C fighter planes, as well as those for the Hispano-Suiza and the Lorraine-Dietrich V8 engines.

French manufacturers afterwards sold licenses to several Japanese companies. Kawasaki Heavy Industry, at the time a shipbuilding company, bought the right to manufacture Salmson aircraft and produced 1,017 examples. Nakajima bought the licenses for the Nieuport 83E2 and the Nieuport 29C1 and built 140 and 608 examples, respectively. Mitsubishi Heavy Industry produced 60 copies of the Nieuport 81E2 as well as the rotary Hanriot engine.

Most of the mission's personnel returned to France at the end of March 1920, but some engineers extended their stay at the request of the Japanese, though this time at Japan's expense. A position of military attaché for aeronautics was created in April 1921 at the French Embassy in Tokyo to continue the work of the Faure mission.

A new, more limited mission led by Commander Marcel Jauneaud (1885-1947) (with two officers) arrived in September 1921 to create an independent air force, an advanced air warfare school, and a department for technical studies, testing, and manufacturing in aeronautics. The first air force of Japan was founded in 1925 on the French model and with equipment of French origin. Another mission, directed by Antoine de Boysson (1892-1946), with six other engineers, arrived in Japan in 1922 and stayed one year on the base at Tokorozawa. Notes on the mission, as well as pictures of one of the engineers, Georges Metz, survive. Later, at their own expense, major aviation companies in Japan such as Mitsubishi, Nakajima, and Kawasaki invited many French engineers who worked on the development of new aircraft until 1935.

## Franco-Japanese Diplomatic Relations, 1919-1925

The Washington Conference on Disarmament (1921-1922) led to a discrete strengthening of relations between France and Japan. If most treaties or alliances, such as the Anglo-Japanese Alliance of 1902 were abrogated, France and Japan, in concert, would maintain the secret clauses of their 1907 arrangement, thus creating an atmosphere of *rapprochement* which would last until 1925. Official or unofficial rumors suggested the possibility of an alliance in the Pacific between the two countries, both political and military. Japan sought, before its isolation, a palliative to its former Anglo-Japanese alliance.[2] Japan wished to turn to France, providing it with assurances of security and peace in this part of the world where it could not maintain major military forces. In order to create this possible *rapprochement*, the two countries redoubled their efforts. France acted via its ambassador to Tokyo, Paul Claudel (1868-1955). In 1923, Japan named as its ambassador to France an important politician, Ishii Kikujirō 石井菊次郎 (1866-1945), a friend of Saionji Kinmochi. France sent Marshal Joseph Joffre (1852-1931) to Japan in 1922, and the governor of Indochina, Martial Merlin (1860-1935) in 1924. Japan in turn sent a mission to Indochina. Of course, the two governments looked at this possibility of alliance, but neither would invoke it or propose to solidify it. The economic dispute between Indochina and Japan was certainly the principal reason which prevented any official negotiation of this 'project'.

2 On the British air advisors in Japan see John Ferris, 'A British "Unofficial" Aviation Mission and the Rise of Japanese Naval Airpower, 1919-1925', in Donald Stoker and Michael T. McMaster (eds), *Naval Advising and Assistance: History, Challenges, and Analysis* (Solihull, UK: Helion & Co., 2017), pp. 87-116.

Paul Claudel used the influence of his friend Alexis Léger (1887-1975), former embassy secretary in Beijing (1916-1921), one of the negotiators at the Washington Conference on Disarmament, and then in 1922 chief of staff of the Minister of Foreign Affairs, Aristide Briand (1862-1932). Léger privately supported all of Claudel's proposals (including the visit of Joffre and Merlin). Briand and the President of Council Raymond Poincaré (1860-1934) thus supported these two projects of visits to Japan.

In his dispatches, Claudel often used the term *'rapprochement'* so as not to frighten the French government, which was anxious to reestablish good relations with the United States and Great Britain. Claudel compared Japan to an 'International Robinson Crusoe' isolated in its corner and observed that the secret clauses of the Franco-Japanese arrangement of 1907 constituted, especially in case of conflict, a genuine military alliance with Japan despite the agreements of Washington since neither France nor Japan had taken the initiative to cancel it. The Japanese press would often mention the imminence of the signing of a new Franco-Japanese alliance, sometimes stating that it would be a military one. Poincaré and Briand continued to describe the relationship as a *'rapprochement'* rather than advancing to a 'military alliance', which would have duplicated the secret clauses of the 1907 arrangement. A virulent American press campaign against the tightening of relations between France and Japan also dampened the enthusiasm of the French government. This 'Project' disappeared definitively with the absence of its French initiator Claudel from Japan for more than 13 months between 1924 and 1925, an absence which brought great disappointment among the relationship's Japanese supporters, notably marshal Uehara Yūsaku 上原勇作 (1879-1933).[3]

## Conclusion

Although France had once again brought to Japan the latest military technologies–this time in aviation–the influence of the United States would prevent the signing of a true military alliance that would have replaced the British-Japanese alliance ended at the Washington Conference of Disarmament in 1922, a conference that saw both Japan and France diminished in terms of maritime power. This conference confirmed the Anglo-Saxon maritime power of the United States and Great Britain.

3 Sources: Refer to the text of the author published in *Sabre et Pinceau, par d'autres Français du Japan (1872-1960)*, (Tokyo: French Chamber of Commerce and Industry of Japan, 2005), pp. 76-151, as well as his doctoral thesis, *La politique Française en Extrêm-Orient et la Japon de 1914 à 1925* (PhD thesis, Hitosubashi University, 1980). For the transfer of technology from France to Japan in the last years of the Shogunate see *Soie et Lumières. L'âge d'or des éxchanges franco-japonais, des origins aux années 1950* (Tokyo: French Chamber of Commerce and Industry of Japan, 2001); see also *Lys et Canon, Images et correspondances retrouvés, 1860-1900* (Tokyo: French Chamber of Commerce and Industry of Japan, 2013).

The pro-French faction of the Japanese army, led by Marshal Uehara Yūsaku, would shrink in influence to the benefit of the pro-German faction. Military relations between France and Japan would be reduced to distant contacts, opening the way to the increasingly important presence of Germany. The two nations drew closer and became allies in 1940. France missed an opportunity to find an ally in Japan, which would have changed Japan's diplomatic strategy.

Colonel Jacques-Paul Faure (1869-1924). (via the Author)

The pilot license of Tokugawa Yoshitoshi. (via the Author)

The members of the mission in Tokyo upon their arrival in January 1919. (via the Author)

The triumphant welcome of the members of the mission to Gifu, with a triumphal arch constructed for the occasion, February 1919. (via the Author)

Gunnery Practice (via the Author)

*Left:* Colonel Faure in front of a Salmson, Gifu, 1919. (via the Author)

*Below:* Japanese Spad (via the Author)

Japanese Dirigible (via the Author)

Japanese Seaplanes (via the Author)

2

# The French Military Aviation Mission in Poland and the Creation of Polish Aviation in the 1920s

*Patrick Facon*

*Translated and Adapted by Nabih Kanbar*

## Introduction

One has to admit that in 1919 the French army was indeed one of the most powerful in the world. Not only had it won the war, but it was also present in Europe and around the world since it had 'to hold the Rhine', wrote Charles de Gaulle, 'occupy Frankfurt, Düsseldorf, the Ruhr, lend a hand to the Poles, to the Czechs, stay in Silesia, Memel, Schleswig, watch Constantinople, restore order in Morocco, control Abd el-Krim, subdue' Taza (an area of Morocco in the Atlas Mountains), 'stand up to the Saharan rebels, take up a footing in the Levant, penetrate into Cilicia, expel Faisal from Damascus, install themselves on the Euphrates and the Tigris, repress the insurrection of Jebel Druze, show strength in all of France's colonies in Africa, America, and Oceania, contain the latent agitation in Indochina, and protect France's establishments in China amidst riots and revolutions'.[1]

Of all the countries mentioned, Poland was the subject of particular attention on the part of France and the Allies. From 1918 to 1919 it appeared, on the one hand, as the best possible bulwark against Russia and the 'Bolshevik contagion', and on the other hand as a key country for squeezing Germany in a pincer and therefore breaking any new attempt at belligerence. In 1919 and during the 1920s in general,

1 Charles de Gaulle, *Le Fil de l'épée* (Paris: Éditions Burger-Levrault, 1932), cited by Jean Doise and Maurice Vaïsse, *Diplomatie et Outil militaire, 1871–1969* (Paris: Imprimerie nationale, 1987), p. 268.

Poland represented therefore high military stakes for France. But it also represented a formidable economic stake because it was rich in various minerals—especially coal—and because of the disastrous state of the mines of the north of France. Poland therefore could help France to recover.

These two factors account for the importance accorded by the French to their military mission in Poland, which would constitute a kind of showcase for French know-how, and in particular for the aviation mission sent there in the spring of 1919 with the Polish army organized in France (APOF).

Indeed, in terms of aviation the French could reasonably see themselves as first in the world. In 1918-1919, French military aviation deployed about 4,500 aircraft in the front line, and the brilliance of French technology was particularly evident in the field of batteries and the engine industry. Besides, its British, American, and Italian allies were very often equipped with French-made aircraft as well as motors from Clerget, Gnome, Hispano-Suiza, Renault, Le Rhône, and Salmson, which were renowned for their robustness and reliability. Thus, in the work of the French Military Mission in Poland (MMFP—*Mission Militaire française en Pologne*), under the command of General Henrys, 'the financial, military and political aspects', writes Pascal Griset, 'were inextricably intertwined'.[2] The MMFP had indeed not only to 'organize a ministry, troops, workshops, establishments, and schools to study the passage to peace path from the warpath',[3] but also to make the Poles purchase French aeronautical equipment and support the economic interests of France in Poland. As Pascal Griset rightly points out, for the first time probably in the history of French aviation, without talking yet about a 'military-industrial complex', relations were being established between the industrial, the military, and the diplomatic worlds.

## The Creation of Schools and the Policy of Prestige: The Promotion of French Aviation in Poland

When the MMFP arrived in Poland at the beginning of 1919, the situation of Polish aviation was fairly tragic. It had only 80 German aircraft, most of them in poor condition, lacking tires or having wooden wheels. As for an aviation industry as such, it did not exist on Polish territory. A test was carried out on the ground in Warsaw by 400 civilian and military workers who, directed by an engineer, began building wings with stocks of equipment left by the Germans. But the results did not live up to expectations.[4]

2 Pascal Griset, 'La Mission militaire française en Pologne: industrie aéronautique et logique militaire', *Revue Historique des armées*, 2 (1987), pp. 93-103, espec. p. 93.

3 Rapport du colonel Chapelet, commandant l'aéronautique de la Mission Militaire Français Pologne (hereafter MMFP), Service Historique de l'Armeé de l'Air, Vincennes, Paris (hereafter SHAA), Mi 26.

4 Ibid.

Polish aviation therefore had to be created entirely from the ground up. Lieutenant-Colonel de Vergnettes and Colonel Chapelet (his second in command), worked based on the idea that personnel trained on a type of equipment subsequently will be inclined to use and advise the purchase of this or related material. This was why the MMFP aviation mission, as soon as it arrived in Poland, and in order to promote French aviation, adopted a systematic policy of setting-up military schools organized on the French model and supervised by French instructors.

Thus, in April 1920, four pilot schools, structured according to the instructions of the military mission, functioned as envisioned. At that time, the 20 French instructors of the Warsaw Elementary Pilot School had already trained 73 pilots, who were then sent to the advanced course in Poznań where they were trained by six French instructors. Several fields of specialty were covered: the Toruń school trained observers under the guidance of five French instructors, and a photography school based in Krakow—two French instructors—completed this training. Again in 1920, a mechanics school was also planned.[5]

After the creation of aviation schools, the promotion of French equipment was also undertaken by organizing air rallies and mock raids. In this field again, France was a great favorite and the aircraft presented, such as the Breguet 14, defended with brilliance the French colors against their Italian and British rivals. This was particularly the case in 1922, when five of the six Breguet 14s with a 300-horsepower engine—and piloted by Polish aviators—finished the race, while only one of the five Bristol fighters lined up at the start did so. This result was welcomed as a great victory by the commander of the MMFP who wrote to the undersecretary of State for Aeronautics: 'As you see, the results of the test constitute a striking success for the French aircraft, which again proved to be superior to all other types of aircraft in service in the Polish Army'.[6] The year 1922 thus marked a certain consecration for the prestige of French wings in Poland, which was further enhanced by the Warsaw-Zurich-Paris cross country 'raid' carried out by three Breguet 14 A.2s of the Polish army.

## The *Raison d'Être* of the MMFP's Aviation Mission: To Sell French Equipment to Poland

In 1919, the demobilization of personnel, the downsizing of the manpower of the aviation industry, and the reduction of surplus equipment were the three main problems facing French military aviation. If the demobilization of personnel was done without great difficulty, the same did not apply to aircraft in service and in stock:

5 Rapport du générale Henrys au ministre de la Guerre, Warsaw, 10 April 1920, Service Historique de l'Armeé de la Terre, Vincennes, Paris (hereafter SHAT), 7N2988.

6 Le commandant de la MMFP au sous-secrétaire d'État à l'Aéronautique, 23 September 1922, SHAT, 17N2992.

What was France to do with 5,000 to 6,000 surplus planes after the dissolution of two thirds of the French squadrons that existed in November 1918? The first solution was to transfer them to civil aviation, which was being organized, or to sell them to private individuals. But since the civilian market did not allow for substantial sales of stocks, the military leaders and industrialists sought rather to develop military missions throughout the world, hoping thus to liquidate with the maximum possible benefits the planes designed during the First World War.

This was probably the true *raison d'être* of the MMFP, but it was a difficult task. Even if France embarked on this adventure from a position of strength—it had won a firm order totaling 8,765,000 francs for 132 of the 382 aircraft intended to equip Polish aviation—foreign competition did exist and was felt. Britain and Italy were confronted with the same problems as France in the post war years, and the work of the French airmen had to be done with extreme caution and diplomacy in order to avoid offending the allies of yesterday by favoring, in too obvious ways, French material. The difficulty lay in how the British and the Italians would be dismissed, and in the way in which the decisions to reject British and Italian planes would be pushed through by justifying them with technical arguments that would have the appearance of perfect objectivity.

In 1919, this task was all the more difficult as the Poles sought to obtain aviation equipment by all means and as fast as possible. Colonel Chapelet gives a very pertinent explanation of this situation: 'A false idea: very much set in their mind, quite rightly, of the considerable work they have done to make something from nothing, are concerned that their labor will disappear and will be ignored. They fear to be swept away by the new material and a new organization. Therefore, they seek by all means to obtain equipment anywhere and regardless of quality to survive in any way possible.... In their desire to get material and to preserve their authority intact, the leaders of Polish aviation, as well as ballooning, approach the head of the mission and ask him: "How much does a squadron cost? ... How much does a company of balloonists cost?" They also solicit the help of some inferior specialists'.[7] Colonel Chapelet also wrote in December 1919: 'A Polish purchasing commission is currently operating in Paris, and perhaps it is necessary to guide it, for the Poles sometimes allow themselves to be too carried away. Not being aware of the conditions under which war units actually work, they are won over by the rather simplistic idea of just buying a "squadron," a system which manufacturers find very advantageous, but which destroys all possibilities for normal resupply and regular maintenance of a unit'.[8]

The British and the Italians were the first to take advantage of this situation and the state of mind of the Poles and provided them very early on with aviation equipment. Indeed, as soon as the Polish-Russian war broke out, the Italians sold Poland 60 observation planes and 15 fighter planes, and about 50 other aircraft were still to

7 Rapport du colonel Chapelet, commandant l'aéronautique de la MMFP, SHAA, Mi 26.
8 Ibid.

be delivered in 1920. In their reports, the French military in Poland did not fail to emphasize that this mission was carried out solely for the purpose of establishing Italian industry in Poland and that it had been able to act through well conducted propaganda, thus attracting the Polish aviation personnel by diverse means, including the promise of employment in the Italian factories of Poland. The British were equally threatening as they also managed to win a contract for the delivery of 80 Bristol fighter aircraft. It must be noted in this regard that the British and Italians did not show the same scruples as the French in ensuring the promotion of their material: 'In a great show', wrote Colonel Chapelet, 'at the Warsaw site, a patrol of French fighter planes performs an impeccable presentation at nearly 2,000 meters, as it is prescribed. At this altitude, savvy connoisseurs are able to appreciate the speed of the evolutions, the maneuverability of the aircraft, and their efficiency in the attacks: a beautiful work, an elegant presentation. Despite that, the presented Italian fighter planes won all the votes by breaking the orders and passing very close to the stands in a spectacular roar'.[9]

In order to counteract foreign competition, MMFP officials put forward very early arguments that seemed well founded, emphasizing the heterogeneity of a military air arm provided by several countries: 'It should be noted that the aviation of three countries was tapped to constitute this supply, which, at first glance, is a fault because it prevents having a homogeneous air arm, at present at least'.[10] For the aviation officials of the MMFP, the Poles bore a part of the responsibility for this situation: 'We have succeeded in getting the Polish leaders to adopt a solid and thoroughly studied framework', wrote Colonel Chapelet in January 1920, 'but their mind is not oriented in practice towards a simple and logical arrangement of their equipment. They do not know how to choose, and only manage to form a fleet of samples in which German airplanes still appear. They are attached to these planes, for many of them have served, and sometimes not without brilliancy, in the German air force'.[11]

In spite of foreign competition, in the early 1920s the work of French airmen was bearing fruit in the supply of equipment. In February 1922, the Minister of War was able to congratulate himself by writing: 'The preponderance of our influence on Polish aviation is indisputable. The Poles have accepted our regulations, our methods, our organization. They gave us very large orders of equipment, totaling for the years 1919 and 1920 nearly 300 aircraft'.[12] This commercial success was further confirmed when General Dupont took charge of the MMFP and speeded up the signing of a military agreement of 19 February 1921, which included in an annex a loan of 400 million francs to enable Poland to purchase French war material.[13]

9 Ibid.
10 Rapport de la MMFP, 13 February 1920, SHAA, Mi 26.
11 Rapport du colonel Chapelet, commandant l'aéronautique de la MMFP, SHAA, Mi 26.
12 Note du ministère de la Guerre, 7 February 1922, SHAT, 17N2992.
13 Georges Soutou, 'La politique économique de la France en Pologne (1920-1924)', *Revue historique* (1974), pp. 85-116, espec. p. 89.

But the best French 'political coup' was realized when the Polish Minister of Military Affairs asked Paris on 15 May 1922—the idea had been suggested to him by General Dupont—to detach a colonel from the French army to head Polish aviation. Colonel Lévèque was then appointed, and as soon as he arrived in January 1923, he endeavored to promote French interests by carrying out 'a fruitful work, thus (engaging) Polish aviation in the process of adopting almost exclusively French devices'.[14] But this 'golden age' did not last because 'under the influence of a real neurasthenia', Colonel Lévèque resigned brutally during the summer of 1924. General Dupont asked naturally for an urgent replacement. A call was even launched in the French press to fill this post! This was in vain.[15] It was finally a Pole, General Zagorsky, who was appointed. From the mid-1920s, France gradually lost the advantages it had gained in Poland.

## Errors, Obstacles, Failures, Decline

The first mistake, the first 'misfire' committed by France in Poland appeared as soon as the MMFP was installed and related to the French schools in Poland, whose results were disappointing in the long-term because of the lack of interest of the aviation officials in France itself. Let us be clear: they did not understand the importance of the schools and neglected to supply them with competent instructors and, especially, with modern airplanes! However, the leaders of the MMFP very soon put their finger on this deficiency: 'It is necessary', wrote General Henri Niessel in December 1920, 'to ensure large development of the Toruń aviation school.... I point out that the school is almost totally lacking airplanes capable of serving'.[16] Here, we agree completely with Pascal Griset when he noted: 'It is particularly damaging for a country that wants to settle in any market to send samples of poor quality. It seems that some officials in Paris saw in the schools created in Poland an easy way to dispose of old stocks more than an effective instrument of promotion. By supplying outdated equipment, the 'showcase' of the schools could only turn against France and disgust forever the Poles disappointed by the French material they use'.[17]

Worse yet, poorly equipped and neglected, the schools were gradually abandoned as the overall personnel of the MMFP were reduced. This was evident as early as 1921, and an inspection report from the Poznań and Toruń schools highlighted the seriousness of the problem: 'too few students attend classes. This is a great danger for the recruitment of aviation personnel.... The planes are old; they do not give a real notion of the value of the French models'.[18] The report went on to stress the urgency of sending them at least two Breguet 14s!

14 Note de MMFP adressée au ministre de la Guerre, 1 September 1925, SHAT, 7N2994.
15 Ibid.
16 Note d'inspection du général Niessel, December 1920, SHAT, 7N2994.
17 Griset, 'La Mission militaire française en Pologne', p. 94.
18 Rapport d'inspection des écoles de Toruń et de Poznań, 6 February 1921, SHAT, 7N2992.

The second French error was the negligence and laxity with which the French equipment ordered by Poland was delivered, as was shown in a report of February 1920 criticizing the organization of French supplies: 'Regarding the equipment to be purchased in France, it is of the utmost importance that this be granted and delivered without delay, and *in excellent condition*, if we don't want to see little by little all the French material replaced by foreign material'.[19] General Henrys added: 'One of the causes of the difficulties we have encountered is certainly due to the discontent, partly justified, of the Polish authorities, and triggered by the very poor condition of the aviation material delivered for the creation of the air service'.[20] Colonel Chapelet's report in this respect is instructive: 'The state of disrepair of the rolling stock and even certain aircraft, not without cause provoked severe criticism among our Polish friends. Arrival of the squadron Br 39 on 25 April 1919 in the afternoon: major difficulties of disembarkment. There is no gasoline on site. I go through a lot to get it; I must beg for it from Polish aviation. There is no oil, and we can't find it here. For the transport of the crates, I would have needed the large trailer. The crates will have perhaps to stay on the platforms where we will have to open them. The rolling stock is used. Some trucks do not look good and their canvas shrouds are completely shredded. That will not produce a good impression. The tires are usually in bad condition. It is essential to anticipate an immediate and substantial resupply of tires. In Poland, we cannot find them, and the squadron that came with me does not even have replacements. There are no tools on the vehicles, not even on the one that came with me. For the assembly of planes we will have to go very slowly because of the lack of specialists. It is hoped that there will be instructions in the boxes for the adjustments since the squadron does not possess any.... In short, we do not receive from France any but very worn-out material, without any supplies'.[21]

In addition to the mediocre quality of the material delivered, France perhaps had not provided the means to achieve its policy with regard to the staff of the mission itself. Thus, as early as the middle of 1919, Colonel Chapelet noted with some bitterness: 'More seriously, as the French mechanics have not found a situation of material interest in Poland, they will almost all abandon Poland after their first commitment of six months. Should we be surprised? Material benefits are low and fraternization between French and Poles is not perfect, especially among noncommissioned officers and troops. Incidents are even frequent enough. It is indispensable to possess abroad qualities of calm and diplomacy, which are not given to everybody. Additionally, it must be said that some French officers have not always given an excellent example'.[22]

As for the lack of dynamism, the passivity and the reluctance of the French industrialists was also strongly denounced by the French military: 'While foreign

19 Rapport de la MMFP, 13 February 1920, SHAA, Mi26.
20 Lettre du général Henrys au ministre de la Guerre, 17 February 1920, SHAA, Mi 26.
21 Rapport du colonel Chapelet, commandant l'aéronautique de la MMFP, SHAA, Mi 26.
22 Ibid.

builders, strongly supported by their governments and military missions in the country, use all means to market their goods, no French maker supported by the government has yet come to do business in Poland'.[23] Colonel Chapelet put up the same negative assessment: 'De Vergnettes does not always understand the difficulties that arise around us, coming from both the Poles and certain members of the mission. He is too often in Paris to deal with industrial issues because the French manufacturers seem to be losing interest in the Polish market that the mission opens for them. They are too accustomed to living without too much effort on the liberalities and orders that the French government ensures them'.[24]

The MMFP thus gave the impression of fighting against the lack of energy of their own country as much as against foreign competition. And even then it seems that it was the latter which at the beginning of the mission at least was the easiest to overcome. Thus, in 1920, General Henrys succeeded, barely, in eliminating the Italians who put pressure on the Polish government to reduce the scope of its order from Breguet: 'After many difficulties and in spite of the strong pressure exerted by the representatives of the English and Italian governments, the Polish government has decided to reserve a large part of its purchases of aeronautical equipment to France.... The struggle has been harsh; it was a near thing to avoid all of the purchases going to the English and Italian governments'.[25]

But these successes were not sustainable. The whole problem stemmed from the fact that no long-term French trade policy was envisioned, a policy that would have given the MMFP the means it required to implement its training plans, thus, to use an expression formulated by Colonel Chapelet, the servicemen of the MMFP often felt as if 'they were making the bed for foreigners'.[26]

Until 1925, this situation could go unnoticed or at least the problems could be solved insofar as the MMFP was strong and the commander of Polish aviation was a Frenchman. But, from the departure of Colonel Lévèque, an irreversible decline began for the place of France in Poland. It was the Poles themselves who gave the *coup de grâce* to French influence when, at the beginning of 1925, the Polish government announced that without further delay, it intended to buy Fokker aircraft and English Bywater tanks—although inferior to the French Mauclaire tanks—rather than French material, which did not fail to worry General Dupont.

Having been thus far in the conqueror's position, the MMFP could now only work from a defensive position and, instead of launching French projects, most of its activity would be devoted to defeating the projects of foreign competitors. This task proved all the more difficult because the French suspected General Zagorsky of receiving bribes from the Fokker company and, as General Dupont noted with some rancor: 'We are

23 Rapport de la MMFP, 13 February 1920, SHAA, Mi 26
24 Rapport du colonel Chapelet, commandant l'aéronautique de la MMFP, SHAA, Mi 26.
25 Lettre du général Henrys au ministre de la Guerre, 17 February 1920, SHAA, Mi 26.
26 Rapport du colonel Chapelet, commandant l'aéronautique de la MMFP, SHAA, Mi 26.

bothering some officers in their games. General Zagorsky is suspected of seeking above all his personal interest'.[27] The only action that General Dupont could then take was of a political nature because in order to counter the Fokker contract he solicited an interview with General Zimiesky and 'pointed out to him that the Fokker factory was German, established in Holland to go around the Treaty of Versailles, certainly subsidized by the Reich and, in these circumstances, able to offer prices lower than those of all its competitors'.[28]

In vain, General Dupont tried again in a second interview, but on 22 January 1925 he had to quickly admit his powerlessness, writing 'French industry is failing along the entire line' when he learned that the Poles had decided to buy three Fokkers for evaluation.[29] Consequently, he considered that he no longer had sufficient means to fight back and remitted to his superiors: 'Our mission is finished with regard to these shady affairs; it is up to the French government to intervene if it considers it appropriate'.[30]

A miracle occurred a dozen days later when the Polish government told him it did not eventually follow up on its order of Fokker aircraft. But General Dupont was cautious and wrote on February 11: 'Let's hope it is true.... I do not know and will never know in what way my protests have influenced the decision of the minister'.[31]

It must therefore be noted that the MMFP was maintained in Poland only because of the relentless work of its members but that it could not count on any assistance from Paris. Worse still, in many cases the plenipotentiary minister in Warsaw, M. de Panafieu, did not accept the military encroaching on his remit and was therefore regularly in conflict with the MMFP. As one prominent witness pointed out, Colonel Chapelet, then squadron commander and the mission's aviation commander, 'instead of forming a united front, these two bodies [the ambassador in Warsaw and the MMFP], one traditional and the other temporary, will always show a certain hostility, and naturally the affairs will suffer sometimes. Abroad, these complications are never good because other nations will have qualified representatives in Warsaw to sell equipment, England and Italy in particular'.[32]

The failure of French aviation in Poland was even more serious and more dramatic in the field of civil aviation. It was evident that the French were quickly displaced by the Germans in this sector. Thus, in January 1927 the newspaper *Mysl. Niepodlegla* revealed that the Aeroflot company, which was largely subsidized by the Polish government, was almost entirely under the control of German companies. Hence,

27 Rapport du général Dupont au ministre de la Guerre, 10 January 1925, SHAT, 7N2994.
28 Note de la MMFP, 30 January 1925, SHAT, 7N2994.
29 Ibid.
30 Ibid.
31 Lettre du général Dupont au ministre de la Guerre, 11 February 1925, SHAT, 7N2994.
32 Rapport du colonel Chapelet, commandant l'aéronautique de la MMFP, SHAA, Mi 26.

of the 95 aircraft it was equipped with, 93 were Junkers. It called for opening an investigation.[33]

Even if it was above all a matter of Polish domestic policy, this affair revealed a certain weakness among the French companies, which did not know how or could not establish a foothold in a market where they nevertheless had undeniable advantages. The investigation quickly revealed that the Junkers were purchased under rather obscure conditions. But it also showed, which is perhaps more serious, that the Junkers aircraft made of metal were very popular in Poland, and that both Polish pilots and the public considered them to be far superior to French aircraft.

It seems, therefore, that in Poland France had placed itself solely on the military ground and that it appeared only tardily and timidly on the commercial ground, whereas Great Britain and Italy had positioned themselves, right from the outset, on the commercial field, leaving aside completely the question of the organization and use of military aviation. As a result, the Poles readily accepted the plans for the organization of their aviation presented by the MMFP, but were rather tempted by foreign countries for the choice of aircraft and their manufacture.

## The Lack of Dynamism of the French Aviation Industry in Establishing Itself in Poland

While the brilliance of French aeronautical technology was particularly evident in 1919, both in the battery and engine industries, shadows were already emerging as the 1920s approached: For example, since 1917 British industry had produced more units than French industry. Upon the armistice of 1918, the latter dropped its production, whereas Great Britain, which had just established an independent military air force—the Royal Air Force—continued to produce almost as many planes as in the course of the First World War. Certainly, French planes like the Spad XIII and Breguet 14 were still popular abroad, but the British, then the Americans, churned-out on their assembly lines more and better performing machines. Another clue should have attracted the attention of the French: when the Germans laid down their arms in November 1918, they ceded to the Allies thousands of aircraft and engines and batteries, testifying to the vitality and power of the German aviation industry, which was only waiting for the advent of a strong political power to be reborn from its ashes.

However, the lack of dynamism of the French aviation industry was just as significant in France itself as abroad. As Pascal Griset notes, 'France, unable to give its planes a firm place on the Polish market, was unable either to set up in Poland an aeronautical industry with French capital and technology, or at least to participate significantly in financing and supervising the Polish aeronautical industry'.[34] This was all the more important because in a country deeply marked by centuries of foreign

33 Dossier de presse réalisé par la MMFP, SHAT, 7N2994.
34 Griset, 'La mission militaire française en Pologne', p. 99.

occupation, the historian adds, 'national independence was a particularly essential value. The import of aircraft was, for the majority of Polish officials, only a temporary means of defending the country, pending the establishment of a national industry. This was to be created in its entirety since the aeronautical industry was virtually nonexistent in the territories forming the new state'.[35]

Of course, attempts were being made, but once again the results were mediocre. The Poles were the first to deplore this situation, such as General Zagorsky, who in a January 1926 speech on the development of Poland's aviation industry said: 'Foreign capital was reluctantly entering Poland, wishing to retain Poland as its market only'.[36]

Although there were Polish aviation factories in Poland, they generally manufactured only foreign licensed equipment. It is true that the Poles relied heavily on the factory of the Franco-Polish Society in Warsaw, which was supposed to allow French capital to participate in the development of a completely Polish industry while giving France a dominant position. But this company was only an empty shell: it was slow to build its factory, and above all it had no program specifying on what projects it would work, which 'shows the lack of realism of the French industrialists and their lack of determination to get established in Poland'.[37] The construction of the factory was, however, underway, but unclear subsidies and construction errors made it an increasingly ruinous undertaking. And in July 1926, General Charpy drew up a very negative assessment of the Franco-Polish Society, noting that despite the advance of four million Swiss francs from the government, nothing had been manufactured: 'The factory is stillborn...it seems destined to disappear shortly'.[38] Finally, as a last evidence of failure, the factory was taken over by Skoda, which was clearly seen by Polish public opinion as an obvious defeat of French influence.

Since 1920, a consortium of French aircraft manufacturers including Breguet, Farman, Blériot, Nieuport, Caudron, Morane-Saulnier, Spad, Renault, Hispano-Suiza, Lorraine Dietrich, and Gnome and Rhône was set up in Poland under Mr. Saulnier's impetus, but these houses had signed an agreement stipulating that all orders obtained by one of the companies could only be made through the consortium as a whole, which would then receive on each order a commission of 10 percent. In October 1922, due to this arrangement, the Polish military procurement mission could only deplore the fact that it could only order French material through this consortium and therefore pay 10 percent more for all of its aircraft![39] Pascal Griset stressed quite rightly: 'This way of proceeding fits more the management of a guaranteed income than a dynamic export policy....This project has never really taken off satisfactorily. In

35 Ibid.

36 Discours du général Zagorsky prononcé le 21 January 1926 devant l'assemblée des techniciens polonaise à Varsovie, *Polska Zbronja*, 2 February 1926.

37 Griset, 'La mission militaire française en Pologne', p. 100.

38 Rapport du général Charpy au ministre de la Guerre, 2 July 1926, SHAT, 7N2994.

39 Rapport du bureau technique de la mission polonaise d'achats, 6 October 1922, (traduction MMFP), SHAT, 7N2999.

addition to the very serious financial problems encountered by French investors due to the fall of the franc, disastrous hesitations concerning the technical choices to be implemented made the initial efforts bog down'.[40]

The absence of the French aeronautical industry in Poland explains perhaps why, when General Józef Piłsudski engaged his country in a resolutely nationalist industrial policy, he met no opposition from France.

## Conclusion

At the end of the 1920s, in spite of all the efforts of the French military mission in Poland, and having failed to integrate economic realities into its diplomatic plans, France was totally excluded from the Polish economic market and lost the supremacy and the military prestige that it had enjoyed among the Poles in 1919.

The acknowledgment of failure is manifest, as Georges Soutou writes: 'the study of concrete cases makes it possible to correct the probably too coherent impression left by the major projects designed in Paris in 1920 and 1921. It appeared very quickly that what could have been a fine example of conquering imperialism, was dissolved amid political uncertainties and economic difficulties'.[41]

Having analyzed the decisions of French diplomacy in Poland in order to underline its contradictions and pious wishes, and trying to pinpoint the reasons for the French failure, the historian goes on to say that French imperialism is not 'the result of the expansionism of the French industry and banking systems. On the contrary, it seems that France's projects far outstrip its financial and economic resources.... Political and military domination is not enough to create economic realities that are otherwise nonexistent'.[42]

The explanation of this state of affairs doubtless comes from the extremely difficult situation. France emerged from the First World War in a disastrous condition demographically and financially, and to quote the title of a work by geographer A. Demangeon published in 1920, contemporary people were beginning to be aware of a certain 'decline of Europe'. Moreover, the old continent was deeply indebted because in order to finance the Great War European countries were forced to borrow, in particular from the United States: in 1919 for instance, France's external debt amounted to 33 billion gold francs, and this deficit would weigh heavily on the settlement of international affairs. No longer having financial superiority, France needed—if it wanted to retain its rank as a power—to hold its place in the world diplomatically and militarily. But from 1919 to 1923, the old allies were divided: on the one hand, tensions increased between the French and the Anglo-Saxons, especially regarding the balance of power in the new Europe, where the British feared

40 Griset, 'La mission militaire française en Pologne', p. 100.
41 Soutou, 'La politique économique de la France en Pologne', p. 86.
42 Ibid., p. 116.

French hegemony; on the other hand, the repayment of the war debt to the United States poisoned Franco-American relations. Indeed, as France multiplied military missions in South America and military interventions in Poland, the Middle East, North Africa, Sub-Saharan Africa, Indochina, and the Pacific, the Americans 'are irritated ... and do not understand how a state can allocate so much money to its military spending in a period of peace while it must repay his war debts'.[43]

Strengthened by their victory in 1918, the French believed that the period of prosperity from before 1914 would resume and that they would find themselves in the position of leaders in international politics. This was not the case because France failed to harmonize its various fields of action in Poland, whether military, financial, or political. In the interwar period, France was forced to practice an 'imperialism of the poor' and the reluctance, the lack of combativeness of its industrialists in the face of foreign competition, the lack of coordination between the military, diplomats, aircraft manufacturers and engine manufacturers, and especially the lack of a long-term policy on the part of the various governments, led to the weakening, not to say disappearance, of the influence and the image of France in a country where it nevertheless had all the assets to establish itself as a model.

43 Doise and Vaïsse, *Diplomatie et outil militaire*, p. 268.

# 3

# 'A poor, confused and late relative': Italian Air Advising in Spain, 1936-1942

*Fabio De Ninno and Jacopo Pili*[1]

## Introduction

Between 1936 and 1939, the Italian Fascist regime tried to take advantage of the Spanish Civil War to establish a long lasting influence over the Iberian country by providing abundant military support to Francisco Franco's Nationalists. This Italian military support eventually turned into direct intervention by the Italian armed forces, and part of their mission was providing military advice to the Nationalist armed forces. Despite the immense body of literature concerning the Spanish Civil War, almost no attention has been paid to this part of the Italian intervention in Spain. This advisory effort failed to play a central role in establishing strong military and commercial relations between Fascist Italy and the young Francoist regime. In particular, the *Regia Aeronautica's* (Italian Royal Air Force) advisory role to Nationalist aviation was soon compromised, depriving Italy and the Italian aircraft industry of becoming privileged partners in Spain's post-war reorganization. The causes of this failure can be traced back to the relationship between the Nationalists and Italy, the more general crisis that the Italian Air Force faced in those years, and the way in which it was

1 Special thanks goes to the Archivio histórico del Ejército del Aire (Madrid) for providing us vital documents and sending them to Italy. We also thank the Archivio dell'ufficio storico dell'Aeronautica militare (Rome), in particular Maresciallo Gaetano Pasqua and Tenente Colonnello Emiliano Barlattani. The first two sections were written by both authors. The section from 'The Italian Air Force and the Spanish Civil War' to 'The Italian Air Force Takes Off' was written by Jacopo Pili. The remaining sections were written by Fabio De Ninno.

employed in the civil war. Most important of all, however, was the growing power of Nazi Germany, and its emergence as the dominant player in European politics.

## Fascist Italy' Relations with Spain, 1922-1936

From its beginning the Fascist movement was imbued with a grand ideological vision calling for the construction of a 'vital space' for Italy in the Mediterranean.[2] This political-ideological project constituted the very basis of Fascist foreign policy and mirrored the path followed by Mussolini in his diplomatic relations with the other states of the region.[3] Spain held a particularly important place in Italy's ambitions because of its dominant geographical position in the Western Mediterranean. Hence, rapprochement with Spain was a goal of the Fascist Regime.[4]

Starting in 1923, when Miguel Primo de Rivera established a pro-Fascist dictatorship in Spain, Mussolini sought to create friendly relations with the goal of shifting the Mediterranean balance of power against France.[5] The Italian armed forces, the navy in particular, calculated the advantages of a possible alliance with Madrid, especially concerning the use of the Balearic Islands as an air and naval base.[6]

The end of De Rivera's dictatorship in 1930, and the subsequent establishment of the Second Spanish Republic (1931-1936), strained the process of reconciliation between the two countries. However, the new Republican regime was characterized by great political and social instability fueled by splits that divided the country, as well as by the political intransigence of leaders of the opposing factions. The constant state of crisis prepared the ground for the outbreak of the civil war of 1936-1939.[7]

Fascist Italy contributed to this process through the contacts established by the Italian government with proponents of the monarchist Right and in the Spanish financial world, whose goal it was to obtain funds and political support against the

2 MacGregor Knox, *To the Threshold of Power: Origins and Dynamics of the Fascist and National Socialist Dictatorships*, Vol. I, *1922-1933* (Cambridge: Cambridge University Press, 2007), p. 297.

3 Enzo Collotti, *Fascismo e politica di potenza* (Florence: La Nuova Italia, 2001), pp. 3-11.

4 Stanley G. Payne, 'Fascist Italy and Spain, 1922-45', *Mediterranean Historical Review*, 13:1-2 (1998), p. 101

5 Giulia Albanese, *Dittature Mediterranee, Sovversioni fasciste e colpi di Stato in Italia, Spagna e Portogallo* (Rome-Bari: Laterza, 2016), pp. V-VII; Marco Mugnaini, 'Italia, Spagna, e la formazione di un nuovo equilibrio mediterraneo, (1923-1928)', *Spagna contemporanea*, 7:14 (1998), pp. 53-77; Ismael Saz, 'Foreign policy under Primo de Riveira', in Sebastian Balfour and Paul Preston (eds), *Spain and the Great Powers in the Twentieth Century* (London: Routledge, 1999), pp. 65-66.

6 John Gooch, *Mussolini and His Generals: The Armed Forces and the Fascist Foreign Politics, 1922-1940* (Cambridge: Cambridge University Press, 2007), p. 110.

7 Stanley G. Payne, *The Collapse of the Spanish Republic, 1933-1936: Origins of the Civil War* (New Haven: Yale University Press, 2006).

Left.[8] The military also established connections with Fascist Italy in order to prepare a possible coup. In the weeks before the Nationalist '*pronunciamento*' (military coup) of 18 July 1936, which would start the civil war, these contacts lead to the signing of contracts for Italian military equipment destined for the rebels. In the aviation realm, in exchange for 39.3 million lire, Fascist Italy committed to supply 15 SM.81 bombers, 24 CR.32 fighters, three Macchi 41 reconnaissance planes, one SM.55X seaplane, and the necessary supporting equipment.[9] Italian support for the Spanish clandestine movement aimed at gaining the friendship of the rebels within the broader context of the Duce's project of Mediterranean expansion.[10]

At the time of the uprising of July 1936, the existing contacts between Rome's military and the Spanish right wing made Fascist Italy the privileged interlocutor supporting the revolt and was the reason why the Nationalists first turned to Mussolini to obtain military aid. On his part, the Italian dictator initially hesitated because Italy was just coming out of the Ethiopian War (1935-1936), which had put the country in a difficult position in both financial and diplomatic terms. While the economic reasons were secondary, an intervention in the peninsula could weaken France by bringing Spain back into the Italian sphere of influence. These traditional power struggles and political goals overlapped with ideological issues, and the intervention became part of a Fascist crusade against the Leftist Popular Front coalition government that came to power in France in January 1936.[11] Most of all, when Mussolini heard of the German intervention, he also thought that by aligning himself with the German policy in Spain this would strengthen the bond between Fascist Italy and Nazi Germany. Lastly, promoting through the 'Fascistization' of Spain the development of a regime ideologically close to the Italian one would have helped the creation of that vital space in the Mediterranean or *mare nostrum* that Rome desired.[12]

## The Italian Air Force and the Spanish Civil War

The *Regia Aeronautica* was the first of the Italian armed forces to arrive in Spain. On 30 July 1936, 12 SM.81 bombers were sent to Franco to transport his troops from Morocco to metropolitan Spain. Three planes were lost on the journey though, and

8 About the contacts between the Spanish Monarchists and the Italian regime see: Ismael Campos Saz, *Mussolini contra la II Repùblica* (Valencia: Alfons El Magnanim, 1986).

9 Data based on Angel Viñas, 'La conniviencia fascista con la sublevaciòn military otros éxitos de la trama civil', in Francisco Sanchez Perez (ed.), *Los Mitos del 18 de julio* (Barcellona: Contrastes, 2013), pp. 79-182.

10 Morten Heiberg, *Emperadores del Mediterráneo: Franco, Musolini y la guerra civil española* (Barcelona: Critica, 2004), pp. 41-44.

11 In particular, Coverdale stressed the importance of the Italian intervention to avoid the consolidation of the Spanish popular front: John F. Coverdale, *I fascisti Italiani alla guerra di Spagna* (Rome-Bari: Laterza, 1977), p. 73.

12 Collotti, *Fascismo e politica di potenza*, pp. 298-300; Brian Sullivan, 'Fascist Italy's Military Involvement in the Spanish Civil War', *The Journal of Military History*, 9:4 (Oct. 1995), p. 702.

most of the aircraft that brought the Nationalist troops to Spain were the Junkers 52s sent by Hitler.[13] This was an unintentional foreshadowing of the general trends that would shape Italian air advising, a situation heavily influenced by the crisis then afflicting the Italian Air Force, as well as the context in which it operated in Spain, specifically German competition.

The *Regia Aeronautica* was established by the Fascist government in 1923 despite the opposition of the other two armed forces. In Italy, the choice to create an independent air force was essentially due to two reasons: 1) the influence of Giulio Douhet's theories on strategic bombing and hence on the necessity of an independent air arm capable of putting this into practice; and 2) the Fascist will to exploit the air force as a propaganda instrument.[14] These two factors peaked during the period in which Italo Balbo was First Undersecretary (1926-1929) and later Minister of Aeronautics (1929-1933). In particular, Balbo turned the air force into an efficient military organization and pushed relevant technological advances that allowed Italian aviation to set many world records and to perform the transoceanic flights that led the Italian planes visiting South America in 1931 and the United States in 1933.[15]

In reality though, these achievements hid some inherent structural weaknesses. In the middle of the 1930s, the Italian aircraft industry entered a phase of technological stagnation: Italian aircraft manufacturers, knowing they could depend on state orders fueled by the Ethiopian and Spanish wars, chose to continue to produce the existing models, sacrificing innovation to profitability.[16] Furthermore, the Fascist wars absorbed resources that were necessary to support Italian rearmament for the coming great European conflict that Mussolini considered unavoidable. At the same time, especially after Balbo's resignation and the nomination of Giuseppe Valle (1933-1939) as Undersecretary of the Air Force, aviation entered a phase of 'doctrinal confusion'. The *Regia Aeronautica* lacked the numbers and technological capability to act as a strategic bomber force. At the same time, the creation of an independent air force had led to growing inter-service rivalry with the army and the navy. These tensions helped contribute to a lack of planes adequate for air-to-ground and air-to-sea missions, and

13 Raymond L. Proctor, *Hitler's Luftwaffe in the Spanish Civil War* (Westport: Praeger, 1983), pp. 11-38.

14 The most accessible account in English about Douhet and his importance in Italy is Thomas Hippler, *Bombing the People, Giulio Douhet and the Foundations of Air Power Strategy, 1884-1939* (Cambridge: Cambridge University Press, 2013), in particular, pp. 115-218; On the use of the air force as a propaganda instrument, see Marco Di Giovanni, 'L'aviazione e I miti del fascismo', in Paolo Ferrari (ed.), *L'aeronautica Italiana una storia del Novecento* (Milan: Franco Angeli, 2004), pp. 203-228; Erich Lehman, *Le ali del potere, la propaganda aeronautica nell'Italia fascista* (Turin: Utet, 2010).

15 Giorgio Rochat, *Italo Balbo aviatore e Ministro dell'Aeronautica* (Ferrara: Boloventa, 1979), pp. 46-144; Claudio G. Segrè, *Italo Balbo, A Fascist Life* (Berkley: University of California Press, 1990), pp. 145-288.

16 Fortunato Minniti, 'La politica industriale del ministero dell'aeronautica. Mercato, Pianificazione, Sviluppo', *Storia contemporanea*, 12:1-2 (Feb-Apr. 1981), pp. 5-55, 271-312.

made it impossible to develop effective tactical ground support and naval air support doctrines.[17] Despite this, in Spain the Italian air force was employed mainly as tactical support for the nationalist ground forces—as well as their German allies—achieving some operational effectiveness.[18]

Another factor causing difficulties for the Italian advising effort was the growing obsolescence of the Italian aircraft, especially when compared to the German ones. For example, at the beginning of the war, Italy effectively employed its Fiat CR.32 fighters. These only had a top speed of 375 kilometers per hour (km/h) in level flight, but were very maneuverable biplanes. Despite its inferiority, CR.32 pilots scored remarkable successes against the more modern Soviet low wing monoplane fighter, the Polikarpov I-16, provided by the Soviets to the Republicans, which had a top speed of 450 km/h. However, starting in March 1937, the first models of Messerschmitt Bf-109 appeared in Spain. The first versions of the German fighter were capable of 470 km/h and had radio equipment that allowed them to be used in formations of two or three aircraft. The Bf-109 rapidly proved far superior to the Soviet I-16.[19] As we will see, the Spaniards were aware of this technical superiority which, combined with the Condor Legion's operational skills, played a decisive role in determining the outcome of Italian air advising in Spain.

## The Early Stages of the Italian Intervention: A Lost Opportunity

After the delivery of the SM.81s, the Italian effort in Spain increased during August and September 1936. Both Italy and Germany sent equipment and military missions, hoping that the Nationalists could manage to quickly conquer Madrid and end the war. Unfortunately for the Fascist powers, the Republican resistance proved far more resilient than expected, and in November the Nationalists were stopped at the capital's eastern outskirts. In December, the rebel offensive ceased. The Nationalist units were now so weak that direct Italian and German intervention seemed necessary to prevent a Republican victory.[20]

17 Giorgio Rochat, *Le guerre italiane, Dall'Impero d'Etiopia alla disfatta* (Turin: Einaudi, 2005), pp. 230-235; Brian R. Sullivan, 'The Downfall of Regia Aeronautica', in Robert S. Higham and Stephen J. Harris (eds), *Why Air Forces Fail: The Anatomy of Defeat* (Frankfurt: University Press of Kentucky, 2006), pp. 135-176.

18 For the narrative of Italian air operations in Spain see: Ferdinando Pedriali, *Guerra di Spagna e aviazione legionaria* (Rome: Usam, 1992); Pedriali's narrative, however, is very able in bypassing all aspects of terror bombing against cities and civilians. For a history of these operations, see Solè I Sabatè, Josep Maria, and Villaroya Joan, *España en llamas, La Guerra civil desde el aire* (Madrid: Temas de hoy, 2003), pp. 23-74, 170-186, 191-197.

19 The best analysis of these aspects is Lucio Ceva, 'L'aeronautica italo-fascista nella guerra civile spagnola (1936-1939)', in Lucio Ceva, *Spagne, 1936-1939: Politica e guerra civile* (Milan: Franco Angeli, 2010), pp. 339-346.

20 Paul Preston, *Francisco Franco, La lunga vita del Caudillo* (Milan: Mondadori, 1993), pp. 207-208; Anthony Beevor, *The Battle for Spain: The Spanish Civil War, 1936-1939*,

The initial Italian assistance consisted of material aid and a small amount of troops to bolster Franco's forces. On 4 September 1936, the Italian Military Mission (*Missione Militare Italiana in Spagna*, MMIS), arrived at Franco's headquarters. Its officers were Lieutenant-Colonel Emilio Faldella, Captain Carlo Sirombo and the *Regia Aeronautica's* Lieutenant-Colonel Pilot Ruggiero Bonomi.[21] Part of the mission's goal was to organize the Italian advisors sent to Spain to train the Nationalist forces in the use of the various military technology provided by Mussolini's regime.[22]

In the air force realm, while the Germans established the Condor Legion (October 1936), the Italians were integrated into a fictional Nationalist unit, the *Aviaciòn del Tercio*, (Tercio Air Force or Spanish Foreign Legion air units) which consisted of the Italian volunteer pilots sent by the *Regia Aeronautica*. In total, by 1 December 1936 118 Italian and 162 German aircraft had been sent to Spain. However, this phase was characterized by the immediate German willingness to provide material to the Francoists. In fact, in mid-November, General Alfredo Kindelán, commander of the Nationalist air force, could count on 12 bombers, three fighters, and nine reconnaissance planes, all provided by Germany, compared with just six reconnaissance planes from Italy.[23] Four Spanish pilots were integrated in the *Aviaciòn del Tercio*, where they were given a brief training course by Italian instructors.[24] This was an early form of air advising, but it was not structured and its only aim was to use the Nationalist pilots to maximize all the available resources for Franco's advance towards Madrid. Indeed, on 8 November 1936 Roatta declared that if some planes had to be given to the Spanish, the bulk of them still had to be used by Italians.[25]

Hitler limited the German involvement in Spain with the aim of prolonging a conflict that he knew would distract the western powers from his moves in Austria and Czechoslovakia. At the same time, he aimed to extend the German economic influence over that country, building informal hegemony, opposed to the one the Third Reich would try to establish over Europe in the imminent global conflict.[26] For that reason, already in December 1936 the German dictator decided that the dimensions of the Condor Legion, the mixed air-land unit sent by the Nazis to Spain, were to remain limited. Even more important, given the need to train the Nationalists

E-edition (London: Phoenix, 2006), ref. 516.

21 Alberto Rovighi and Filippo Stefani, *La partecipazione italiana alla guerra civile spagnola*, Vol. 1, *Dal luglio 1936 alla fine del 1937* (Rome: Ussme, 1992), p. 129.

22 Alcofar Nassaes and Josè Luis, *CTV, Los Legionarios Italiano en la guerra civil espanola, 1936-1939* (Barcelona: Dopesa, 1972), pp. 42-46.

23 Coverdale, *I fascisti italiani*, pp. 101-2; Pedriali, *Guerra di Spagna*, p. 138.

24 Alfredo Logoluso, *Gli Assi del Fiat CR.32 nella guerra civile Spagnola* (Gorizia: Leg, 2012), pp. 77-80.

25 Stefani Rovighi, *La partecipazione italiana*, Vol. I, documenti, n. 13, MMIS al Ministero della guerra, Servizio informazioni militari, per cc. Ministeri F.A. e Esteri, Salamanca 8 novembre 1936, p. 67.

26 Pierpaolo Barbieri, *Hitler's Shadow Empire, Nazi Economy and the Spanish Civil War* (Cambridge, MA: Harvard University Press, 2015), p. 3.

in the use of the armaments Germany had provided, the Germans started to train some officers of the Francoist army.[27]

In contrast, after it became clear that Madrid was not going to fall, Mussolini's priority was to end the conflict as soon as possible. Hence, in November a clear escalation of the Italian intervention began. On 7 December 1936, the *'Ufficio S'* (Office S for *Spagna/Spain*) was established at the Ministry of Foreign Affairs to manage the contacts between Rome and Franco. Meanwhile, the *Comando*—later *Corpo—Truppe Volontarie* (CTV) (Voluntary Troops Command, later Corps) was created to unite all Italian military forces involved in Spain. Between the end of November 1936 and February 1937, 49,332 men, as well as 554 artillery pieces and 81 light tanks, reached Spain. The Italian Air Force was strengthened as well, with the constitution of the *Aviazione Legionaria* (Legionary Air Force) on 28 December 1937. The new air unit was independent from the Tercio air force and was supplied with a total of 21 bombers, 86 fighters, and 23 planes of other types. Its mission was to support land operations, both Spanish and Italian. All Italian units, both air and land, were under the command of General Roatta in order to promote inter-service cooperation.[28]

It must also be said that the Spaniards, at least for the time being, were not so much interested in being advised as in receiving airplanes. The Nationalist rebels had succeeded in keeping the control of the bulk of the army, but the navy and the air force had largely remained on the Republican side. In July 1936, Spain's Air Force had 241 operational aircraft and another 71 in reserve, mainly old French-made Breguet-XIX bombers.[29] When the civil war began, the air ministry's leaders and the 1st Air Fleet, which was made up of the largest and most modern units, were in Madrid or its surrounding areas—a fact that enabled the Republicans to assume their control.[30] As for the pilots, some two-thirds of these lined up with the Republicans while the remainder chose the Nationalists, the latter could thus immediately count on a small number of highly trained fighter pilots.[31]

27 Robert H. Whealey, *Hitler and Spain: The Nazi Role in the Spanish Civil War, 1936-1939* (Frankfurt, KY: University Press of Kentucky, 1989), pp. 50, 55-56, 67-68.

28 Stefani Rovighi, *La partecipazione italiana*, I, pp. 151, 180-181; Coverdale, *I fascisti italiani*, p. 248.

29 Sole I Sabate, Villaroya, *España en llamas*, p. 15.

30 George Esenwein, 'Spanish Civil War: Franco's Nationalist Army', in Wayne H. Bowen and José E. Alvarez (eds), *A Military History of Modern Spain, From the Napoleonic Era to the International War on Terror* (Westport: Praeger, 2007) p. 76; Rafael A. Permuy López, *Air War Over Spain: Aviators, Aircraft and Air Units of the Nationalist and Republican Air Forces, 1936-1939* (Hersham: Ian Allan, 2009), pp. 10-11.

31 Jesus Salas Larrazabal, *Air War Over Spain* (London: Littlehampton, 1974), pp. 45-46; Michel Alpert, *The Republican Army in the Spanish Civil War, 1936-1939* (Cambridge: Cambridge University Press, 2007), p. 235. In 1937, only 65 officers of the Republican air forces were from the pre-war ranks of the Spanish Air Force, while in February 1937, 333 air force officers were dismissed from the ranks, many of whom were with Franco.

The Francoists therefore initially had more trained pilots than available planes, which resulted in less need for Italian personnel to carry out training and advising. This was illustrated by a 31 December 1936 meeting at the Nationalist HQ in Salamanca In the presence of the commander of the *Aviazione Legionaria*, General Vincenzo Velardi, Franco, and General Kindelán, the latter insisted upon receiving 15 to 20 Ro.37 reconnaissance planes, in addition to the six he had already been provided. He did not want any Italian pilots, claiming 'he had the necessary Spanish pilots'.[32]

The Italians, for their part, avoided discussing the issue. Mussolini was interested in winning the quickest victory possible and the direct employment of the Italian units was surely more expedient than an effort to form Spanish ones. In fact, on 4 January 1937 Undersecretary Valle, while discussing the issue with the dictator, highlighted that it was necessary to provide the Spaniards with the planes they had requested because it would free-up Italian and German air force units. In particular, Valle was willing to cede to the Spanish some fighters and reconnaissance planes (20 CR.32, 2 CR.20, 4 Cant, and 15 Ro.37), some with dual controls for training Nationalist pilots. The intent was to give the Spaniards some autonomy to conduct minor operations, in particular reconnaissance flights for the Nationalist army and navy, a type of operation considered of minor importance in the Italian air doctrine. In the end, the Duce approved the transfer in order to concentrate the *Aviazione Legionaria* on the conduct of more decisive air operations.[33]

For the moment, the MMIS had duties that were essentially operational, so the Italian aviation officers focused their efforts on how to work and coordinate with the Spanish and German units that were part of Nationalist Aviation. In fact, in Valle's opinion 'there is no need to set up a training course for the Spanish pilots since they have managed well so far'.[34] Substantially, in order to ingratiate themselves with the Spaniards, the Italians trusted in advising less than in 'a totalitarian use …that would give the Spanish government a taste of the Italian Air Force potential'.[35]

As a result, the possibility of establishing their first 'bridgehead' for the organization of the Nationalist Air Force was lost, limiting the training provided for the Spanish to the few pilots of the first CR.32s dispatched to the Nationalists. This is in marked contrast with the Italian Naval Mission (MNI—Missione Navale Italiana) established in Cadiz on 3 October 1936, which was also officially under the control of the MMIS. However, due to its greater autonomy, and the fact that it was less directly involved in

32 Archivio storico dell'Aeronautica militare (ASAM), Operazioni militari Spagna (OMS), Sottoserie (SS.) 7, busta (b.) 76, fascicolo (f. 11), Relazione sulla riunione del 31/12/36 al quartier generale spagnolo, p. 2.

33 ASAM, OMS, SS7, b. 76, f. 15, Ministero dell'Aeronautica, Gabinetto Prot. n. 197 'OMS', Promemoria per il capo dell' US, Decisioni di S.E. il Capo del governo, 4 January 1937, p. 3.

34 ASMAE, Gabinetto del ministro e del segretario generale, 1923-1943, b. 1207, Verbale della riunione a Palazzo Venezia del 6 dicembre 1936, p. 9.

35 ASAM, OMS, SS7, b. 124, n. 4, Missione compiuta in Spagna dal 24 al giorno 29 dicembre 1936, p. 15.

military operations, it could focus more on naval advising, and this reduced German competition. Also, from the outset the naval advisory effort envisaged a reorganization of the Nationalist navy on a long-term basis.[36]

## Italian Air Advising Takes Off

In Mussolini's opinion, the massive delivery of aid and the creation of the CTV would be enough to launch a winning offensive against Madrid. However, the Republicans at Guadalajara (8-23 March 1937) stopped the CTV's offensive against the capital. The Italian defeat tarnished the country's international prestige and induced the Fascist leaders not only to persist in the intervention, but it also created a desire for revenge by strengthening their direct support for the Spaniards.[37]

The Italian Air Force activity in Spain also enlarged its objectives, employing the Douhetian strategy of terror bombings launched against Spanish cities, especially from 1938.[38] The aforementioned 'totalitarian' use of aerial warfare seems to have been superficially applied in the spring of 1938 through the bombing of Barcelona (16-18 March 1938), which caused over 1,100 deaths and 2,000 injuries. However, not only did the bombing fail to cause the morale of the Catalan population to collapse as expected by the Italians, it also brought protests from Franco.[39] As we will see, this had important consequences for Italian air advising.

The growing Italian support to Franco's military forces led also to an increase in the Italian advising efforts. In April 1937, in the aftermath of the Guadalajara battle and after learning of similar German initiatives, the CTV command decided to establish some 'Italian training courses for Spanish officers' (*Corsi italiani addestramento ufficiali spagnoli*, CIAUS). In the words of the director of the courses, Colonel Emilio Battisti, the aim of the initiative was:

> To take part in the direction of the training and the preparation of the Spanish officers and, under a broader and more forward looking point of view, to pave the way to put Italian officers into the heart of the work of reorganization of what

36 See Fabio De Ninno, 'The Fascist Naval Missions to Persia, China, and Spain: Commerce and Strategy in Mussolini's Navy, 1933-1940', in Donald Stoker and Michael T. McMaster (eds), *Naval Advising and Assistance: History, Challenges, and Analysis* (Solihull: Helion, 2017), pp. 175-200.

37 Collotti, *Fascismo e politica di potenza*, p. 319; Coverdale, *I fascisti italiani*, p. 256.

38 Heiberg, *Emperadores del Mediterraneo*, pp. 118-135.

39 Coverdale, *I fascisti italiani*, pp. 323-324; The details of the operations are in Pedriali, *Guerra di Spagna e aviazione legionaria*, pp. 351-355; however, Pedriali insists that the bombardments were aiming at military targets, but this statement is not reliable according to the leading historian of the Italian air force, Ceva, *L'aeronautica italo-fascista nella Guerra civile spagnola*, pp. 330-337, Heiberg contested Pedriali as well, cfr. Ivi, p. 134.

> tomorrow will be the army of Nationalist Spain, introducing doctrine, methods, procedures, arms and materials.[40]

Clearly, the CTV command had understood the long term advantages that could be obtained with such an initiative, so from a realistic perspective it appears that the members of the MMIS clearly were aware of the opportunities offered by military advising. On the whole, in the course of the entire civil war this activity greatly expanded. The Italians held 156 courses for Spanish personnel, preparing 260 senior officers, 5,000 junior officers, and 20,000 troops, 10,000 of which received specialized training. The courses included basic training for infantry, cavalry, and artillery, and a school for radio-telegraphers and telephone operators. Groups of instructors also were dispatched to the Nationalist military academies.[41] In comparison, the air advising effort was developed far more slowly and was smaller, a sort of 'poor cousin' in comparison with the army.

In the same month in which Italy launched courses for the army, the *Aviazione Legionaria* offered to start an air training initiative for the Spaniards. On 1 April 1937, Minister of Foreign Affairs Galeazzo Ciano told Roatta that it was possible to have Spanish pilots trained in Italy. However, for the moment the Italians did not follow-up on this proposal, and when a couple of weeks later Franco asked for 20 CR.32 fighters and four BA.65 bombers that had just arrived in Spain, Ciano answered that the planes would be available to the Nationalists but only 'with Italian personnel'.[42]

Essentially, a window had opened, but while the army was trying to exploit it, the air force was blocked by the persistent Italian reluctance to transfer material to the Nationalists. Furthermore, the difficulties in starting any advising activities were reflected in the relative coolness of the relationship between the Nationalists and the Italians in those months. Franco in particular had welcomed with a certain satisfaction the Italian defeat at Guadalajara for it had let him escape perceptions of excessive Italian influence that the presence of the CTV risked creating.[43] At the same time, the differences among the policies of the Italian Army, Navy, and Air Force about advising was a clear manifestation of the lack of cooperation and reflected interservice rivalry among the three services at an institutional level; each of them essentially operated on their own.

40 ASMAE, Gabinetto del ministro e del segretario generale, 1923-1943, b.1207, Direzione corsi addestramento ufficiali spagnoli, N. 1333 di protocollo CIA, Progetto riordinamento CIAUS, 2 settembre 1937, p. 2.

41 Alberto Rovighi and Filippo Stefani, *La partecipazione italiana alla guerra civile spagnola, 1936-1939,* Vol. II, *Dall'autunno 1937 all'estate 1939* (Rome: Ussme, 1993), p. 480.

42 ASMAE, Gabinetto del ministro e del segretario generale, 1923-1943, b.1207, Ciano a Colli, Telegramma in partenza n. 842, 14 aprile 1937.

43 Stanley G. Payne and Jesùs Palacios, *Franco: A Personal and Political Biography* (Madison: University of Wisconsin Press, 2014), p. 177.

As the war continued through the spring and the summer of 1937, the general conditions of the conflict changed dramatically. In June 1937, the Nationalists managed to conquer Bilbao, but during the summer the Republicans launched their offensives around Madrid and in Aragon, proving that their army had managed to reorganize effectively.[44] Though the offensives could not break the Nationalist front, they were used by the Nationalists to ask for additional assistance from Italy, including a submarine campaign against Republican sea lines of communication as well as more planes. Furthermore, it was Franco's strategy to slowly and methodically conquer Spanish territory, which made a continuous expansion of his armed forces necessary. The Nationalists increased their pressure on Rome to deliver more planes to bolster Italian involvement in the Spanish Civil War in order to provide at least some air cover over all their forces. Indeed, according to the Francoists the lack of planes was 'the root of the precarious situation of the Spanish Air Force, which cannot draw from its own resources, so that it needs the constant help of the Italian formations'.[45]

At the same time, Mussolini had decided to support Franco at any cost and now was willing to provide him with what he asked for.[46] Another relevant factor was that the economic relations established between Nationalist Spain and Italy, which now seemed to favor the transfer of Italian military equipment to the Nationalists. In fact, until that moment part of the Italian opposition to supplying material support was due to Spain's difficulty in paying for the supplies. On 21 December 1936, the Nationalists made a clearing agreement with Rome (to avoid having to transfer funds) according to which the material already sent to the Spaniards was to be paid for with shipments of food and raw materials. However, the Spaniards often defaulted, making the Italians not very inclined to keep sending their military supplies, at least until a new agreement was reached between Ciano and Franco on 11 August 1937 specifically addressing the transfer of armaments.[47] In particular, the Italian aeronautic industry was taking advantage of the civil war to install itself inside the Spanish market, a move that allowed them to displace the French in the dominant role. In March 1937 an agreement between FIAT and Hispano-Suiza for the transfer of licenses for the repair, assembly, and construction of the CR.32 in a Seville factory was signed. Later, in the summer of 1938, that agreement lead to the transfer to the Spanish firm of the license for the building of 100 CR.32s; the fuselages were built in Spain and the engines imported from Italy.[48] Meanwhile, fear of German competition grew in

44 Alpert, *The Republican Army*, p. 258.

45 ASAM, OMS, SS7, b. 76, f. 12, Cuartel general del generalissimo, Estado Mayor 3 Secciòn al Generale Mancini (Roatta), Jefe de la Mision Italiana, Salamanca, 25 septiembre 1937.

46 Rovighi, Stefani, *La partecipazione italiana,* I, p. 374.

47 Felice Guarnieri, *Battaglie economiche tra le due grandi guerre,* Vol. II, *1936-1940* (Milano: Garzanti, 1953), pp. 130-134.

48 Gianluca Balestra, 'L'industria aeronautica italiana in Spagna, 1936-1938', *Spagna contemporanea*, 2:3 (1993), pp. 82-83; Larrazabal, *Air War Over Spain*, p. 241.

the spring of 1937 since the Germans had sent some 50 military advisors to serve at the Falangist training schools for junior combat officers. The following April, these German advisors were incorporated into the Nationalist army training facilities.[49] These concerns were recorded in a May 1937 report drafted by a Ministry of Foreign Affairs delegate after his return from Spain. He reported the growing effectiveness of the Nazi penetration of the aeronautic field, explaining that the Germans were not just focusing on the war. They were also working hard on economic penetration of Spain. All the purchases of German material reported to a single agency, named HISMA (Hispano-Maroqui de transportes/Spanish-Moroccan transport society). In the field of aeronautics in particular, not only did they need to provide good bombers and decent fighters for the battlefield (their task had been made easier by the availability of the fast Messerschmitt), they had managed to obtain all that they wanted from the Spanish government in terms of long-term economic penetration.[50]

The new circumstances drove a rapid expansion of the Nationalist Air Force via Italian material. By 2 September 1937, the Spaniards had been provided with a total of eight SM.79s, eight CA.135s, 10 CR.32s, six Ro.37s, and eight Cant Z.501 seaplanes.[51] Also, on 15 November, another eight SM.79s had been sent to the Nationalists, as well as a second tranche of 16 planes that were in the process of being shipped.[52] At the end of 1937, the Spanish Air Force had 150 frontline planes. These included earlier versions of German Junker-52 bombers, new Italian SM.79s and SM.81s, and four squadrons of CR.32 fighters.[53]

Such a massive dispatch of material to the Spaniards put an emphasis on the needed training of the personnel for combat and maintenance. Consequently, in October 1937, Ciano took advantage of the situation to force the Nationalists to send some of their personnel to train in Italy, telling them that such things would prove essential in the event, now still uncertain, of an evacuation of the Legionary air forces. The Italians also repeatedly told Franco to establish his own air force by sending cadets to Italian schools. 'If he had done that', Ciano insisted, 'today he would already have a remarkable pilot corps. While much time has been wasted, please talk to Franco again about the issue, and advise him to prepare a group of Spanish pilots as soon as possible'.[54]

49 Payne, *Franco and Hitler*, p. 28.

50 ASMAE, Gabinetto del ministro e del segretario generale, 1923-1943, b. 1264, Rapporto del mag. Casero a S.E. il ministro, Legnano, 12 maggio 1937, pp. 2-3.

51 ASMAE, Gabinetto del ministro e del segretario generale, 1923-1943, b. 1264, Ministero dell'aeronautica, Gabinetto del Ministro, Aeroplani della R. Aeronautica inviati in OMS a tutto il 22 settembre 1937.

52 ASMAE, Gabinetto del ministro e del segretario generale, 1923-1943, b. 1264, Valle a Ciano, visto da Mussolini, 15 November 1937.

53 Beevor, *The Battle for Spain*, ref. 847, 2; Larrazabal, *Air War Over Spain*, p. 204.

54 ASMAE, Gabinetto del ministro e del segretario generale, 1923-1943, b. 1264, Ciano a Berti, Telegramma in partenza n. 2598, 17 ottobre 1937.

Indeed, on 5 October 1937 the first 25 Spanish pilots reached the aerial training schools of Arezzo, Falconara, Firenze, Grosseto, Lucca, Pescara, Pisa, Pistoia, and Parma, and another 50 arrived in December.[55] Overall, by September 1938, Italian air schools had awarded 92 pilot licenses to Spanish aviators.[56]

In November, as an exchange and with the obvious goal of remaining as free from the MMIS as it could, the *Jefatura del Aire* (Air Directorate—The Nationalist analogue of an Air Ministry) asked for the dispatch to Spain of specialists for the training of pilots and the preparation of 1,100 technical personnel.[57] By 29 November, Mussolini had approved the dispatch of the required instructors, and in December the specialists departed for duties in Spain. Additionally, the Ministry of Aeronautics dispatched four fighter pilots as instructors at the fighter school of the Spanish Nationalist government. Also, 60 specialists were seconded to the Spanish Air Force as coverage for the current deficiencies of that arm, and a good number of these personnel were employed as instructors at the specialist training school of Franco's air force. Finally, 50 Spanish pilots were sent to Italy for training in addition to the 50 already there.[58]

At this point, after a year and a half of troubles, Italian air advising had finally begun to gather momentum, proceeding with the instruction of Spanish pilots and specialists. The majority of these flew or worked on the CR.32 fighters forming the bulk of the Nationalist fighter force, or the new SM.79 bombers provided by Italy. In addition, 60 Italian specialists had to serve under the direction of the *Jefatura* under the terms of special contracts similar to the other Italian military missions serving foreign governments; these were identical to those of the MNI.[59]

In the wake of the successes of the *Aviazione Legionaria*, however, the Italians underrated the weight of looming German competition. Colonel Drago, the commander of the air advising units, was well aware of the danger, however. By 2 December 1937, he had proposed expanding the existing instructional facilities before the Germans did so first:

> About the schools, while considering that the installation of proper schools requires much time, it should not be difficult to send in the meantime an

55 ASMAE, Gabinetto del ministro e del segretario generale, 1923-1943, b. 1264, Telespresso n. 9175, Ministero dell'aeronautica a ministero degli esteri, 15 ottobre 1937; ASMAE, Gabinetto del ministro e del segretario generale, 1923-1943, b. 1264, Telespresso 12437, Allievi piloti spagnoli nelle scuole di pilotaggio 30 dicembre 1937.

56 ASMAE, Gabinetto del ministro e del segretario generale, 1923-1943, b. 1264, Ministero dell'aeronautica a Ministero degli affari esteri, Allievi Piloti di nazionalità spagnola istruiti in Italia, prot. 22057, 7 settembre 1938.

57 ASMAE, Gabinetto del ministro e del segretario generale, 1923-1943, b. 1264, Promemoria per il mistero degli affari esteri, Ufficio 'S', 12419, 4 dicembre 1937.

58 ASMAE, Gabinetto del ministro e del segretario generale, 1923-1943, b. 1264, Appunto per Ciano, Ufficio Spagna, 2 dicembre 1937.

59 ASMAE, Gabinetto del ministro e del segretario generale, 1923-1943, b. 1264, Prot. 13105, Personale specializzato presso reparti Spagnoli, 18 dicembre 1937.

> officer and some specialists to each Spanish squadron in order to prepare the Spanish personnel to receive our material in the shortest time possible. It is my opinion, however, that it is necessary to already have something down on paper concerning the proper schools, both for training pilots and specialists, in order to avoid the Germans preceding us. (Today an officer of the German Air Ministry left for Berlin by air after having long consulted with General Kindelán about that issue). I will inform the Ambassador about that tonight.[60]

In the middle of May 1938, General Giuseppe Valle also sent a note to Ciano in which he underlined that intelligence sources had informed him that the arrival of a German air advisory mission was imminent. Valle suggested that Franco should ask for an Italian mission:

> I am receiving these days trustworthy reports about negotiations and measures in course between the Spanish and German governments regarding some important tasks that would be trusted to the latter concerning the post-war military reorganization.
>
> I do not need to highlight to you Italian aviation's extremely effective contribution, in both action and value, in Spain…I just believe it would be convenient to add value to such a contribution and to its recognition by trying to counterpoise our penetration effort to the ones of other nations. If, as I believe, you agree, I hope you would ask our ambassador in Salamanca to address the Spanish government so that Generalissimo Franco would officially ask for the dispatch to Spain of an aeronautic mission which, since now or since the end of the operations, should provide for the reorganization of Nationalist aviation.[61]

The issue involved Mussolini as well, who on 5 July 1938 demanded news about 'the means of the *Regia Aeronautica's* penetration in Spain'.[62] Pressured by the Air Ministry and by the Duce, the Minister of Foreign Affairs asked the ambassador to Nationalist Spain, Count Viola di Campalto, to investigate the status of the relations between the Germans and the Spaniards on air advising. The ambassador replied that any negotiation between the Burgos government and the Germans concerning the latter's post-conflict role about air-advising could be excluded.[63] According to Campalto the

60 ASAM, OMS, SS7, b. 76, f. 8, Promemoria per il Sig. Generale Comandante, T. Colonnello Pilota, Carlo Drago, Salamanca, 3 novembre 1937, p. 1.

61 ASMAE, Gabinetto del ministro e del segretario generale, 1923-1943, b. 1231, Valle a Ciano, 14 maggio 1938.

62 ASMAE, Gabinetto del ministro e del segretario generale, 1923-1943, b. 1264, Ministero dell'Aeronautica al ministero degli esteri, Ufficio 'S', Prot. N. 14505, 5 luglio 1938.

63 ASMAE, Gabinetto del ministro e del segretario generale, 1923-1943, b. 1231, Telespresso 3604/1135, Viola di Campalto a Regio ministero degli affari esteri, 25 luglio 1938, p. 1.

Italian materials, the fighters in particular, were considered vastly superior to the German ones, and Italian instructors were prevalent in all the schools established by the Nationalist air force.[64]

The ambassador's argument was not unfounded. Since 1937, the air advising work of the *Aviazione Legionaria* had been greatly increased following Drago's proposal on the expansion of the schools. A July 1938 report, drafted as an answer to Mussolini's demand, described the status of the 'Specialist School of Málaga'. This training facility was launched in March 1938 with the support of General Kindelán, to train 500 selected specialists in five month courses with Italian instructors for motor, mechanical, electrical, and radio equipment.[65] Also, by early 1938, a 'Fighter School' was established at Gallur to train Spanish pilots.[66] In both schools Italian personnel trained the Spaniards in substantial numbers:

| The Composition of the Schools Established by the *Aviazione Legionaria* (July 1938)* | | |
|---|---|---|
| | Specialist School of Malaga | Fighter School |
| Officers | 1 Colonel (School Commandant); 1 pilot major; 5 troop specialists (instructors); | 1 pilot major; 4 instructor pilots |
| Non-commissioned officers and troops | 12 non-commissioned officers; 20 troop specialists | N.A. |
| Material available | Mostly didactic material | Planes: 16 Ro.41, 6 CR.20, 1 CR.30. Various replacements for planes and engines |
| Number of cadets | ca. 500 | 20 |

* Data based on: ASMAE, Gabinetto del ministro e del segretario generale, 1923-1943, b. 1264, Mezzi di penetrazione della R. Aeronautica in Spagna, Appunto per il Duce, 5 luglio 1938, p. 1.

According to the report, the Spanish officers, who often visited the schools, were satisfied with the progress. Most importantly, it was highlighted how the two schools,

64 Ivi, p. 2.

65 Archivio Historico de l'Ejército del Aire (AHEA), SIG. N 2730-3, Estado Mayor del Aire, Nota confidencial sobre la creaciòn y puesta in funcionamento de una scuola de mecanicos y especialistas de aviacion con profesorado italiano en Malaga, 2 May 1938.

66 ASMAE, Gabinetto del ministro e del segretario generale, 1923-1943, b. 1211, Relazione finale dell'attività dell'ufficio Spagna, 1939, Appunto per il ministro Pietromarchi, Aviazione Legionaria, p. 2.

'If conveniently and promptly expanded, could, once the war was over, create all these other air force institutions that the Italian government, in agreement with the Spanish one, would esteem as appropriate and convenient to install'.[67]

There was also a workshop for the inspection and repair of aircraft, engines, and flight instruments at Tablada, in which both Italian and Spanish personnel worked together. Finally, the report highlighted the importance of the negotiations between FIAT and the Hispano-Suiza, as well as the presence of the 60 Italian specialists dispatched to the Spanish units.[68] Overall, it was hinted that in order to outline an effective penetration strategy for the air advising group, it was necessary to link training to the future shipment of equipment to the Nationalist Air Force.

Italian air advising had now reached a great scale and attained significant importance. However, in its report to the Duce, the Air Ministry underlined that in order to properly exploit the success obtained up to then, it was necessary to plan an actual aviation mission independent from the *Aviazione Legionaria* and hence exempt from operational tasks.[69] At this point, what's surprising is that although the *Regia Aeronautica* actively advocated the necessity of creating a proper air advising mission and then keeping it separated from the *Aviazione Legionaria*, Campalto concluded this analysis by excluding the option to dispatch a mission that was detached from the MMIS for the reason that:

> It appears then doubtless that the future Spanish military air force will want to organize itself—as it already shows—according the model of our own aviation. Hence, this embassy...does not believe that we should insist for the Spanish to welcome an Italian aeronautic mission whose official role could not avoid to be considered—as things are today—premature and hence not appropriate.[70]

As an alternative, he proposed to send a technical advisor to Franco's government to negotiate air force issues.[71] Even more surprising was the reaction of the Undersecretary of the Air Force. On 17 August 1938 he claimed to completely agree with the ambassador's analysis, de facto going back on what he had said until that

67 Ivi, p. 2.
68 Ivi, pp. 2-3.
69 Ibid. The Ministry official wrote in capitals in the original document in order to express the urgency of the matter: 'Regardless of the measures that will be implemented to add value to the means and the activities indicated above, it is essential that, from now on an Italian aeronautic mission will be dispatched to Spain in agreement with the Spanish government, with the goal of establishing and maintaining consistent contact with the national authorities, that would guarantee us in the future.'
70 ASMAE, Gabinetto del ministro e del segretario generale, 1923-1943, b. 1231, Telespresso 3604/1135, Viola di Campalto a Regio ministero degli affari esteri, 25 luglio 1938, p. 2.
71 Ivi, p. 3.

moment both in regard to supposed German competition, and on the issue of the creation of a separate advising mission.[72]

It is clear that there was an inconsistency between the analysis of the *Aviazione Legionaria's* officers and that of the diplomatic personnel, partially caused by the problems of Italian intelligence in Spain. In the Iberian country, the *Servizio informazioni militari* (SIM), the main Italian intelligence agency, answered to the MMIS, then to the 'S' office of the Ministry of Foreign Affairs, but its activity was very limited and mostly focused on the Italians fighting on the Republican side. At the same time, the CTV established its own 'I' (Information) service, which had an aviation section with the task of collecting and decoding military and political information on both the Republicans and Nationalists.[73] Since the CTV reported the information to the Italian military authorities, the supposed news regarding the Germans reported by Valle originated from this source.

It was a chaotic and ineffective organization anyway, which explains the inconsistencies between the information coming from the air force and that provided by the ambassador. However, given the expansion of the training program for ground personnel and the great dimensions that it reached, it should not be assumed that the authorities did not understand the potential of aviation advising to influence the future development of the Spanish Air Force. This is also confirmed by Valle's pressure to expand this effort through the dispatch of an independent mission.

The rejection of the Air Ministry's proposals was probably due to an incorrect political-military analysis by the Italian government, which was convinced that the direct employment of the air force was an advertisement internationally, particularly in Spain, and a better one than an air advising mission. Indeed, according to the Duce, the terror attacks on Spanish cities contributed to exalting the idea of the Italians as people that 'evoke horror for their aggressiveness instead of pleasure as mandolinisti [mandolin performers]'.[74] The Italian use of air power against the civilian population contrasted to the German approach focused on tactical support and damaged Italy's relationship with Franco. One of the main problems for Italian air advising was the lingering myth at the highest levels of the Fascist government that the Italian air force was a potentially decisive strategic weapon.[75]

72 ASMAE, Gabinetto del ministro e del segretario generale, 1923-1943, b. 1231, Telespresso 19737, Ministero dell'aeronautica a ministero degli esteri ufficio S, risp. F. 24634, 17 agosto 1938.

73 Heiberg, *Emperadores del Mediterraneo*, pp. 172-180; Giuseppe Conti, *Una guerra segreta, Il Sim nel secondo conflitto mondiale* (Bologna: Il Mulino, 2008), pp. 37-39; Andrea Vento, *In silenzio gioite e soffrite, Storia dei servizi segreti italiani dal Risorgimento alla Guerra Fredda* (Milan: Il Saggiatore, 2010), pp. 189-190.

74 Ciano, Galeazzo, *Diario 1937-1943, a cura di Renzo De Felice* (Milan: Rizzoli, 1980), 20 March 1938, p. 115.

75 Gooch, *Mussolini and His Generals*, p. 376.

## The Slow Decline of Italian Air Advising

Italian air advising played a key role in turning Spanish Nationalist aviation into an effective force. However, by the end of the civil war, a wide gap existed between the operational qualities of the Condor Legion and the *Aviazione Legionaria*, with relevant consequences for the long run. First of all, given the limited size of the German contingent, the air units of the Condor Legion mostly acted as a support for the Nationalists, while the *Aviazione Legionaria* mainly worked with the CTV. Such a difference had a decisive role in how the Germans managed to win the favor of Franco's generals. The technical factors should be considered as well. Most of the Francoist pilots flew the CR.32, but by the end of 1937 it was increasingly clear that the Bf-109 dominated the Spanish sky. The introduction of dive bombing following the arrival of the Ju-87 'Stuka' in March 1938 marked another decisive demonstration of the technological superiority of the Condor Legion and German aviation equipment.[76]

German superiority was especially clear in the field of tactical cooperation, something for which the Spanish Civil War was a training ground for developing a German air doctrine far superior to the Italian one. The operations which led to the conquest of the north between March and October 1938, and all of the following Nationalist advances repeatedly confirmed the image of the Condor Legion as much more effective than the *Aviazione Legionaria*. Finally, the German military presence was never quite as politically intrusive as the Italian intervention: Wolfram von Richthofen, the commander of the German air forces in Spain from 1 November 1938 (and cousin of the famous Red Baron), was persuaded that the credit for the victory had to be bestowed on Franco for that alone would grant him the legitimacy he needed to rule the country.[77]

Despite the important role exercised by Italian air advising in the expansion of Franco's air force, growing German influence, in combination with Italian complacency had a remarkable influence on the future cooperation between the *Regia Aeronautica* and Nationalist Spain.

The end of the civil war on 1 April 1939 marked the transition to the next phase of Italian air advising as Fascist Italy had now to face the problem of how to capitalize on the political, military, and economic investment it had made during the intervention. Indeed, both Italy and Germany aimed to strengthen their respective relations with Franco, provide military support, and at the same time ensure the Spanish armed forces' dependence on their armaments.[78]

In such a context, military advising was mostly a tool which Rome counted on in order to strengthen the political and economic ties between the two countries. That

76 Details of the operations in Proctor, *Hitler's Luftwaffe*, pp. 117-150.
77 James S. Corum, 'The Luftwaffe in the Spanish Civil War', in John Gooch (ed.), *Air Power, Theory and Practice* (London: Routledge, 1995), pp. 73-80.
78 Preston, *Franco*, p. 325.

was made clear by the creation in July 1939 of a military mission of 60 officers, 90 junior officers, and 50 civilians under the command of General Gastone Gambara, the former chief of staff of the CTV.[79] The importance of the mission was underscored by the fact that Gambara was appointed ambassador to Spain at the end of the summer of 1939.[80]

In the spring of 1939, when the Nationalist victory was near, the opportunity arose to expand the influence of the Italian air force and thus the penetration by Italian aeronautic firms into the Spanish market. In a note drafted in the first quarter of the year, the Air Ministry admitted that the excessive attention given to operations over advising was proving harmful in the long run. Indeed, now that Franco had won, the Italian efforts to penetrate Spain's air force and market were damaged by the *Aviazione Legionaria's* focus on military operations, and its scant consideration for the possible industrial development of postwar Spain. In particular, a spring 1939 report by the Air Ministry underlined the danger that Italian industry might be completely excluded by the future of the Spanish Air Force, despite the paramount role that Fascist Italy expected to play because of its contribution in men and material during the war. The report underlined the interest of the Spanish government in building an autarchic air industry by maintaining the control of the property assets of the Spanish factories, including airplanes and spare parts.[81]

## Trying to Secure the Italian Position

During the last month of the war, in an attempt to regain lost time, the Air Ministry studied a project for collaboration with 'a totalitarian character' with the Spaniards. It was proposed that the installations, materials, and some Italian personnel were to remain in Spain to develop cooperation. The goal was to establish a mission similar to the one then operating in China (1934-1938) where Italian advisors had exploited their role as advisors for Chiang Kai-Shek's air force to convince the Chinese to favor the purchase of equipment from a group of Italian manufacturers.[82]

In early April 1939, a mission formed by one air force officer and one delegate from the 'Consortium of aeronautic exportations' (the organization established by the

79 ACS, Ministero dell'aeronautica, Gabinetto 1939, b. 89, Ministero della guerra a ministero affari esteri, Ufficio 'S' e Ministero delle finanze, Costituzione di una missione militare in Spagna, 24 luglio 1939.

80 Gennaro Carotenuto, *Franco e Mussolini, La Seconda guerra mondiale vista dal Mediterraneo: i destini diversi di due dittatori* (Milan: Sperling & Kupfer, 2005), p. 26.

81 ACS, Ministero dell'aeronautica, Gabinetto 1939, b. 89, Organizzazione industriale aeronautica in Spagna, memo without date, c.a. spring 1939.

82 ACS, Ministero dell'aeronautica, Gabinetto 1939, b. 89, Iniziativa per industria aeronautica in Spagna, prot. 23018, 15 marzo 1939. On the Italian air mission in China, see: Giancarlo Montinaro, 'La missione aeronautica in Cina', in Romain H. Rainero and Paolo Alberini, *Missioni militari italiane all'estero in tempo di pace, 1861-1939* (Rome: Ussme, 2001), pp. 373-394.

Fascist government to gather Italian producers into one cartel), was dispatched to Spain. Thanks to the contacts established by Lieutenant-Colonel Rocco Appignani, the liaison officer of the MMIS at the Nationalist command, the mission was received by Kindelán, the Minister of the Spanish Air Force, and was assured that it was the Spanish government's intention to maintain a 'relative balance' between German and Italian cooperation.[83] The following month, Appignani was appointed the air attaché to Madrid. Valle pressured the Ministry of Foreign Affairs to hasten his appointment:

> Considering the normalization of the Spanish situation, and given the necessity to maintain the friendly relations between the Italian and Spanish air forces after the foreseeable withdrawal of the *Aviazione Legionaria*, this Ministry deems it essential to immediately appoint the *Regia Aeronautica* attaché at the Royal embassy in Spain. The appointment seems even more essential given that the air force attaché, maintaining the current relations with the Spanish authorities, would have the chance to closely follow their [Spain's] air force's necessities and could then positively influence the aviation supplies that will certainly be needed, directing them to the Italian market.[84]

In the following two years, the situation turned against the Italians, mostly because of the autarchic orientation of the new regime, as well as of the pro-German attitude adopted by the senior leadership of the Spanish Air Force following the conflict. This prevented the chances of greater Italian penetration of the Spanish air force.

The Italian companies' attempts to establish an industrial partnership were immediately impeded by the agreements of the new regime in favor of technical cooperation with Germany and by Spain's desire to keep the Spanish aviation industry in Spanish hands. In the spring of 1939, negotiations between Fiat and Hispano-Suiza to start the production of the CR.32 and of its successor the CR.42, succeeded. Even though the Spaniards had shown interest in Siai-Marchetti building the SM.79 bomber in Spain, they would later use Cadiz's Costrucciones Aeronauticas S.A. (CASA) to start the licensed production of 36 Heinkel 111 bombers, followed by the production of the Heinkel 112 fighter. Furthermore, the Spaniards refused to let the Italians buy parts of their companies, preferring to accept their technical expertise while leaving the property in the hands of the government in Madrid.[85] Those choices

83 ACS, Ministero dell'aeronautica, Gabinetto 1939, b. 89, Telegramma cifrato in arrivo, 6/4/ XVIII

84 ASMAE, Gabinetto del ministro e del segretario generale, 1923-1943, b. 1231, Ministero dell'aeronautica a Ministero degli esteri, Ufficio 'S', Nomina dell'addetto aeronautico presso il governo spagnolo, 19 maggio 1939.

85 Gianluca Balestra, 'L'industria aeronautica italiana in Spagna, 1939-1941', *Spagna contemporanea*, 2:4 (1993), pp. 109-113.

were connected to the new regime's broader orientation, which aimed to progressively nationalize the key industries of the defense sector.[86]

The contrast between Italian and Spanish interests was also fueled by the reorganization begun by the Spanish Air Force after the conflict. In the spring of 1939, both the *Aviazione Legionaria* and the Condor Legion left their equipment in the hands of the Nationalists, who also acquired what was left of Republican aviation assets. Overall, the new Spanish Air Force could count on about 1,400 planes from various countries, of which at least 250 were obsolete. The greater part of the fighters were made up of CR.32s, and to a lesser extent Bf-109s, while their bombers were largely a combination of Ju-52s, SM.79s, and He-111s. In the summer of 1939, the new Air Minister, Juan Yagüe, started an important reorganization process. In August, the Air Ministry was established and the air forces were distributed among five air regions and three autonomous aerial zones. The process peaked on the 1 October 1939 with the setting up of the *Ejército del Aire*, the new air force of Francoist Spain.[87]

On 3 October 1939, an impressive project was introduced which envisaged the purchase of 3,200 planes as part of a ten-year air force expansion plan. During the period in which this plan was debated, the initial German victories in World War II contributed to strengthening the pro-German feelings of the Spanish air force leaders. By observing the German operations in Norway, Yagüe himself, together with his successor Vigòn, claimed to be convinced that the *Luftwaffe* would have destroyed the Royal Navy.[88] Then, the Spanish Air Force's attention turned definitively from the *Regia Aeronautica* to the *Luftwaffe*, and in May 1940 a Spanish aviation mission went to Germany to ask for technical assistance. Despite the German claim to not being able to support the Spaniards, the Minister's plan was, however, officially approved by the government on 21 June 1940, right after the fall of France.[89] The Spanish Air Force's pro-German orientation was further strengthened by the fall of Yagüe, who was replaced in June 1940 by Juan Vigón, Franco's Chief of Staff during the war and one of the Nationalist officers most respected by the Germans. A short while later, the Germans were allowed to install two meteorological stations in Spain, which also worked as radio beacons for the *Luftwaffe*, while at the same time providing technical assistance to the Spaniards.[90]

Despite the shift in favor of Nazi Germany, Franco's benevolent feelings towards Mussolini did not diminish, and the relationship between the two dictators remained cordial throughout the 1939-1940 period. When Italy joined the war on 10 June 1940, Franco, pressured by the Duce, declared that Spain was a 'non-belligerent power' and

86 Jordi Mollas-Gallart, *Military Production and Innovation in Spain* (Chur: Harwood Academic Publisher, 1992), p. 46.
87 Larrazabal, *Air War Over Spain*, p. 305.
88 Preston, *Franco*, p. 20.
89 Stanley G. Payne, *Franco and Hitler: Spain, Germany and World War* (New Haven, CT: Yale University Press, 2008), p. 52.
90 Ivi, pp. 117, 236.

assured Mussolini that despite the country being forced into neutrality by economic difficulties, he was willing to provide all the assistance he could. From the spring of 1940, the Spaniards started negotiations with the Germans concerning the possibility of their entry into the war, trying to obtain military support for a possible Spanish attack against Gibraltar and the promise of colonial gains in North Africa. Vigón met the Germans in France at the end of June 1940. Convinced that the *Wehrmacht* was invincible, he asked for support for the re-equipping of Spanish forces. These contacts culminated in the meeting between Franco and Hitler at Hendaye on 23 October 1940, where Spain signed a convention promising to join the war on the Axis side when the Germans deemed it appropriate. However, relations between the two countries remained partially cold because of the Spanish requests for colonies in Africa, in particular the request to expand Equatorial Guinea at the expense of Cameroon, a former German colony Berlin wanted to get back after the war. Furthermore, the Germans asked to install a naval base in the Canary Islands, picturing a future conflict with the United States, but Franco and the major Nationalist officers refused.[91] Moreover, in order to make their armed forces efficient, Spain required massive German support, which the Germans proved, however, unwilling to provide, disliking 'last-minute volunteers for a war which they were convinced was already won'. Later, by the summer 1941, a combination of British economic pressure, acknowledgment of Spain's weakness and the limits of German power, induced Franco's establishment to be more prudent, despite the fact that by this time the Axis dictators wanted Spain to enter the war on their side.[92]

Nevertheless, about military support it was clear that Spain was definitively turning to Germany. The strengthening of the pro-German attitude translated almost immediately into a setback for the Italian hopes of penetration in both the air advising and industrial realms. Indeed, according to a report by the Italian Ministry of Foreign Affairs from August 1940, Vigòn's directives on the future of the Spanish Air Force were to reorganize the Spanish aeronautic industry through the intervention of the state. The Germans would have provided the technology to rebuild the Spanish industry. Hence, other foreign interferences had to be removed. Finally, all the Italian materiel was to be used until exhausted without replacement and with the least necessary maintenance. These trends were confirmed by the news that Vigón was on a mission in Germany at the end of June.[93]

The Spanish decided to renounce Italian support because Rome was only able to provide obsolete fighter planes—like the CR.42 biplane or the G.50 monoplane—inferior in performance to the new production series of the German Bf-109. The

91 Gerhard L. Weinberg, *A World At Arms, A Global History of World War II* (Cambridge: Cambridge University Press, 1994), pp. 177-178.
92 Preston, *The Politics of Revenge*, pp. 53, 57.
93 ACS, Ministero dell'aeronautica, Gabinetto 1940, b. 195, Ministero degli esteri a Ministero aeronautica, Telegramma in partenza n. 22444 P.R. Riorganizzazione industria aeronautica spagnola, 15 agosto 1940.

same was true when it came to dive-bombers. The German campaigns in Poland, Scandinavia, and France had proved the efficiency of the Ju-87 dive bombers, while Italy was unable to produce a comparable plane. The only sector in which there was some competition was level bombing, but even here the *Luftwaffe's* successes thwarted Italy's ambitions. In September 1940, three months after Italy had joined the war, the Siai Marchetti, the producer of the SM.79 bomber, let the Italian Air Ministry know that Vigòn's directives were driving sales to the German aviation industry.[94] In the following years, the Spaniards would sign contracts for the construction of 200 He-111 bombers, 100 Ju-52 transports, and 200 Bf-109 fighters. In the end, few licensed planes were produced because of difficulties in the German war economy. However, the Spanish Air Force's preference for German aircraft was clear because even if the terms of payment were more demanding, as historian James Corum pointed out, 'German technology and industrial assistance were considered to be well worth the price'.[95]

After the start of the war, the Italians continued to exercise their advising roles via courses at the school in Málaga and the fighter school at Reus, and the presence of personnel in Spanish air units. Indeed, in July 1939, soon after the creation of the *Ejército del Aire*, the *Regia Aeronautica* and the Spanish Air Force reached an agreement on the permanent stationing of the Italian personnel.[96] However, at this point Italian advising was starting to operate in an unfavourable context and its functions were reduced in the following two and a half years.

The Spaniards took the first step toward their emancipation from Italian aviation advising at the end of the summer of 1939 when they took control of the 'Specialist School' in Málaga. The training facility had become very important and effective, and in August 1939 had 24 Italian officers and 30 non-commissioned officers serving as instructors. The school was co-directed by a Spanish Commander, Joaquin M. Vara Del Rey, and Italian Colonel Rainieri Spada, with both jointly in charge of the curriculum.[97]

On 1 September 1939, the *Ministerio del Aire* asked Franco for the authorization to transfer the control of the school and arrange the return home of the Italian instructors, arguing that it would be better for the Spanish Air Force if the training was provided by their own personnel.[98] By the end of September, the first Italian

94 ACS, Ministero dell'aeronautica, Gabinetto 1940, b. 196, Promemoria per l'eccellenza il sottosegretario di stato, Trattative Savoia-Marchetti per la collaborazione industriale in Spagna, 19 settembre 1940, p. 2.

95 Corum, 'The Luftwaffe in the Spanish Civil War', p. 81.

96 AHEA, SIG A1500, Estato mayor del Arie, 5a seccion secretaria a sub-seccion detall y contabilidad, 13 July 1939.

97 AHEA, SIG N 936-5, Relacion nominal del personal Legionario Destinado en esta escuola en el dia de la fecha, Clasificado por destinos y specialidades, Malaga 28 de agosto 1939.

98 AHEA, SIG N 936-5, Ministerio del Aire al Exelentisimo Senor Generalissimo de Los Ejerctios Nacionales Y Jefe del Gobierno Espanol, 1 September 1939.

instructors were leaving Spain, and by January 1940, after 22 months of activity, the 'Specialist School' in Málaga, where 1,500 Spanish air force personnel were trained, was closed.[99] Despite the closure of the 'Specialist School', the Italian presence was still noteworthy. According to an Italian report, at the end of 1939, 129 officers, noncommissioned officers, and enlisted personnel continued carrying on instruction and support duties:

| R.A. Personnel in Service with Spanish Aviation (late 1939)* | | | | |
|---|---|---|---|---|
| | | Officers | Non-Commissioned Officers | Enlisted Personnel |
| | Pilots | 3 | 4 | |
| Reus Fighter School | Specialists | | 5 | 16 |
| Centro Meterologico delle Baleari | Specialists | | 2 | 1 |
| | Officers | 2 | 19 | 77 |
| Spanish units | Specialists | | | |
| Totals | | 5 | 30 | 94 |

* ACS, Ministero dell'Aeronautica, Gabinetto 1940, b. 196, Allegato alla relazione dell'addetto aeronautico al ministero dell'Aeronautica, Personale della scuola Caccia di Reus, 12 gennaio 1940.

The Italian presence was spread through the entire structure of the Spanish Air Force, and was also supported by 93 civilian specialists employed mainly in the Spanish workshops for maintenance and repair services. Civilian personnel were the first ones removed because in December 1939, the *Subdirección de material personal civil* (the sub-directorate for material and civilian personnel) of the Spanish Air Staff believed that maintaining these Italian specialists was too expensive.[100] In spring 1940, the Spanish asked Appignani to organize their departure, and by June 1940 the number of these specialists was reduced to 20 and was progressively reduced to zero in the following year.[101]

99 Guido Mattioli, *L'aviazione legionaria in Spagna* (Rome: L'Aviazione, 1940), p. 423.
100 AHEA, SIG A1500, Subdireccion de material personal civil, num 3601 to Director general de material, 5 December 1939.
101 AHEA, SIG A1500, Ministero del Aire, Seccion Servisios Material Negociado de Personal, Relacion del personal comprendido en el Escrito n. 863 que se enquentra prestando servizio en las maestranza que se indicas, Madrid, 4 June 1940.

In the same period, the *Ministerio del Aire* asked the Italians to start removing their instructors from the fighter school, though the tenure of the Italian instructors in the fighter school was renewed in July 1939 when the institute moved to the Catalan town of Reus. The work of the Italian instructors was greatly appreciated by the Spanish. For example, the commander of the school, Pilot Major Guido Nobili, was considered an officer of 'extraordinary valor'. According to his Spanish successor as director of the school: 'He worked in a tireless manner' and 'the technical organization of the school is a model of good technique and knowledge of all aspects of pilotage'.[102]

Similar opinions were also held for the other Italians that worked at Reus. Despite this, at the end of October 1939, right after Yagüe outlined his expansion plan, Nobili was informed that the Spaniards were going to take control of the courses at the end of the current training cycle. Nobili went to the *Ministerio del Aire* in order to define some procedures concerning the Fighter School in Reus, but was informed by the Spaniards of their intention of taking over the school at the end of the current course.[103]

This move was justified by the European and international situation. During the summer of 1939, mobilization disclosed the cracks within the Italian armed forces. The air force was in a catastrophic state because of the intervention in Spain, and in September only possessed 847 effective modern planes, of which 240 were undergoing maintenance. The Second World War had begun in September 1939 and Italy had chosen neutrality by declaring itself a 'non-belligerent'. However, after the autumn, hopes for a negotiated peace between Germany and the Allies waned rapidly and Mussolini took the first steps in readying his military for combat. Unfortunately for Italy, both the army and the air force were in a dire situation. The state of his military apparatus led the Duce to replace both the Undersecretaries for War and the Air Force on 31 October 1939 in order to accelerate readiness for the Italian entry into the war.[104] The aforementioned General Pricolo replaced Valle. He was aware by now that there was little prospect of long-term penetration of Spain, and was conscious of the necessity of putting his air force back in order. For this purpose, the experience of the personnel still present in Spain was very valuable. A progressive Italian disengagement followed. Considering this situation, in November 1939, the new Italian Undersecretary of the Air Force, General Francesco Pricolo, highlighted that the diplomatic benefit of continuing the advising activity at all costs was not worthwhile and ordered that at the end of the current course the Italian personnel should return home.[105]

102 AHEA, SIG. N 1243-4, Infome sobre el Maggiore pilota, Nobili Guido, Aerodromo de Reus, 23 Julio de 1940.
103 ACS, Ministero dell'Aeronautica, Gabinetto 1940, b. 196, Ufficio dell'Addetto aeronautico, n. 856, Promemoria per S.E. il Capo di Gabinetto, 31 ottobre 1939.
104 MacGregor Knox, *Mussolini Unleashed, 1939-1941: Politics and Strategy in Fascist Italy's Last War* (Cambridge: Cambridge University Press, 1982), pp. 55-59.
105 ACS, Ministero dell'Aeronautica, Gabinetto 1940, b. 196, Pricolo a Ufficio dell'addetto aeronautico presso la R. Ambasciata d'Italia, Madrid, n. 88824, Scuola caccia Reus, 15

The Spaniards took control of the fighter school at Reus, but due to difficulty in getting German support, in January the *Ministerio del Aire* decided to lengthen the stay of five flight instructors (one officer and four non-commissioned officers) and of all Italian technical specialists.[106] In the end, Pricolo allowed these last advisors to stay in Spain and continue to carry out their functions, even after the school at Reus had been closed and its personnel shared out between the schools at Jerez de la Frontera and Tablada.[107]

By that time though, the courses were under Spanish direction as Nobili had returned to Italy in May 1940.[108] The simultaneous departure of General Gambara to Italy was a sign of Italy's forthcoming entry into the war and signaled a reduced ability to maintain key personnel in Spain since their service was most urgently needed at home.[109]

With the departure of Nobili, the Italian air advisory effort lost all of its autonomy. This put an end to attempts to use it as an instrument to actively influence the development of the Spanish Air Force. Despite this, and the opposition of the Italian Air Force that required the return of its personnel, even in the spring of 1941 the Spaniards managed to maintain some instructors (one Pilot Captain, two weapons specialists, five motor specialists, and one assembly specialist), arguing that without them their training would have been severely curtailed.[110] Only one year later, in June 1942, the Spanish could rely on sufficient numbers of qualified instructors, which allowed most of the Italians to depart. The last instructors, one weapons specialist and one motor specialist, were in Spain until September 1942.[111]

## Conclusions: Delusions of Grandeur

Despite the appreciation of Spanish officers for the work of the Italian instructors and technicians, the mission failed. Indeed, the Italian air advising effort in Spain took place in a particular context in which the Italian services participated in the

novembre 1939.

106 ACS, Ministero dell'aeronautica, Gabinetto 1940, b. 196, El Jefe del Estato Mayor del Aire to Sr. Coronel Appignani, Agreado Aereo a Madrid, 11 de Enero 1940, 11 gennaio 1940.

107 ACS, Ministero dell'aeronautica, Gabinetto 1941, b. 153, Appignani a Ministero dell'aeronautica, Telespresso n. 273, Trasferimento della scuola da caccia di Reus, 11 febbraio 1941.

108 Logoluso, *Gli assi dei Fiat Cr.32*, p. 170.

109 Carotenuto, *Franco e Mussolini*, p. 74.

110 AHEA, SIG. A4142, Ministerio del Aire, Subsecretaria, Direccion general de instruccion, n. 2919, el General, director general de instruccion, to the general subsecretario, Madrid, 29 April 1941.

111 AHEA, SIG. A4142, Ministerio del Aire, El General Jefe del estato mayor del Aire Eduardo G. Gallarza to General subsecretario de este ministerio, Num. 486, 6 August 1942.

fighting while also competing for influence with their German allies. In the long-term the Germans prevailed, partly because of the superiority of their technology and military doctrine. However, what contributed more to undermining the Italian air advisory effort was the poor state of the Italian Air Force, the political nature of Fascist intervention, and its impact on Italy's relationship with Nationalist Spain's military.

The first problem of Italian air advising in Spain was that this operation depended and reflected the general problems of the Italian strategy during the Spanish Civil War. Until at least spring 1937, Mussolini relied on achieving a quick victory, believing that a massive Italian intervention would produce an immediate and decisive impact on the conflict. In this phase advising tasks were limited since a long-term reconstruction of Nationalist forces didn't occupy first place in the Italian list of priorities, thus the chance of securing from the beginning the lead position of influence over the Nationalist Air Force was lost. The changing conditions of the conflict and the defeat at Guadalajara transformed the nature of Italian intervention, which was now simultaneously compelled to chase victory in order to regain lost prestige, while building the relationships necessary for a future political and economic infiltration of the country. However, German competition was growing stronger because of their ability to limit their involvement in military operations while developing a coherent strategy of economic penetration in the country. The Italian failure to win political and economic benefits from military advising came from their lack of planning for a long-term penetration of Spanish affairs.[112]

However, an analysis based on only this point would be misleading because of how the political nature of Italian intervention conditioned all aspects of the Italian presence, not least that of air advising. Indeed, Italy's intervention in the Iberian Peninsula was dictated by the goal of turning Spain into a Fascist country, and to have it play a part in the Italian plan to build its own 'living space' in the Mediterranean. By intervening, Mussolini intended to take out a 'complete mortgage' on Spain, and to get it he displayed an enormous economic and military generosity towards Franco. In fact, Italy supplied the Nationalists with massive amounts of aid, even if they proved to be unable to pay for it, and in the post-civil war period, despite his ministers' opposition, in an amazing 'act of largesse', the Duce lowered the Spanish debt from eight to five billion lire. These were seen as necessary steps for gaining Spain's favor. For the Italian dictator, economics was a tool of politics.[113]

However, to speed up this project Mussolini also tried to win a leading role for the Italian military in Spain. Between July 1936 and March 1939, 76,241 men from the army and militia, and 5,700 men from the air force saw service in Spain. The losses or those killed in action were, respectively, 3,266 and 200, while the material supplied included, among other things, 1,930 artillery pieces and 764 airplanes. The

112 This is Barbieri's thesis, *Hitler's Shadow Empire*, pp. 197-217.
113 Carotenuto, *Franco e Mussolini*, pp. 26-27.

Germans sent about the same number of planes to Spain, while the number of men was around 19,000, 298 of whom died.[114] Believing they had carried the greater burden of operations, officials at the highest levels of the Italian government thought this guaranteed clear Italian preeminence in the future Francoist regime, including influence in the development of Spain's armed forces. This proved in many respects true because during the civil war and the first years of the regime (1936-1940) Franco mainly looked to Italy as a political model.[115]

The Italian evaluation of their position in Spain was not objective since it was generated by a typical case of 'victory disease'. First, the victories won in Spain convinced Italian leaders that they were in possession of efficient and modern armed forces.[116] For example, this explains why the Italians continued to deem the CR.32 and CR.42 biplanes reliable even after the civil war, and offered them to the Spaniards. Being convinced that they had an air force at the developmental forefront, the Italians did not take advantage of their experience in Spain to update their tactics and aircraft. Nobody in the Italian air force and government questioned the assumption that the few hundred killed in the air raids on Barcelona were the best demonstration of the Italian Air Force's power, and what it could offer to the future Spanish Air Force. Indeed, as the Danish historian Morten Heiberg noted, a part of Mussolini's strategy in Spain explicitly included the use of terror bombing in order to finish the Republic.[117]

Being sure of their preeminence in the peninsula thanks to the massive military intervention, the leading figures of the Italian government, both military officers and diplomats, developed a false feeling of self-confidence.[118] Consequently, they overlooked the warnings of Italian advisors who maintained the necessity of forestalling German competition by extending the presence of Italian air advising. It should be added that the massive Italian presence, instead of exercising a positive influence, ended up provoking some friction with the Spanish military because the Italians, particularly before the battle of Guadalajara, insisted on having leading roles in military operations, which would automatically undermine the authority of the new government, particularly that of Franco.[119] Consequently, relations between MMIS and Francoist commands were marked by a strong sense of superiority on the part of the Italians. Additionally, because of the excessive attention-seeking behavior of CTV, Italian accomplishments were often enhanced by Italian propaganda, which caused tensions with Nationalist military officers.[120] Hubris and the lack of unbiased

114 Coverdale, *I Fascisti italiani*, pp, 368-370; Proctor, *The Luftwaffe in Spain*, p. 253.
115 Payne, *The Franco Regime*, p. 254; Javier Tusell, *Spain from Dictatorship to Democracy, 1939 to the Present* (Malden-Oxford: Wiley-Blackwell, 2007), p. 12.
116 Giorgio Rochat, *Le guerre italiane, 1935-1943,* p. 130.
117 Heiberg, *Emperadores del Mediterráneo*, p. 214.
118 Payne, *The Franco Regime*, p. 160.
119 Preston, *Franco*, p. 235.
120 Ranzato, Gabriele, *L'eclissi della democrazia: La guerra civile spagnola e le sue origini* (Turin: Bollati-Boringhieri, 2004), pp. 557-558.

judgments contributed to create the premise for the swift decline of the influence of Italian advisors in the aftermath of the Nationalist victory.

However, to these problems must be added German competition. During the war, the Spanish military—above all the members of the Nationalist Air Force—realized that the Condor Legion was superior both technologically, operationally, and tactically to the *Aviazione Legionaria*. However, since their equipment was largely Italian, particularly their fighters, the Francoists accepted air advising from the *Regia Aeronautica*. But in 1939-1940 it became clear that the old CR.32 and CR.42 biplanes produced by Italy no longer measured up to the German planes. This belief was considerably strengthened by Nazi victories in Poland, Scandinavia, and France in 1939-1940, which made the professional and personal inclinations of the leaders of the *Ejército del Aire* lean decisively towards Germany. Yagüe and Vigòn, the two chiefs of the Nationalist Air Force in the aftermath of the civil war, indeed proved to be clearly in favor of the Germans and were convinced—particularly Vigòn—that the Italian regime was inherently weak compared to the Nazi one.[121]

In the end, despite the positive judgment of the Italian advisors' work, the Spanish assessment of Italy's military capacity proved valid, and is further proof that the failure of Italian air advising has to be considered within the context of an Italian Air Force that was falling rapidly behind the *Luftwaffe*. This in turn reflected the growing inability of Fascist Italy to keep pace with Mussolini's ambitions. Indeed, the failure of Italian advising was just one of the many signs of the impending military crisis of Fascist Italy, which became evident with the Italian defeats in Greece and in the Mediterranean in 1940-1941, and fed a growing subordination to Nazi Germany that saw Rome become Berlin's satellite.[122]

121 Corum, 'The Luftwaffe in the Spanish Civil War', p. 81.
122 Knox, *Mussolini Unleashed*, p. 271.

4

# A Measure of Success? Soviet and American Military Advising in Yugoslavia, 1945-1957

*James Horncastle*

## Introduction

Yugoslav ambassador Vladimir Popović in a 1952 meeting with General Joseph Collins, the US Army Chief of Staff, highlighted what was the most important aspect of American military aid to Yugoslavia: the construction of a modern air force in order to counter the Soviet Union and its allies' material superiority.[1] For Yugoslavia, its air force was the most glaring weakness in its efforts to resist a possible Soviet attack. Yet, it also proved to be the most contentious area in Yugoslavia's efforts to acquire aid from the United States. The American Military Assistance Staff, Yugoslavia (AMAS), the name for the US advisory mission, remained, as Lorraine Lees notes, the most quarrelsome part of the strategic relationship between the two countries in the 1950s.[2] The tension between the Yugoslavs and foreign nations over their air force, however, was not a new phenomenon, and extended back to the country's irregular warfare campaign in the Second World War.

This chapter examines how Soviet and American military advisors managed to transform the Yugoslav Air Force (YAF) into a modern combat arm and, in so doing, obtain political benefits for their respective countries. When the Soviets began their reform efforts of the YAF, it was a marginalized military entity. The Soviet advisory mission, nevertheless, managed to reform the YAF into a Soviet-style force capable of supporting its political ambitions before larger political concerns, namely the

1 Lorraine M. Lees, *Keeping Tito Afloat: The United States, Yugoslavia, and the Cold War, 1945-1960* (University Park, PA: The Pennsylvania State University Press, 2010), p. 110.
2 Ibid.

Tito-Stalin split, caused the USSR to scrap the mission in 1948. Three years later, the United States took up efforts to reform the YAF. The US did so with the purpose of supporting the Yugoslav People's Army in its efforts to resist possible Soviet aggression. When AMAS began its mission, the YAF was not in a position to perform many of the functions, such as air superiority and ground support, called for in its Soviet-designed doctrine. By the end of AMAS' mission, however, the YAF, while still significantly outnumbered by the Soviet Union and the surrounding satellite states and possessing fewer jet aircraft, was in a position to contest the initial dominance of the air in a localized war. Both Soviet and American military aid, in other words, demonstrated the ability of an international advisory mission to shape the YAF and obtain political advantages in the process.

## Historiography

The historiography on military aid missions, while extensive, suffers from several major limitations. The first is that as aid missions are an ongoing matter of policy, analyses typically focus on whether a particular mission succeeded or failed. For example, William H. Mott, in *United States Military Assistance: An Empirical Perspective*, created a formula by which we can assess the success or failure of US military assistance programs.[3] While assessing the successes and failures of these missions is important, the weakness of Mott's methodology is that in his efforts to quantify success the numbers he assigns detract from a nuanced understanding of these missions. Mott's work on military assistance is not an isolated example of policy dictating analysis. George M. Guess, in his analysis of foreign military aid, takes the Department of Defense's vague definition that 'The success of US arms sales via Foreign Military Sales (FMS) is measured by its contribution to strengthening the professional military establishment'.[4] While there is a place for such generalizations within the field, one must place them against a background of case studies. A point on which these authors deserve particular credit, however, is their focus on the political dimension. Taking this insight, and using specific case studies, one can elucidate the specific dynamics that lead to success and failure, which a quantitative analysis cannot provide.

The second major issue within the field is that examining the Soviet and American military aid missions will help resolve the tendency within the field to focus on a specific number of case studies.[5] AMAS' role in contributing to US foreign policy objectives in the region was significant to not only American policy goals as a whole, which historian Donald Stoker notes is a key component of military aid, but also provides an example

3 William H. Mott IV, *United States Military Assistance: An Empirical Perspective* (Westport, CT: Greenwood Press, 2002), p. 64.

4 George M. Guess, *The Politics of United States Foreign Aid* (London: Routledge, 1987), p. 3.

5 A notable exception which, while dated, still offers a balanced insight into early US military aid is James A. Huston, *Outposts and Allies: US Army Logistics in the Cold War, 1945–1953* (Cranbury, NJ: Associated University Presses, 1988).

of a successful military aid program.[6] The problem that most analyses of both Soviet and American military aid encounter, however, is that they rely on several specific case studies. For example, Mott focuses his analysis on Thailand, Israel, Iran, Egypt, Ethiopia, Somalia, Japan, and the Philippines.[7] While an extensive list, Mott did not mention Yugoslavia. These case studies, while important, create a skewed perspective on US military aid missions by assuming the exceptional issues encountered in these cases are in fact the standard, and largely ignoring examples in Europe and Latin America. Guess, likewise, focused his analysis on Latin America and Asia—further skewing the tendency to view these limited case studies as instructive for the field as a whole, while minimizing ones that fall outside their narrow geographic definition.[8]

Finally, examining both Soviet and American aid efforts will overcome the tendency in the English literature to concentrate solely on American aid. The literature's focus on American aid, given US prominence in the post-Second World War era, makes sense. Problematically, however, this gives only one country's perspective on military aid. One can reach a more complete understanding of military aid by combining an examination of US military aid with that of the Soviets.

## Soviet Advisory Efforts

At the end of the Second World War, Yugoslavia firmly situated itself within the Soviet camp. The Partisans, a Second World War resistance movement dominated by the Communist Party of Yugoslavia (CPY), managed through its wartime success to exploit its popularity and military strength to become the leading communist movement outside the Soviet Union. Tito's personal prestige within the communist camp, in fact, was second only to Joseph Stalin's.[9] Furthermore, amongst the countries behind what Winston Churchill would term the Iron Curtain, none was more aggressive in promoting communist expansion than Yugoslavia as its involvement in the Greek Civil War (1946-1949) demonstrated.[10] Thus, it appeared that Yugoslavia was not only a member of the Soviet Bloc, but in fact its most fanatical member.

One of the critical aspects of Yugoslav military culture that has often gone unnoticed in the West was the desire of Yugoslavia to break away from its irregular

6 Donald Stoker, 'The History and Evolution of Foreign Military Advising and Assistance, 1815-2007', in Donald Stoker (ed.) *Military Advising and Assistance: From Mercenaries to Privatization, 1815–2007* (London: Routledge, 2008), pp. 1-2.

7 Mott, *United States Military Assistance*, p. 300.

8 Guess, *The Politics of United States Foreign Aid*, pp. 87-143.

9 Barbara Jelavich, *History of the Balkans: Twentieth Century* (Cambridge: Cambridge University Press, 1983), p. 384.

10 That Yugoslavia pursued an independent policy with regard to Greece was not recognized by the United States and outside powers, which instead subsumed it under the perspective of a Soviet plot to expand its influence. As Mastny shows, however, this simply was not the case. See Vojtech Mastny, *The Cold War and Soviet Insecurity: The Stalin Years* (Oxford: Oxford University Press, 1998).

warfare past. In part, one can attribute Yugoslavia's desire to the common association of prestige that comes with a conventional army. In the case of Yugoslavia, however, there exists a readily apparent spark for why the CPY, in the aftermath of a highly successful partisan campaign, sought to transition from an irregular to a conventional force. Stalin, upon meeting Tito in early 1945, badgered him about the performance of the Yugoslav Partisans relative to the Bulgarian Army, which had recently occupied Yugoslavia. Stalin,

> Teased Tito with obvious deliberateness—in a manner that had in it as much malice as jest. He did it by speaking unfavorably of the Yugoslav Army while flattering the Bulgarian Army. That previous winter Yugoslav units including many recruits who were engaged for the first time in very serious frontal attacks had suffered defeats, and Stalin, who was apparently well informed, took the opportunity to point out the Bulgarian Army is better than the Yugoslav. The Bulgars had their weaknesses and enemies in their ranks. But they executed a few score—and now everything is in order. The Bulgarian Army is very good—drilled and disciplined. And yours, the Yugoslav, they are still Partisans, unfit for serious front-line fighting. [...]
>
> [...] When Stalin said that the Bulgarian Army was better than the Yugoslav, Tito could not stand it, and shouted that the Yugoslav Army would quickly rid itself of its weaknesses.[11]

Tito, who transformed what was a failing communist party into the most successful resistance organization in Europe, took Stalin's comment as a personal affront.[12] Tito was, at the very least, an egotist about his and the party's accomplishments.[13] Yugoslavia had to eliminate weakness, in this case the inability of the army to perform conventional operations as effectively as the Bulgarians. While Tito certainly considered other factors when reforming his armed forces along conventional lines, such as a conventional army's greater utility in an offensive war, we should not underestimate Tito's ego in our assessment of the Partisans' transformation into a conventional force.

The Soviets advising the Yugoslavs was not a new development. The Soviets reached the decision to militarily advise the Yugoslavs as early as 13 December 1943.[14] The

11 Milovan Djilas, *Conversations with Stalin* (London: Harcourt, Brace, Jovanovich, 1962), p. 89.

12 The extent of Yugoslavia's resistance movement to the overall success of Second World War remains a controversial topic.

13 Milovan Djilas, *Tito: The Story from Inside* (New York: Harcourt, Brace, Jovanovich, 1980), pp. 7-15.

14 'Soviet Decision to Send a Military Mission to the Partisans, 13 December 1943', in Stephen Clissold (ed.), *Yugoslavia and the Soviet Union, 1939-1973* (New York: Oxford University Press, 1943, 1975), pp. 160-161.

Yugoslavs, though grateful for the Soviet interest, largely ignored the advisors.[15] The CPY-led Partisans were highly competent at irregular warfare. The Partisans, as Stalin pointed out, however, were highly deficient at conventional warfare. Tito recognized this, and obtained agreement from the Soviet Union soon after Stalin's criticism for Soviet trainers to start transforming the Partisans into a conventional force.[16] The Soviet advisors, whom the Yugoslavs once looked upon with disdain, became a key part of Yugoslavia's transformation.

The area where the Red Army trainers had perhaps the largest influence was in constructing the YAF. Soviet trainers and advisors proved critical in transforming Yugoslavia's air force into a powerful actor capable of offensive operations. The Partisan Air Force in the Second World War had limited capabilities and the Yugoslav Partisans relied on the Balkan Air Force, a multinational organization, and their liaison officer, William Deakin, to coordinate activities with ground forces.[17] The Yugoslavs considered the Balkan Air Force a blow to Yugoslav prestige, and they sought at the first opportunity to build their own indigenous air force. Yugoslav officials, in constructing their conventional force, sought to ape the Soviet model.[18]

The Soviet Union, in seeking to expand its influence in the Balkans, was only too happy to oblige the Yugoslav officials. The actions of the Soviet advisors though (apparently they acted in an arrogant manner and were paid between 30,000 and 40,000 dinars, whereas the highest ranks of the Yugoslav armed forces were only paid between 9,000-11,000 dinars), eventually formed a sore point in Soviet-Yugoslav relations.[19] Furthermore, there was internal resistance to the roles of the Soviet advisors. Colonel-General Koča Popović, the Yugoslav Chief of Staff, had requested a large-scale reduction in the number of advisors as early as 1946.[20] His reasons, however, were related to professional rivalry more than any legitimate issue. The fact that the CPY did not heed his advice, despite his influence, speaks to how seriously the politicians wanted the Soviet inspired reforms. Thus while Yugoslav military professionals such as Popović likely rejected the Soviet officers' utility out of professional pride, and the CPY politicians later used their arrogance in their case about Soviet domination, it is quite clear that in the interim they not only willingly accepted the Soviet advisors, but embraced them.

15 In World War Two the Yugoslavs even greeted Soviet advice about conventional operations with trepidation. Djilas, *Wartime*, trans. Michael Petrovich (New York: Harcourt, Brace, Jovanovich, 1977), pp. 404-405.

16 R.J. Crampton, *The Balkans since the Second World War* (New York: Routledge, 2014).

17 For Deakin's account of his appointment and role, see William Deakin, *The Embattled Mountain* (London: Oxford University Press, 1971), pp. 265-266.

18 Crampton, *The Balkans since the Second World War*, p. 33.

19 Rinna Kullaa, *Non-Alignment and Its Origins in Cold War Europe: Yugoslavia, Finland and the Soviet Challenge* (London: I.B. Tauris, 2011), p. 47.

20 Ibid.

Soviet officers, and the CPY's fascination with all things Soviet, resulted in the construction of an air force based on Soviet doctrine. Soviet Air Force doctrine and practice differed significantly from the methods taught by the later American advisors. For example, the YAF followed the Soviet structure of divisions, regiments, and squadrons. This was simply the most obvious distinction. In terms of doctrine, the Soviet air force during this period dedicated its operations to, as Lieutenant-Colonel Leslie Drane notes, 'using large aircraft formations to maintain control of the air and to provide massed aerial artillery'.[21] In fact, Colonel General Sudets, the Chief of Staff of the Soviet Army Air Force, wrote in 1948 that 'the training of air force units is planned so that they can first of all provide direct assistance to the ground forces'.[22] This was different from the United States Air Force, which in 1947 officially became distinct from the United States Army, and increasingly pushed to develop doctrine independent of the other armed service branches.[23] Thus, while Soviet doctrine in the late 1940s was very much tied to combined arms and supporting the ground forces, American doctrine was moving in the opposite direction towards an air force capable of conducting independent operations. It is important to note that this distinction caused significant tensions in the 1950s between the American reformers and their Yugoslav pupils.

Soviet trainers facilitated the YAF's transformation by providing them with surplus war materiel. The YAF received 213 Ilyushin Il-2 fighter-bombers that were largely surplus from the Red Army's 1944-1945 advance into Eastern Europe and Germany.[24] Soviet designs were complimented by a limited number of German designs, specifically the BF-109G, seized from Bulgarian, German, and Croatian sources, and British planes, primarily Supermarine Spitefires, acquired from the Balkan Air Force.[25] The YAF's air compliment was certainly heterogeneous, but this decision allowed for a rapid buildup in an effort to match the air forces' capabilities to the ground army.

The Soviet advisors, in many ways, were too successful in training the YAF. Throughout 1947 the Soviet trainers brought the YAF to a high enough level of competency that the Yugoslavs felt they could replicate Soviet instruction elsewhere in the Balkans, specifically in Albania.[26] Tito, for reasons that remain debated, sought to deploy two divisions to Albania, allegedly under the auspices of protecting Albania

21 Leslie R. Drane Jr., 'Soviet Tactical Air Doctrine', Professional Study (Mawxell, AL: Air University Press, 1976), p. 21.

22 Cited in Raymond L. Garthoff, *Soviet Military Doctrine* (Glencoe, IL: Free Press, 1953), p. 174.

23 Lieutenant-Colonel Dik Alan Daso, *US Air Force: A Complete History* (Washington, DC: The Air Force Historical Foundation, 2006), pp. 284-323.

24 Robert Michulec, *Il-2 Il-10: Monografie Lotnicze* (Gdansk: AJ-Press, 1999), p. 29.

25 Bojan Dimitrijevic, *Jugoslovensko Ratno Vazduhoplovstvo, 1942-1992* (Beograd: Institut za savremenu istoriju, 2009), p. 356.

26 For an analysis of these policies from the Albanian perspective, see Albina Dranqoli, 'Tito's Attempt to Integrate Albania into Yugoslavia, 1945-1948', *History Studies: International Journal of History*, 32 (2011), pp. 191-196.

from 'monarcho-fascist aggression'.[27] The Yugoslavs, in accordance with Soviet air doctrine, deployed an air regiment to Albania first so that the ground forces possessed adequate air support. This deployment, as Djilas recounted, created a sore point in Soviet-Yugoslav relations.[28] Nevertheless, the YAF's ability to perform such a task demonstrated that Soviet instruction helped transform it into a modern air force.

## Yugoslavia's Diplomatic Shift

The Tito-Stalin split, however, interrupted the Soviet efforts to install their conception of an air force upon the Yugoslavs. In fact, the Soviets, realizing that the Yugoslav armed forces were critical to the regime's stability, made them their first target in their efforts to unseat Tito. On 18 March 1948, General Aleksei Barskov, the head of the Soviet military mission, informed the Yugoslav authorities that he had received word that the Soviet Union would immediately withdraw its military advisors in the country due to the fact they were 'surrounded by hostility'.[29] Tito, desperate to maintain the military advisors for both political and practical reasons, conducted an investigation in the wake of the letter that turned up no evidence of their systematic mistreatment.[30] Nevertheless, the Soviet Union refused to keep the advisors in Yugoslavia, and upped the pressure on the CPY regime. These actions eventually culminated in a full break on 28 June 1948 with the expulsion of Yugoslavia from the Cominform, the Soviet-controlled internationalist organization designed to coordinate the policies of the world's socialist countries.[31] Over the next few years the Soviet Union and its satellite states renounced their treaties with Yugoslavia and initiated a series of border incidents intended to topple Tito's regime.[32] That said, the Yugoslav armed forces, in large part due to the training they had received and their loyalty to Tito, provided a pillar of stability for the regime.[33] The Yugoslavs, due to their prior alienation of the United States and the West, were alone in a hostile world.

27 Hoxha claimed in 1957, post facto, it was a Yugoslav plot to take control of Albania. This point, however, is open to contestation. See Enver Hoxha, *The Selected Works of Enver Hoxha*, Vol. 2 (Tirana: Nentori Publishing House, 1982), pp. 655-724.

28 While there were other reasons for the rupture in Soviet-Yugoslav relations, the YAF's attempt to replicate the Soviet Union's role in the Eastern Bloc in Albania proved an additional source of tension. Djilas, *Conversations with Stalin*, p. 133.

29 'Tito Protests to Molotov Against the Withdrawal of Russian Advisers and Enquires the Reasons for Soviet Displeasure, 20 March 1948', in Stephen Clissold (ed.), *Yugoslavia and the Soviet Union, 1939-1973: A Documentary Survey*, (New York: Oxford University Press, 1975), p. 169.

30 Ibid., 170.

31 Ibid., pp. 202-207.

32 Svetozar Rajak, *Yugoslavia and the Soviet Union in the Early Cold War: Reconcilation, Comradeship, Confrontation, 1953-1957* (New York: Routledge, 2011), p. 49.

33 Ivo Banac, *With Stalin Against Tito: Cominformist Splits in Yugoslav Communism* (London: Cornell University Press, 1988), p. 155.

The American government initially did not believe the Tito-Stalin split was legitimate. For them, it made no sense that the USSR would turn against what until that point had been their most faithful disciple.[34] Eventually, however, the American government realized the practical utility of using Yugoslavia against the Soviet Union. After they confirmed it, the Americans were more than willing to support Yugoslavia.[35] This recognition led to increased ties between the two countries as early as late 1949.

For both the Yugoslavs and Americans, by 1951 the YAF was the one branch in desperate need of US military aid. The ground forces, while short of parts for the mechanized units, were at least sufficient in small arms as Yugoslavia's domestic industry was capable of meeting the country's needs.[36] Given that the United States, contrary to the view of the Yugoslavs, believed that the ground forces should prepare for a partisan campaign, this meant that Yugoslavia, from the US perspective, had the tools at hand for a protracted conflict.[37] The Yugoslav Navy, perhaps the service most neglected by the Yugoslav authorities, was the least important for halting a Soviet advance. The navy, designed as a coastal defense force, was more useful for halting a potential NATO landing on the Dalmatian coast than opposing a Soviet invasion from the north and east.[38] Unlike the Yugoslav Navy, the YAF had an important role to play against any invasion of the country. Its ability to perform that role, however, was limited. An American military assessment from January 1952 declared:

> The Yugoslav air force (YAF) has 649 aircraft, of which 408 are assigned to tactical units. The YAF is a balanced air force designed not only to fight over Yugoslav territory, but also to carry out limited offensive missions outside the border of Yugoslavia. Most of the aircraft are of German or Soviet World War II design and construction, and [the] lack of modern equipment would make it difficult for the YAF to accomplish its missions, both within Yugoslavia and beyond the Yugoslav frontiers.[39]

The YAF, in other words, was more a paper tiger than a viable combat arm. Furthermore, the YAF also had as part of its doctrine a focus on offensive operations,

34 Lees, *Keeping Tito Afloat*, pp. 43-82.
35 Ibid., pp. 43-80.
36 'National Intelligence Estimate, Probability of an Invasion of Yugoslavia in 1951', in Nick Ceh (ed.), *US Diplomatic Records on Relations with Yugoslavia During the Early Cold War, 1948-1957* (Boulder, CO: East European Monograph Series, 2002), p. 274.
37 Ibid.
38 The Central Intelligence Agency, when it examined the ability of Yugoslavia to resist a potential Soviet invasion in 1951, only examined the army and air force in relation to this question. See: Nie-29/1 Review of the Conclusions of Nie-29, 'Probability of an Invasion of Yugoslavia in 1951', 4 May 1951, https://www.cia.gov/library/readingroom/document/cia-rdp79r01012a000800020029-9.
39 'National Intelligence Estimate', p. 331.

a legacy of the previous period that was now a liability. The YAF's heterogeneous equipment dating from the Second World War, their limited spare parts supplies, their opponents' growing strength, and their antiquated doctrine meant that it would be of limited use in a conventional conflict against the Soviets.[40]

The Yugoslavs realized their tactical and strategic deficit and sought to increase their ties with the United States. In the immediate aftermath of the Tito-Stalin split, these efforts were limited to economic aid to make up for the disruption caused by the Soviet bloc's blockade of the country and to counter the agricultural shortcomings due, in part, to Yugoslavia's collectivization efforts. Nevertheless, in late 1950 Vladimir Velebit, a former Partisan Major-General and trusted diplomat, conducted unofficial talks with the Americans whereby the latter promised aid to the beleaguered Yugoslavs.[41] These talks progressed quite well, although American concerns about Yugoslavia prompted officials to downplay developments on the matter. For instance, on 6 March 1951, when news leaked that it was considering the export of combat planes, the State Department quickly noted that the shipments would not amount to much in volume due to the weakness of the Yugoslav economy.[42] The American populace's ongoing resentment towards Yugoslavia, compounded by the emergence of McCarthyism in American domestic politics, caused the State Department to deliberately downplay the significance of such a move.

In June, these informal talks transformed as the Yugoslavs formally requested aid under the provisions of the 1949 Mutual Defense Assistance Program (MDAP).[43] Although both sides faced significant obstacles in reaching an agreement, Yugoslavia and the United States concluded the *The Military Assistance Pact* on 14 October 1951. Tito, on signing the pact, made clear that Yugoslavia's goal was for 'the United States to supply us with capabilities that we do not possess. Above all, [the provision of] heavy artillery and aircraft'.[44] Yugoslavia desired, in other words, that the YAF be one of the major beneficiaries of the new policy. As such, any assessment of American success regarding the mission must heavily consider the role of air force assistance, for it was the basis of Yugoslav involvement. This does not mean that American military aid had to fulfill Yugoslav demands in this area, but rather the importance of it provides a benchmark for the program as a whole.

40 The Soviet Satellite states' increased air capabilities are explored in Ceh (ed.), *US Diplomatic Records on Relations with Yugoslavia During the Early Cold War, 1948-1957*, p. 332.

41 Lees, *Keeping Tito Afloat*, p. 98.

42 'Allies May Sell Military Aircraft to Tito to Bolster Yugoslavia Against Aggression', *New York Times*, 7 March 1951, p. 20.

43 'Mutual Defense Assistance Act of 1949', *The American Journal of International Law*, 44:1 (1950), pp. 29-38.

44 *Titova Rec U Publikacijama, 1941-1980* (Beograd: Centar za vojnonaučnu dokumentaciju i informacije, 1980), p. 400.

## AMAS' Efforts at YAF Reform, 1952-1957

The American Military Assistance Staff, Yugoslavia, was the US instrument for guaranteeing that Yugoslavia used the military training and equipment that it received to further American interests. AMAS' role was one of the thorns in US-Yugoslav relations. The Yugoslavs, seeking to exploit the ambiguity of the treaty with the US, argued that the role of American military advisors should be limited to inspecting the equipment upon receipt and providing guidance on a limited number of training grounds.[45] When the Americans insisted that the military mission possess the right to inspect and advise the Yugoslavs on the employment of the arms, the latter attempted to use the (imagined) role of the Soviet military advisors in the split as justification for their reluctance.[46] The Yugoslavs, nevertheless, bowed to American pressure after the latter made it clear that the point was non-negotiable.[47] Given that American domestic pressure was very much opposed to the deal, agreeing to give arms to Yugoslavia without oversight was politically impossible.[48] This agreement permitted the Americans to ratify *The Military Assistance Pact*, but it meant that what would become AMAS, which was founded in December 1951 and consisted of 30 officers commanded by Brigadier-General John Harmony, was already viewed with suspicion by the Yugoslavians. Fortunately for AMAS, the results arising from the delivery of American military aid soon eliminated such concerns.

The first goal of the AMAS was stabilizing the armed forces so that the country would not immediately fold in the face of external aggression. With the YAF, this meant that they needed to replace nearly the entire inventory of aircraft due to their inability to acquire replacement parts. The Western powers demonstrated their concern about the YAF's inability to perform its functions when even before the official signing of *The Military Assistance Pact* it dispatched 140 Mosquito light-bomber/night fighters to Yugoslavia. They quickly followed these deliveries with F47-D Thunderbolt fighter-bombers, which Yugoslavia started to receive on 31 December 1951.[49] While these assets still left Yugoslavia at a quantitative disadvantage to their potential Eastern Bloc adversaries, the Yugoslavs greeted them with great fanfare.[50] The YAF encountered considerable logistic issues in converting over to the Anglo-American planes, including such basic issues as the differing measurement systems used in America and Europe.[51] Nevertheless, the AMAS greatly facilitated the matter, and

45 C.L. Sulzberger, 'US Ready to Sign Tito Arms Accord', *New York Times*, 11 November 1951, p. 14.
46 Ibid.
47 Ibid.
48 Lees, *Keeping Tito Afloat*, p. 108.
49 Bojan Dimitrjevic, 'The Mutual Defense Aid Program in Tito's Yugoslavia, 1951-1958, and Its Technical Impact', *The Journal of Slavic Military Studies*, 10:2 (1997), p. 25.
50 Ibid.
51 Ibid.

the Yugoslavs were happy to possess the problem of figuring out how to install new parts rather than the previous one of having no parts at all.

AMAS's most important task was transitioning the YAF from a piston-air force to the jet age. The AMAS staff recognized the significance of the YAF obtaining jet aircraft from not only a military perspective but also a political one and responded appropriately. AMAS coordinated with the Yugoslav authorities to obtain the maximum political effect from American deliveries. The Yugoslavs themselves needed no prompting and in 1953 images of the newly acquired T-33a jet aircraft covered the newspapers and filled press releases throughout the country. The *New York Times* covered the delivery in detail and George V. Allen, America's ambassador to Yugoslavia, plainly stated that 'the impact of this event (the jet-aircraft delivery) will be understood not by us alone… It will be well understood by anyone who desires to deprive Yugoslavia of its sovereignty and independence'.[52] The Americans, in short, intended the delivery to represent their commitment to Yugoslavia and serve as an example—and a warning—to the USSR. The Yugoslavs intended it to represent their modernity. Even though the T33a was simply a trainer, and would possess limited utility in a war with the Soviet Union, the delivery was as much about the political as practical. Symbolism, in other words, was a key facet of American policy in Yugoslavia, and one must judge AMAS' efforts in Yugoslavia in such a manner.

While the initial shipment of jet-aircraft was quite small, it fundamentally altered the YAF's organization. The US first had to train the pilots to fly the much more technologically intensive aircraft, which AMAS facilitated. In September 1952, AMAS sent three Yugoslav pilots to France to learn the finer points of jet aviation, and 10 more pilots joined them in December once they confirmed the success of the initial trial.[53] Although these individuals became the first jet-instructors in the YAF, the United States demonstrated its concern for their proper training and employment by having the USAF major who delivered the initial jets to Yugoslavia remain with AMAS for 90 days in order to instruct them on the finer points of their operation.[54] Training, however, was not the only area where the Yugoslavs needed improvement. AMAS helped instruct the Yugoslavs on building the proper infrastructure needed for such a shift, such as specialized storage facilities and longer runways, to turn these new assets into effective combat planes.[55] For the Americans, even if the symbolism of US military aid to Yugoslavia was of equal significance to the military, they still had to guarantee that if the Cold War turned hot that Yugoslavia performed to expectations.

The best assessments of the United States' progress in turning the YAF into a capable force are American intelligence reports from this period. The National

52 Jack Raymond, 'US Delivers Jets to the Yugoslavs', *New York Times*, 11 March 1953, p. 7.

53 Dimitrjevic, 'The Mutual Defense Aid Program in Tito's Yugoslavia, 1951-1958, and Its Technical Impact', p. 29.

54 Raymond, 'US Delivers Jets to the Yugoslavs', p. 7.

55 Dimitrjevic, 'The Mutual Defense Aid Program in Tito's Yugoslavia, 1951-1958, and Its Technical Impact', p. 26.

Security Council (NSC) in particular kept track of AMAS' efforts at modernizing the YAF. Its February 1954 assessment, made two years after the US deliveries began, was promising. The NSC noted:

> Although the Yugoslav air force has approximately 1,000 World War II type aircraft, its present capabilities are negligible for its two principal missions of air defense and tactical support of ground forces. However, air force capabilities are gradually increasing as a result of technician and pilot training under MDAP and will be further enhanced by the scheduled addition in 1954-55 of some 200 late model F-84 jets.[56]

It is important to note the transition that NSC acknowledged in the YAF's doctrine during this period. The YAF no longer fixated on performing tactical operations in support of the ground forces as it had in 1951.[57] Instead, the report acknowledged that the YAF's new primary mission was strategic air defense. This point, in particular, indicated AMAS' influence within the country. Air defense, in short, was critical to the US strategy of Yugoslavia being a key flank guard to the southern NATO countries. No mention was made of the YAF's offensive capabilities.[58] In short, American doctrine concerning air power during this time seemingly wedded itself to Soviet and Yugoslav doctrinal norms and needs.

AMAS' objective of modernizing the YAF encountered a significant roadblock in the aftermath of the Belgrade Declaration of 1955. The Belgrade Declaration, given by Nikita Khrushchev in the summer of 1955, normalized relations between the governments of Yugoslavia and the Soviet Union. Yugoslavia, however, did not rejoin the Cominform or the Soviet-led Council for Mutual Economic Assistance (COMECON).[59] The agreement between the Yugoslavs and Soviets, however, did cause consternation on the part of American politicians about continued aid to Yugoslavia in the face of the new political status quo.[60] While Eisenhower and the State Department, to a certain extent, felt betrayed by these actions, they recognized the political game that Yugoslavia played in this period.[61] Yugoslavia sought to balance both the United States and the Soviet Union in an effort to participate in the burgeoning Non-Aligned Movement.[62]

56 'NSC Staff Study on United States Policy Towards Yugoslavia', in Ceh (ed.), *US Diplomatic Records on Relations with Yugoslavia During the Early Cold War, 1948-1957*, p. 401.
57 'National Intelligence Estimate', in ibid., p. 331.
58 Ibid., p. 401.
59 In fact, Khrushchev acknowledged Soviet guilt in the alienation.
60 Lees, *Keeping Tito Afloat*, p. 172.
61 Ibid., pp. 172-173.
62 Svetozar Rajak, 'No Bargaining Chips, No Spheres of Interest: The Yugoslav Origins of Cold War Non-Alignment', *Journal of Cold War Studies*, 16:1 (2014), p. 152.

The president and his advisors, practicing carrot and stick politics, sought to use the issue of jet fighter planes as a means of guaranteeing that Yugoslavia adhered to its previous political stances. In particular, the F-86E Sabre was one of the premiere fighter aircraft in the mid 1950s, and America's deliveries of the plane to Yugoslavia were intended to transform the YAF. Nevertheless, by mid-1956 the United States had only delivered six of the F-86Es to the YAF before suspending the shipments because of Yugoslavia's new embrace of the USSR.[63] The Yugoslavs responded appropriately. As the 1956 report by the Operations Coordinating Board, notes 'the recent suspension of F-86E deliveries has resulted in a Yugoslav decision that additional assignments to AMAS should be held up pending determination of the status of military aid to Yugoslavia'.[64] AMAS, in short, became a political battleground between the United States and Yugoslavia.

The Yugoslav decision to apply pressure on the AMAS demonstrates the important symbolism that it had for the Americans and Yugoslavs. AMAS, in many ways, was a means of the Yugoslavs and Americans resolving their differences without escalating to a serious political breach. The Yugoslavs, in their efforts to use AMAS to demonstrate their newfound political independence in the aftermath of the Belgrade Declaration, equivocated. As James Riddleberger, the American Ambassador to Yugoslavia reported in a 19 April 1956 telegram: '[Yugoslav Foreign Minister Srdia Prica] remarked that discussion between Yugoslav military and AMAS were now underway which would establish exact status of approved programs. In these circumstances, Yugoslav Government would prefer to postpone a definite answer until present technical talks were concluded'.[65] The Yugoslavs no longer felt the pressure of immediate invasion from the Soviet Union. Instead, they now sought to obtain political gains from the Americans where they once acquiesced to the United States. As American Secretary of State John Foster Dulles noted in the spring of 1956 in response to the Yugoslav decision to back out of an October 1955 agreement about increasing the number of AMAS staff: 'although AMAS staffing not vital matter itself, as Yugoslavs well know, it became during [their] talks [a] symbol and measuring rod [of] US-Yugoslav military relations'.[66] The American's trump card to Yugoslav pressure, however, were the material needs of the YAF.

While the United States was able to exert political pressure upon the Yugoslavs through halting military aid, the delay in 1956 threatened to undo the work that AMAS had accomplished in transforming the YAF into a modern western air force.

63 'Report Prepared by the Operations Coordinating Board', in *Foreign Relations, 1955-1957* (hereafter *FRUS*) (Washington, DC: United States Government Printing Office, 1956, 1992), Vol. 26, p. 745.
64 Ibid.
65 J.W. Riddleberger, 'Telegram from the Embassy in Yugoslavia to the Department of State', *FRUS, 1955*-1957, Vol. 26, p. 719.
66 John Foster Dulles, 'Telegram from the Department of State to the Embassy in Yugoslavia', in *FRUS, 1955-1957*, Vol. 26, p. 721.

Ambassador Riddleberger, who was responsible for coordinating between AMAS, Eisenhower, and the Yugoslavs, was grim in a 12 March 1957 report to the State Department:

> Turning to the Yugoslav air force it is noted that the benefit of their successful F-86-E training program wherein 227 pilots and 711 technicians were produced is being lost. The 5 flyable aircraft are insufficient to provide proficiency training for more than 15 pilots and 50 technicians, because of complexity and high performance type of aircraft. While not as acute problem, same situation exists with respect to F-84G aircraft where 109 are now flyable of the 132 delivered. YAF reports and AMAS has verified the number of qualified pilots and technicians available in excess of those required to activate the three remaining fighter-bomber (F-84G) squadrons to bring YAF up to the planned 9 fighter-bomber squadrons contained in the force goal. Spare parts and equipment are available in Yugoslavia for one wing of 75 F-86E and are not interchangeable with other YAF aircraft.[67]

AMAS, in other words, had delivered upon its task of training the YAF to partake in modern combat operations. Ironically, given initial Yugoslav opposition to the idea, their direct role in building up the YAF ensured that even if the United States did not deliver the planes, as was the case in 1957, they possessed the foundation for a strong and independent air force.

Despite AMAS' excellent job in preparing the YAF, as Ambassador Riddleberger noted, American and Yugoslav politics threatened to undo the positive work accomplished. In the same report, Riddleberger noted:

> Deterioration of spares and equipment in storage is not a serious problem but follows a normal course and must be expected. The delivery of these spares to YAF has been interpreted as an indication of future deliveries of F-86E aircraft. Storage of programmed but undelivered aircraft is another problem, however, in that this 'flyable storage' would be at great expense to the US. Yugoslavia has approximately eight months of good flying weather per year, most of which lies immediately ahead. The present lack of aircraft denies YAF that training which could be executed during the March-October period and pushes further in the future the ultimate attainment of the planned force goal of providing Yugoslavia with an equipped and trained fighter-bomber and day fighter capability to support its conventional ground and sea forces. Over the MAP years YAF has provided funds and worked in an orderly fashion to have adequate ground facilities (seven modern jet aircraft fields), pilots and technicians prepared to

67 James W. Riddleberger, 'Telegram from the Embassy in Yugoslavia to the Department of State', in *FRUS, 1955–1957*, Vol. 26, p. 766.

> receive the programmed aircraft. YAF is now capable of absorbing aircraft and equipment deliveries at the maximum rate of delivery believed attainable by USAF.[68]

In short, American and Yugoslav political machinations threatened to undo AMAS' efforts to transform the YAF into a modern institution. One can glean the efficiency of AMAS' work, however, by the fact that the YAF was now capable of absorbing the new aircraft as quickly as the United States could provide them. Thus, while political decisions outside of AMAS' control may have overtaken their efforts, they nevertheless managed to accomplish the task set out for them. The YAF, an air force incapable of using jet aircraft when AMAS' mission began in 1951, now had abundant competency in that area. Yugoslavia, even if it would not immediately employ this expertise in the 1950s, now possessed a solid base for future success.

A brief détente in American-Yugoslav relations allowed for the temporary continuation of aircraft delivery in 1957, but political developments once again hindered the process. In part, the American decision to reinitiate deliveries was pragmatic. Ambassador Riddleberger noted that maintenance of the aircraft earmarked for Yugoslavia proved to be a significant cost for the Americans.[69] It made sense, instead, to make political capital off them before the planes were obsolete, as the F-86E was transitioning from a frontline fighter to being obsolete in the aviation renaissance that occurred in the 1950s. Nevertheless, Yugoslavia's decision to recognize East Germany on 15 October 1957 caused Secretary Dulles in a 22 October 1957 telegram to the American Embassy in Belgrade to order a November halt in deliveries of the planes.[70]

The political considerations at work in Yugoslavia make it one of the more difficult military assistance missions to analyze, particularly in the critical area of AMAS' air force assistance program. While all military assistance missions have a political calculus, in few instances are the states that the United States supported pursuing a foreign policy that, in many ways, was at odds with American policy and underwent such significant fluctuations as that of Yugoslavia.[71] Yugoslav recognition of East Germany, and the inability of the United States to use military pressure in the section of the Yugoslav armed forces most in need of support, demonstrates the limitations of using military aid in pursuit of foreign policy goals. Granting military aid, and the threat of it ending, is only an effective carrot and stick approach if the international and domestic arena makes it conducive for the receiving state to adhere to the assisting state's direction. By late 1957, the stabilization of Yugoslavia's domestic and international position, and its desire to pursue an independent foreign policy, meant

68 Ibid.

69 Ibid.

70 John Foster Dulles, 'Telegram from the Department of State to the Embassy in Yugoslavia', *FRUS, 1955-1957*, Vol. 26, p. 792.

71 For alternative examples see Mott, *United States Military Assistance: An Empirical Perspective.*

that the United States had less leverage than in the past. The Americans themselves recognized this fact when on 18 October 1957 Assistant Secretary of State Charles Elbrick contacted Dulles with his recommendation that the US halt jet deliveries to Yugoslavia while continuing all other military aid.[72] The YAF and AMAS' training program, as the most contentious support issue between the two parties, was the first to go. It, like AMAS itself, proved to be a barometer of American-Yugoslav intentions, and although AMAS' mission officially continued until 25 August 1959 when both parties agreed through mutual consent to terminate it, the air force component of the mission had effectively ended in 1958.

## Conclusion

Soviet and American military aid to Yugoslavia, despite political obstacles, succeeded in transforming the Yugoslav Air Force into a powerful arm of the Yugoslav People's Army. In both instances, the outside power succeeded in influencing the doctrinal development of the Yugoslav Air Force, particularly through 'carrot' based incentives. Negative pressure, however, had mixed results. Both American and Soviet threats to withdraw their military advisors, while greeted with consternation by the Yugoslav authorities, did not succeeded in altering Yugoslavia's political course. Nevertheless, both the Soviets, and in particular the Americans, succeeded in deriving temporary political gains from their military aid missions.

72 Elbrick, 'Memorandum from the Assistant Secretary of State for European Affairs (Elbrick) to the Secretary of State', in *Foreign Relations, 1955-1957* (Washington, DC: United States Government Printing Office, 1957, 1992), p. 789.

# 5

# 'Fly Me to the Cold War': The United States and the Modernization of the Spanish Air Force in the 1950s[1]

*Lorenzo Delgado Gómez-Escalonilla and Pablo León-Aguinaga*

## Introduction

In May of 1950, Frank Sinatra became one of the first American stars to pay a visit to the Spain of General Francisco Franco, the pariah country *par excellence* of postwar Western Europe due to its cooperation with the defeated Axis nations. At the time, the US government did not even maintain full diplomatic relations with the Iberian country. A few months later, however, Washington announced its intention to exchange ambassadors with Madrid. From that moment on, visits from American stars like Sinatra became habitual, helping to 'normalize' the image of the Iberian country and put it on the map of the growing international tourist industry.[2] Even so, the majority of Americans who arrived in Spain in the 1950s were from the US military. They were there not to liberate the country from Francoism as some would have liked, but to operate the joint military bases and installations that the Spanish government had ceded to the United States under the auspices of three bilateral accords that were

1 This work is part of two research projects: 'Modernization of the Spanish Educational and Scientific Establishments in the International Context, 1953–1986' (MINECO, HAR2014-58685-R), and 'The International Factor and the Transformation of the Armed Forces (1953–1982): Defence Diplomacy and Technology Transfer' (CUD-Zaragoza, 2014-09). The archives used and their abbreviations include: Archivo Histórico del Ejército del Aire (AHEA); Archives du Ministère des Affaires Étrangères, France (AMAE-F); Centro Documental de la Memoria Histórica, Archivo Fundación Nacional Francisco Franco (CDMH-AFNFF); National Archives of the United States, College Park (NACP); Service Historique de la Défense, Ministère de la Défense (SHD-MD).

2 See Neal M. Rosendorf, *Franco Sells Spain to America: Hollywood, Tourism and Public Relations as Postwar Spanish Soft Power* (New York: Palgrave Macmillan, 2014).

signed in September of 1953. The agreements included a US commitment to assist and advise on the modernization of the Iberian country's defense infrastructure and the three branches of the armed forces.

By 1964, the year that Frank Sinatra recorded his hit song 'Fly Me to the Moon', the Spanish Air Force (SAF), though still light years away from the countries that were in the space race and their main allies, had effected a considerable leap in capability with the crucial aid of the US military. This chapter identifies and contextualizes the main milestones in that process, the implementation of US military assistance and advising, and the evolution of the SAF. It does so with documents from the civilian and military archives of Spain, the US, and France, the latter being of great value as the Gallic country was the second most important international actor influencing Spanish defense relations in the Cold War.

## An Inauspicious Start

When the Spanish Civil War ended in 1939, the SAF was put together with equipment from diverse origins with unequal capabilities. The disparity of material and the shortages of spare parts were accompanied by tight budgetary constraints, which prevented the necessary program of standardization and hampered operational capacity. To overcome these difficulties, Spain sought the technical and military assistance of the Axis countries, seeking to obtain licenses for the construction and import of Junker, Heinkel, and Fiat aircraft components. World War II slowed down this process while also causing severe limitations in the availability of fuel. Spanish pilots had fewer and fewer flying hours, focusing their efforts on the organizational structure and on teaching. Only the members of the squadrons that fought with the *Wehrmacht* on the Eastern Front maintained close contact with the revolutionary changes that were taking place in aviation during those years.[3]

The precarious situation of the SAF became evident after the end of the war, by which time the gap that Spain suffered with respect to the considerable technical progress achieved by the modern air forces had increased. Solutions were explored, such as purchasing licenses and materials in several countries and attracting German aeronautical engineers, but without success. The inability of Spain's industrial sector to respond to the technological challenges of modern aviation was coupled with the lack of economic resources. To these factors would be added the embargo of military supplies that the main Western countries were imposing on the Spanish regime. At the start of the 1950s, reports coming out of both US and French military sources described the SAF as obsolete. The shortage of combat material and technical know

3 *Historia de la Aviación Española* (Madrid: Instituto de Historia y Cultura Aérea, 1988), pp. 248–267.

how hampered both its operability and the formation of its cadres, making Spain highly vulnerable should it ever have to confront modern forces.[4]

In the face of its internal incapacity for undertaking the modernization of material and training required by the SAF, it proved essential to seek foreign aid. If the Franco regime's camaraderie with the Axis nations made this process difficult in the years following the world conflict, the dawning of the Cold War proved a game changer. The Pentagon took notice early on of the strategic value of Iberian territory, and although various political, diplomatic, and even ethical considerations would delay temporarily the bilateral approach, the United States finally made itself an indispensable partner in launching the desired upgrade of Spain's defensive potential. It was an improvement that, in any event, was mainly focused on US interests, which did not fail to foster resentment among the Spanish leaders who, despite voicing disagreement on a few occasions, had to go along with what was offered. Nevertheless, it is also important to recognize that this strategic link provided the Spanish military with a set of resources that allowed it, though more slowly than it wished, to get out of the backward state that it had fallen into.

From late 1948 Spain became a required stop on the increasingly frequent tours made by US military and political delegations to Western Europe. In September 1949, for the first time since Spain's civil war, a small squadron of US warships arrived in Spanish ports. In these excursions American officials evaluated the willingness of local authorities to take part in US military overseas deployments in exchange for eventual American aid.[5] At the same time the Spanish military made some attempts (though they bore little fruit) to obtain US resources to modernize its capacity for combat and instruction, to improve the training of their cadres, and to keep themselves reasonably informed of military advances. The Spanish air attaché in Washington, in particular, had undertaken unsuccessful efforts to send technicians to the United States to expand their preparation, obtain permits to sell patents for engines and jet fighters, and to purchase spare parts such as engines and propellers for Spanish aircraft. Even gaining access to military manuals and regulations was a proposition not without

4 'Synthèse sur l'organisation générale de l'Aéronautique militaire espagnole', 2 May 1951, and 'Le potentiel militaire espagnol au printemps 1951', 25 May 1951, SHD-MD, GR 14 S 57 y 12 S 110; 'Spain' and 'Annex: Summary and Evaluation of Spanish Armed Forces', 22 June 1951, NACP, RG 59, Lot Files, Office of Western European Affairs (LF-OWEA) 1942–58, Spain, Box 10.

5 'Voyage de la Commission militaire et navale américaine à Madrid', 'Visite de l'Amiral Hillenkoetter à Madrid', 'Visite d'une Délégation de la Commission des Forces armées de la Chambre des Représentants américaines à Madrid', 2 and 18 October and 29 November 1948; 'Visite de l'Amiral Richard L. Conolly et l'escadre américaine de l'Atlantique Est et de la Méditerranée', 'Visite en Espagne de parlementaires américains', 14 September and 4 October 1949, AMAE-F, Amérique, Etats-Unis 1944–52, vols. 185 and 186, and Europe, Espagne 1944–1960, Vol. 81; 'Nota para su Excelencia', 24 September 1948, 11 and 22 August 1949, CDMH-AFNFF, docs. 8907, 12081, and 12069.

its difficulties. In the Pentagon there was a fair amount of receptiveness to these entreaties, but they were met with the barriers imposed by the State Department.

The outbreak of the Korean War in the summer of 1950 altered the balance of forces in favor of those who gave priority to reinforcing the anti-Communist block over other considerations. The results were felt at the UN, which rescinded the diplomatic sanctions adopted against the Spanish government four years earlier, with the United States voting in favor. The Truman White House, at first hostile and then reticent, authorized the start of preliminary talks to evaluate Spanish availability to join the Western defense alliance structure. Contacts for establishing American military bases in Spain marked the bilateral agenda for the short-term.[6]

Until the start of 1951, delays and evasions concerning Spanish requests were a constant, but that attitude would change in the years that followed. Early that year, exploratory talks with Spanish leaders began. The US government was starting to acknowledge openly the expedience of linking the Iberian country more closely with the defense of Western Europe, and at the same time was beginning to reassess Spain's inclinations and capabilities toward that end. In March, a first estimate was made of the Spanish military potential. The conclusions were fairly eloquent: the Spanish armed forces were only estimable in numerical terms. The troops were not receiving professional training comparable to that of the Americans; they were 'poorly paid, fed, clothed, and housed'. The quarters were considered 'uncomfortable and unhealthy'. Many high-ranking officers gave the appearance of being outdated in their knowledge, and military training relied heavily on pre-World War II methods. Instruction put more of a premium on courage than on planning, knowledge of modern material, or training. The SAF was in even worse condition than the Navy or the Army, with a few outdated airplanes and no modern technology, which made it operationally incapacitated for both offensive and defensive action. The words used most often to define the Spanish military contribution in case of war were 'nil' and 'insignificant'.[7] Subsequent US missions sent to provide a more exhaustive study of the situation would observe with reference to the SAF: 'At this time the state of organization, training, and equipage requires a complete rehabilitation in order to produce an effective air arm capable of conducting modern combat operations.'[8]

6 Two recent accounts on the Truman White House's approach to the Spanish Question are Xabier Hualde, *El cerco aliado. Estados Unidos, Gran Bretaña y Francia frente a la dictadura franquista (1945-1953)* (Bilbao: Universidad del País Vasco, 2016), and Wayne H. Bowen, *Truman, Franco's Spain, and the Cold War* (Columbus: University of Missouri, 2017).

7 'Capability of Spain to Defend the Spanish Pyrenees Line, Including an Analysis of Terrain Northeast of the Ebro River', 1 March 1951, in 'Spain', and 'Annex: Summary and Evaluation'.

8 'Historical Data Report on Military Assistance Advisory Group, Spain', 13 November 1954, NACP, RG 334, MAAG Spain, Security Classified Correspondence (SCC), 1952–1962, Box 1.

In that first half of 1951, the SAF were interested in acquiring US military training films, which began arriving, albeit in very limited quantities, at the training centers.[9] A tour of American aeronautical science centers by personnel of the *Instituto Nacional de Técnica Aeronáutica* (INTA), led by its director general, was also organized during this time, followed soon after by a visit to INTA's facilities by a large military delegation from the US.[10] Of greater public impact was the visit of a squadron of F-84 fighter jets from its bases in occuppied Germany, which conducted exhibitions in Seville and Madrid. Spanish leaders responded with lavish hospitality.[11] Something similar was to occur that same spring when Spain joined the exchange set up by the US Civil Air Patrol. The Air Ministry sent out orders to show 'the maximum possible attention and deference' toward the American visitors.[12]

The military rapprochement between the two countries reached an even higher level with the invitation made in July 1951 to the Spanish Air Minister, General Eduardo Gonzalez Gallarza, to travel to the United States and visit the major air bases and aeronautical construction centers in California. He was the first Spanish minister to make an official visit to the US after the establishment of the Franco regime. During his trip, he made clear in his statements that Spain was ready to strengthen military relations with the United States in dealing with the common enemy, communism.[13] At the end of that month, Franco met with Admiral Forrest P. Sherman, who was acting as a representative of the Department of Defense and the Joint Chiefs of Staff (JCS). The terms of eventual military cooperation between the two countries were

9 Arrangements for the acquisition or assignment of such films in AHEA, N61/3, N66/3, and N67/3. Since World War II, through the American House of Madrid, the US Information Service had been loaning documentary films of all kinds to the military ministries and various units of Madrid. The 'Aviation' section was one of the fixed categories of the USIS Spain Film Catalog from the 1950s to the mid-1960s. See Pablo León-Aguinaga, S*ospechosos habituales. El cine norteamericano, Estados Unidos y la España franquista* (Madrid: CSIC, 2010), pp. 410-432.

10 Contacts with INTA were made at the invitation of Theodore von Karman, President of the Advisory Group for Aeronautical Research and Development (AGARD). AHEA, N61/3, N66/3, and N67/3. Following these visits and other collaborative initiatives with the California Institute of Technology, INTA researchers began receiving funds from the USAF Air Research and Development Command and grants from the NASA-ESRO (National Aeronautics and Space Administration) and European Space Research Organization). See José M. Sánchez Ron, *Cincel, martillo y piedra. Historia de la ciencia en España (siglos XIX y XX)* (Madrid: Taurus, 1999), pp. 382–387.

11 'Milton M. Towner, Agregado Aéreo de los EE.UU., a Antonio de Rueda Ureta, Jefe de la 2ª, Sección del E. M. del Aire', 1 May 1951. The documentation for such visit in AHEA, N61/3.

12 'Estado Mayor del Aire', 4 July 1951, AHEA, A10584.

13 'États-Unis-Espagne. Le Ministre de l'Air espagnol est invité par l'Etat Major américain', 27 June 1951, AMAE-F, Amérique, Etats-Unis 1944–52, Vol. 187; Dispatch from the Oficina de Información Diplomática (OID), 2 July 1951, CDMH-AFNFF, doc. 6889. More information on that visit is in AHEA, N61/3.

starting to be defined. Successive missions undertook more in-depth studies of the country's conditions and its military installations, and of how they might be employed in support of US security objectives.[14] Meanwhile, in autumn of that year, the United States passed the Military Security Act, which aimed to coordinate the various foreign aid and assistance programs towards defense objectives in the face of the communist threat, which was already being viewed in global terms.

The vicissitudes of the Spanish-American negotiation process are well covered in the academic literature.[15] The most important talks occurred in the orbit of the two-man association formed by Juan Vigón of the Spanish general staff and United States Air Force (USAF) General August W. Kissner. The heightened Spanish requests for equipment were substantially cut-down by US negotiators. Ultimately, as General Vigón remarked ruefully at one point, an agreement was reached that comprised 'the double aspect of a concrete military pact for one of the sides, and a benevolent political declaration of vague military content for the other.'[16] The accords signed on 26 September 1953 sealed a commitment destined to last for several decades: financing and American military and technical assistance in exchange for a full Spanish pledge to give the United States *carte blanche* for the use of Spanish territory as needed.[17]

From the US point of view, the agreement was dictated by mere convenience and was conceived as a commitment limited to the military sphere. Moreover, although there was no association of Spain with NATO, the US military installations in the Iberian country would be used 'in support of and in consonance with NATO defense plans'.[18] Without participating in the design of the Atlantic defense strategy, the placement of bases in Spain implied that one way or another its territory would be at NATO's service.[19]

14 'Details of Spanish Base Negotiations', 26 September 1953, NACP, RG 59, LF-OWEA 1942–58, Spain, Box 3. See also Ángel Viñas, *En las garras del águila. Los pactos con Estados Unidos, de Francisco Franco a Felipe González (1945–1995)* (Barcelona: Crítica, 2003), pp. 142-149.

15 For a reconstruction of the negotiations for the 1953 Agreements see Viñas, *En las garras del águila*, pp. 159-207; Antonio Marquina, *España en la política de seguridad occidental 1939–1986* (Madrid: Ediciones Ejército, 1986), pp. 498-574; Boris N. Liedtke, *Embracing a Dictatorship: US Relations with Spain, 1945–53* (Houndmills: St. Martin's Press, 1998); Arturo Jarque, *¡Queremos esas bases! El acercamiento de Estados Unidos a la España de Franco* (Alcalá de Henares: Universidad de Alcalá, 1998); Jill Edwards, *Anglo-American Relations and the Franco Question, 1945–1955* (New York: Oxford University Press, 1999).

16 'Details of Spanish Base'.

17 A detailed annalysis on such concessions in Viñas, *En las garras del águila,* pp. 243-268.

18 'Background on Spanish Agreements', 13 October 1953, NACP, RG 59, LF-OWEA 1942–58, Spain, Box 3.

19 'Conséquences stratégiques et politiques de l'accord hispano-américain', 10 November 1953, AMAE-F, Europe, Espagne 1944–1960, Vol.166.

## An Emphasis on Training, Human Resources, and Material Management

When Spanish-American military cooperation got underway at the end of 1953, the deficiencies of the Spanish armed forces were just as they had been reported a few years earlier. Of the three services, the SAF was the one that needed the most attention; in the postwar period it had become a 'totally unusable' force.[20] It had 634 obsolete planes in service, 32 of which were cataloged as fighters but could scarcely have been used as such.[21] The pilots were faced with the material impossibility of training under proper conditions as the wearing-out of their equipment was coupled with a lack of spare parts. The only factor likely to favor SAF modernization was US aid, but such a contribution would take years to make an appreciable difference.[22]

To oversee the construction of the American bases, the Joint United States Military Group (JUSMG) was created, while the Military Assistance Advisory Group (MAAG) was tasked to oversee the supply and training program. General Kissner, chief negotiator of the military portion of the 1953 pacts, assumed the leadership of both parts of the US military presence in Spain. Kissner's vision reflected the priorities of the Pentagon in Spain: the Iberian Peninsula became the springboard for the Strategic Air Command and USAF Europe (USAFE) in the Euro-Mediterranean theater. Similarly, both MAAG and JUSMG were under the supervision of the Secretary of the Air Force and not of CINCEUR (Commander in Chief, Europe) as was the case with their counterparts elsewhere in Europe.[23] The United States did not delay in the deployment of that operation. Just one month after the signing of the agreements, at the end of October, Harold Talbott arrived in Madrid, paying a visit to the sites intended for the air bases in the company of Kissner and General Lee B. Washbourne, USAF director of installations. With him in Spain was General Nathan F. Twining, Chief of Staff of the USAF, who had also been dispatched to Spain to supervise these beginning steps.[24]

According to the American strategic design, Spain's principal contribution would be that of putting its geographical position at the service of the deployment of the Western alliance. It was hoped to make use of its advantageous location, to benefit from the internal 'stability' provided by the Franco regime, and to take advantage of the freedom of movement in the euphemistically cataloged bases of 'joint operation'. The participation of the Spanish military in this design would be very limited. In

20 'Situation des forces armées espagnoles', 7 January 1953, SHD-MD, GR 14 S 57.

21 *Historia de la Aviación*, p. 279.

22 'Le potentiel militaire des pays de la Péninsule Ibérique en 1954, 1e Partie: L'Espagne', 6 November 1954, SHD-MD, GR 12 S 110.

23 'Terms of Reference of Joint United States Military Group (Spain) and Military Assistance Advisory Group (Spain)', 14 January 1954; 'Organization and Terms of Reference for Spain: JUSMG & MAAG', 1954, NACP, RG 59, LF-OWEA 1942–1958, Spain, Box 3.

24 'Télégramme', 3 November 1953. AMAE-F, Europe, Espagne 1944–60, Vol. 166.

A group of Spanish Air Force officers during their visit to General Thomas D. White, Vice Chief of Staff, USAF, in the Pentagon, 12 November 1953. (Courtesy of the US National Archives at College Park, Still Pictures, RG 342)

the plans established by the JCS, the first objective of the *Mutual Defense Assistance Program* (MDAP, later called *Military Assistance Program*, MAP) was: 'Air defense forces (radar, interceptor aircraft, antiaircraft artillery) protection of (1) air bases (2) naval bases and (3) main governmental, communications, and industrial centers'.[25] The American deployment contemplated the establishment of its bases in Torrejón de Ardoz (Madrid), Valenzuela (Zaragoza), and Morón de la Frontera (Seville), plus the naval base of Rota (Cadiz). To these were added the depot at San Pablo (Seville) and a series of radar stations in Inoges (Zaragoza), Rosas (Girona), Elizondo (Navarra), Villatobas (Toledo), Alcoy (Alicante), and Soller Constantina (Seville). The 'modernized' or MDAP/MAP units of the SAF were to be located mainly on the bases at Talavera la Real (Toledo), Manises (Valencia), Son San Juan (Majorca), Villanubla (Valladolid), and Getafe (Madrid).

The bulk of the program was to be concentrated in the first quadrennium (1954–1957), with the transfer to the Spanish armed forces of most of the material and armaments envisioned, as well as the establishment of a teaching and training circuit.

25 Memorandum for the Operations Coordination Board (OCB), 'Implementation of the US Aid Program for Spain,' 21 November 1955, and 'Memorandum B. Facts Bearing on the Problem', NACP, RG 218, Geographic File (GF), 1954–56, Box 33.

The expectations placed on the arrival of this new equipment proved considerable, while at the same time it generated much uncertainty since management of the equipment would require advance training prior to use. US military officials, aware of the logistical and instructional deficiencies of their Spanish counterparts, soon emphasized the linkage of the sending of supplies and material with the training of the personnel who would be in charge of their use and maintenance. These training programs would be essential to ensure the optimal incorporation of the material and armaments given to the Spanish, a difficult task given the country's lack of resources and its considerable educational and technological backwardness at the time. Spain would, in fact, have to send a portion of its personnel to be instructed in US training centers. They would also need to increase their knowledge of English.[26] Moreover, candidates for training programs would have to be prepared for a lifestyle and education system that differed in many respects from what they knew in their home country: the work demands, strict schedules, regimented meals, deference along the chain of command, the nature of the living quarters, etc.[27]

Although American aid had been eagerly sought and viewed as the essential tool for lifting the armed forces out of its organizational, technical, and operational atrophy, no short- or medium-term projections had been made of the effects that such aid would bring. In the first round of cooperation by the Spanish military with the premier Western power, there was much improvisation, ignorance, and inertia, leaving it to the United States to write the script and set the pace of the process. Later on, there was no shortage of lamentation at having thus proceeded.

At the start of 1954, the American military material began to arrive. Of the three branches, the SAF received the most advanced equipment, which represented a major training and logistical challenge. Training aircraft such as the Lockheed T-33 were initially provided to instruct Spanish pilots on jets. Eventually, over 300 jets would be provided, mainly Sabre F-86F fighters as well as T-33s and T-34s. Maritime rescue and training helicopters were also included, as well as propeller airplanes of various types. Simultaneously, the refinery at Escombreras was refurbished to produce aviation gasoline. The magnitude of the challenge—the leap into the modern fighter jet era—explains the intensity with which the AF Training Program began.[28] The goal was to furnish personnel to nine interception wings, to which Sabre aircraft would be assigned: pilots, mechanics, flight controllers, and other cadres capable of meeting the operational, logistical, and technical requirements related to the new material and its proper maintenance.[29] To that end, many spots were reserved for directors and

26 See Francisco Escribano e Isabel Herrando, 'La implantación del inglés como lingua franca en el Ejército de Tierra español (1953–1989)', *Ayer*, forthcoming.

27 'Datos sobre la vida militar en EE.UU.,' 23 December 1953, AHEA, N67/2.

28 1,801 members of the SAF were trained under the MDAP in 1954-1957. 'Weekly Activity Report for MAAG, Spain, for the Ambassador', 8 December 1956, NACP, RG 334, MAAG Spain, SCC, 1952–1962, Box 6.

29 'Modernisation de l'Armée Espagnole', 2 November 1954, SHD-MD, GR 14 S 57.

mechanics in the SAF schools: Jet Aviation (Talavera la Real), Basic Flight (Matacán), Aircraft and Engine Mechanics (León), Communications and Electronics (Cuatro Vientos), and the General Academy of the Air (San Javier).

Throughout that year, the transit of missions was constant: senior leaders, officers, and NCOs from the SAF visited military training centers in the United States or took extended stays there to study, while their American counterparts who traveled to Spain to either inspect the construction of the bases or to instruct their Spanish colleagues in the operation and maintenance of the military equipment supplied. The future teachers of the *Escuela de Reactores* (Interceptor School) located in Talavera and founded in December 1953, were first trained at Fürstenfeldbruck air base in the German Federal Republic, where they received several courses in modern aeronautics. In the months that followed, other USAF facilities in Europe became common destinations (Ramstein, Rhein-Main, Bitburg, Hahn, and Kaufbeuren in West Germany, and Châteauroux in France). In the United States, the courses took the Spanish military to USAF bases throughout the country (Lackland, Amarillo, and Bryan, Texas; Chanute, Kansas; West Palm Beach, Florida; Williams, Arizona, etc.). In most cases, the training received was focused on specialties such as piloting, maintenance, weapons, construction, electronics, communications, and meteorology, to which English language courses were added.[30] That same year, training flights in Spain began in Talavera, under close consultation with the USAFE instructors. Somewhat later, after acquisition of the American material and training from the courses abroad, adjustments were made to the organizational structure under the MAAG's advice, with special emphasis on the creation of the Basic Flight Training School and the School of Air Traffic Control (both in Matacán).[31]

The formative itinerary was expanded and consolidated in the years that followed (in 1955, Spanish officers began to attend courses at the USAF Air Command and Staff College in Maxwell, Alabama), with constant inspection visits to keep on improving the workings of the machinery. The Air Minister, General González Gallarza, crossed the Atlantic again, accompanied by the Air Chief of Staff, General Francisco Fernandez Longoria, and other officers. For almost a month they met with their American colleagues (Talbott and Twining) as well as visited air bases and aeronautical facilities. Also on that trip were representatives of several Spanish aeronautical industries (Fábricas Hispano de Sevilla, ENMASA, Fábrica de Hélices para Aviación, CASA, and AISA), who evaluated prospects in the United States for the modernization of their sector. The possibility that Spain could build jet aircraft under American license, raised at that time, was ruled out on account of the inadequacy of Spanish technical resources and human capital. Also, General Fernandez Longoria visited the American air bases in West Germany, where Spanish pilots were trained in the handling of jet aircraft. In turn General Orval R. Cook,

30 'Historical Data Report'.
31 *Historia de la Aviación*, pp. 280–299.

Pilots of the SAF receive a briefing from Captain Encinias (far right), USAF, Officer in Charge of the MAAG training school at Talavera la Real, Spain. Second from right is Captain Malcom Agnew, USAF, a pilot instructor, 10 June 1954. (Courtesy of the US National Archives at College Park, Still Pictures, RG 342)

A group of foreign air force pilots, including four Spanish Captains, check in at Lackland air base for their MDAP funded training, 1956. (Courtesy of the US National Archives at College Park, Still Pictures, RG 342)

USAFE deputy commander, traveled to Spain to see firsthand how the program was being developed.[32] Members of INTA were also invited to visit research and development centers in the United States.[33]

By the end of 1954, the American authorities regarded the prospects of cooperation with the Spanish regime as excellent, even 'in many cases more satisfactory than in other European countries.'[34] Thus was ratified the intent of keeping US military machinery in Spain autonomous from the US European Command (EUCOM): the main operational force in Spain, the JUSMG Air Section, converted in July 1956 to the Sixteenth Air Force (16th AF) and based in Torrejón de Ardoz, was not made part of the NATO-attached forces in Europe. Likewise, it was also noted that the ability of the Spanish military to absorb the armaments and equipment supplied under the MDAP had been limited, hence a 'slow down' policy emerged in the allocation of military aid funds, except for personnel.[35] Some of their Spanish counterparts understood the situation:

> In general, relations with the people of the American Mission go very well. Almost all of them are very competent, are animated by the best will and take great interest in helping us. The difficulties lie mainly in the difference of organization, with the consequent difficulties of synchronizing our small forces with their gigantic ones, and also the lack of preparation and work rhythms of many of our people.
>
> Where more deficiencies are observed is in matters of material, which are naturally the most complicated and where our lagtime is greater. In this respect, unfortunately, we are giving an impression that is not entirely satisfactory.[36]

32 'Application des Accords hispano-américains: Livraison de matériel de guerre d'instruction. Construction de bases', 27 March 1954; 'Télégramme', 1 May 1954; 'Application des Accords hispano-américains. Missions militaires, voyages d'études, bases', 4 May 1954; 'Application des Accords hispano-américains. Visites du Général Gallarza et d'une mission militaire espagnole aux Etats-Unis. Bases', 1 June 1954, AMAE-F, Europe, Spain, 1944–60, Vol. 167.

33 Spain even had the possibility of having a permanent delegate in the AGARD, though this did not ultimately come to pass because the country did not belong to NATO. AHEA, N67/3.

34 Office of Political Adviser, EUCOM, American Embassy-Paris to Director, Office of European Regional Affairs, Departement of State, 27 December 1954, NACP, RG 59, LF-OWEA 1942–58, Spain, Box 3.

35 For this, $6 million was allocated. 'Nota para S.E. sobre ayuda militar a España en el año fiscal 1955', 23 December 1954, AHEA, N67/3.

36 General Francisco Fernández Longoria, Chief of Staff of the Air, to Colonel Julio Salvador Díaz Benjumea, Air Attache to the Embassy in Washington, 10 March 1955, AHEA, N67/3.

Meanwhile, high-level military exchanges continued apace. The Air Force Secretary returned to Spain in April 1955.[37] Two months later the Sabre fighter planes began to arrive in Spain, forming in September the First Fighter Wing in Manises. To expedite this process, officials relied on the advice of an F-86 Mobile Training Detachment, which had to devote more time to the task than expected due to the Spanish tendency 'to return to the bad habits of the past'.[38] This concern was addressed at the follow-up meetings between the MAAG and the Liaison Committee of the SAF (CEFFAA), as was that of the misuse of staff trained under the MDAP. The MAAG insisted that the staff attending the training courses were being sent fairly frequently to destinations that had no connection to the development of the program.[39] Dealing with this faulty use of human resources consumed a good deal of the MAAG's advisory energy in its early years as it aimed to standardize and professionalize the selection of F-86F pilots and aviation equipment.

The resources of the MDAP and the Technical Assistance Program (TAP) were combined to convince the Air Ministry of the necessity of introducing modern methods into its human resources policies. The USAFE sent a Personnel Classification Training Team to Madrid, which together with members of the local Higher Council for Scientific Research (CSIC) and the National Institute of Applied Psychology and Psychology (INPAP), were in charge of preparing a selection method adapted to the needs of the SAF. The latter, 'after 27 months of continuous pressure' by the MAAG, eventually integrated it into what the Americans described as one of their most precious achievements. From that point on, the Air Ministry would support the selection of pilots and navigators by the Department of Experimental Psychology of the CSIC. It also represented a 'great victory for the development of psychology in Spain', and one of the earliest examples of the transfer of knowledge to the civilian world derived from US military assistance and advising in Spain.[40]

Around the same time, Spanish military officials had begun to express initial feelings of discontent with the type of military aid received and the procedures for its award. Their displeasure with the insufficiency of and delay in the supplies was cloaked in friendly tones in the course of successive visits of high-ranking American military leaders to Spain. Likewise, it was emphasized that economic assistance to

37 'Un nouveau passage en Espagne de M. Talbott, Secrétaire américain à l'Air', 26 April 1955, AMAE-F, Europe, Espagne 1944–60, Vol. 169.

38 MAAG Spain to the Assistant for Mutual Security, USAF: 'Request for Changes to UMD and Training Mission, Air Force Section', 25 March 1957, NACP, RG 334, GC, Box 5.

39 'Weekly', 17 November 1955, NACP, RG 334, MAAG Spain, SCC, 1952–1962, Box 2, 'Nota informativa para el Excmo. Sr. General Jefe del Estado Mayor del Aire, sobre conversaciones con el General Kissner, Jefe del MAAG en Madrid', 1 February 1956, AHEA, N67/3.

40 'Weekly', 14 April 1955 and 15 March 1956, NACP, RG 334, SCC, 1952–1962, Box 2 and 4; José Germain, INPAP to Miguel Orduña López, Colonel Chief of the 2nd Section of the High Staff of the Air, 13 November 1961, AHEA, A10908.

Spain was much lower than what had been granted to other countries through the Marshall Plan.[41] Behind this discontentment was the fact that the Spanish military had begun to take a 'bath of reality' and to become increasingly aware of the role assigned to them by their American colleagues. It was partly because of the excessive expectations placed on collaboration with the United States as a means of achieving the desired modernization of the Spanish military, partly because of their own ignorance of the legal regulations governing US military deployment, and partly because of their inability to convey an image of efficiency as they received the agreed-upon aid.

The Spanish complaints centered around the slow arrival of the equipment, the poor quality of some of it, and the limited amount of choice regarding the materials delivered.[42] The final say over the type and quantity of material and its economic value rested almost exclusively with the Americans. What was more, the costs of sustaining the equipment delivered—including fuel—would be borne by the Spanish budget at a time when Spain's government faced serious problems in international trade due to its lack of foreign exchange. Because it was not a NATO member, Spain's bargaining position with Pentagon leaders was more limited than that of other European partners of the United States. It was increasingly evident that the funding and assistance coming from the United States were being tailored to suit that country's own interests.[43]

MDAP officials acknowledged that the proffered endowments would not be completed in the first biennium, justifying the wait by pointing to the long time it took to deliver equipment that had a high cost per unit, especially the F-86F sabres.[44] At the start of 1956 the Spanish Air Ministry added some additional requests not originally included in the aid program. The American response was that this material could only be received in return for giving up other items.[45] When the Spanish negotiators reiterated their requests, General Kissner advised them to accept without protest what was assigned in the original plan:

> Later on, when the time comes that Spain has shown that it can work with the material planned for delivery at present, it will be able to ask for more material

41 'OCB Discussion May 18 of Slowdown in MDAP Deliveries to Spain', 17 May 1955. NACP, GR 59, LF-OWEA 1942–1958, Spain, Box 5; 'Bases américaines en Espagne', 19 July 1955, and 'Application des Accords hispano-américaines (visite en Espagne du Secrétaire à l'Air des Etats-Unis et de diverses personnalités américaines – 2ème anniversaire des Accords)', 15 October 1955, AMAE-F, Europe, Espagne 1944–60, Vol. 169.

42 'OCB Discussion May 18 of Slowdown in MDAP Deliveries to Spain', 17 May 1955, NACP, RG 59, LF-OWEA 1942–1958, Spain, Box 5.

43 Air Attaché in Washington to Chief General of the High Staff of the Air, 20 October and 16 December 1955, AHEA, N67/3.

44 'OCB. Progress Report in Spain (NSC 5418/1)', 8 December 1955, NACP, RG 59, Lot File 62 D430, Box 32.

45 'Agregado Aéreo en Washington al General Jefe del Estado Mayor del Aire', 5 January 1956, AHEA, N67/3.

> with a moral force that it now lacks.... I am afraid that, due to the shortage of trained specialists and knowledge of the logistical problems posed by modern flight technology, you will not be in a position to maintain the material to be received under the current plan at a sufficient level of efficiency and flight service.[46]

The head of the American mission further insisted on the urgency of organizing an Air Defense Command in Spain, on solving the serious problems that existed with radio transmissions, and on the 'importance of the problem of the preparation of specialist personnel, as well as that of logistical support.' The improvisational styles and lack of knowledge shown by the Spanish military in the initial stages of the bilateral relationship took their toll. The poor understanding of the modalities and mechanisms of US military assistance, together with the reduced efficiency in receiving the agreed upon aid, allowed less room for maneuver. The way in which the Spanish leaders were trying to accelerate military modernization met with firm resistance from the Americans, who did not see it as viable or necessary. It would not be easy to overcome US reservations to authorize new military aid when it was not clear that the material given thus far was being used efficiently.

## A Positive Contribution Not Free of Friction

Three years after the signing of the 1953 accords the SAF was in the process of transition, trying to incorporate the modern logistical and tactical concepts of its North American counterparts, but its military effectiveness was still considered nil. When the time came that the foundations were completed and an organization built in the American mold, those forces would have 'a limited defensive capability'.[47] Up to that point, the SAF had received from the MDAP a dozen F-86F fighter jets, T6D and T33A training aircraft, H-19B rescue helicopters, and SA-16 rescue aircraft, along with some C-119F transport planes. In addition, the US had provided machinery for the construction of airports, transmission equipment, engines and spare parts for flight equipment, armaments, tools and auxiliary facilities, specialist training equipment, vehicles, firefighting equipment, fuel tanks, language laboratories, etc.[48] At the same time, the TAP had made it possible to accelerate the training of flight controllers as well as military and civilian meteorologists in modern techniques and systems.

46 'Nota informativa para el Excmo. Sr. Gral. Jefe del Estado Mayor del Aire, sobre conversaciones con el General Kissner, Jefe del MAAG en Madrid', 1 February 1956, AHEA, N67/3.
47 'The Spanish Armed Forces', 27 August 1956, NACP, GR 59, LF-OWEA 1942–1958, Spain, Box 7.
48 A complete list in 'Material recibido en el Ejército del Aire con cargo al MDAP hasta el día 22 de febrero de 1956', AHEA, N1247/4.

With the objective of achieving greater bilateral coordination, and following the suggestions of their American partners, the Air Force continued its reorganization with the creation in April 1956 of the Air Defense Command, one of MAAG's main priorities. In its charge would be the air combat squadrons, the alert and control network, antiaircraft artillery (which concentrated a large part of the resources that MDAP allocated to the Army), and other forces or services assigned to it. Its purpose was the air defense of the territory, including defense against an eventual Soviet attack against the US bases. The operational collaboration between the two countries in this area was destined to increase gradually, as were the risks posed by the presence of these bases should there be a confrontation with the USSR. For this reason, the Spanish leaders did not refrain from seeking more means to modernize and increase the deterrent capacity of the Spanish military, with special emphasis on ground-to-air and air-to-air missiles, which were initially excluded from the agreed aid. Their American counterparts, while making no concrete commitment to financing, showed themselves generally willing to study the Spanish positions on improvement of the aid machinery.[49]

That year the Second Fighter Wing in Zaragoza, equipped with Sabres and some T-33A aircraft, and the Third Fighter Wing in Villanubla, with T-6D aircraft and later some T-33As as well, were launched. The training of Spanish pilots in jet aircraft was largely carried out in Spain once the personnel and means were available. This decision was partly motivated by the shortage of foreign exchange in the Spanish economy, which led to a decline in traveling abroad for courses in subsequent years. The Spanish military leaders stressed this problem to their American colleagues, also pointing out the complications that the language barrier continued to cause and the negative repercussions that the stark contrast with the American resources and armaments had on the morale of the participants.[50] The MAAG follow-up reports provided numerous examples of this feeling of frustration upon returning to Spain and getting reacclimated to the outdated equipment and the many deficiencies of the Spanish military. However, the reports also noted that teaching systems and methods of instruction were becoming more efficient and practical, thanks to the continuous guidance of the MAAG and the incorporation of teachers trained in USAF methods and with experience at USAF schools and bases.[51]

The Spanish leaders returned to their position of entreating an increase in military and economic aid, justified by necessity in the face of the inflation generated by

49 Interviews between Lieutenant-General Francisco Fernández-Longoria, Chief of Staff of the Air with the President of the JCS, Admiral Arthur W. Radford, and with General Nathan F. Twining, Chief of Staff of the USAF, 10 and 11 April 1956, AHEA, N67/3.

50 Meeting between the Minister of the Spanish Army and Brigadier-General Dahlen, 21 November 1956, NACP, RG 334, MAAG Spain, SCC, 1952–1962, Box 1.

51 The members of the Air Force in the contingent of the MAAG bound for Spain were almost half of the total (51 of a total of 105), 'Informe especial. España y la ayuda norteamericana', 4 April 1957, CDMH-AFNFF, doc. 21847.

the construction of the bases and the costs derived from the implementation of the MDAP.[52] They gave an accounting of their own financial burdens borne for 'the extraordinary expenses of the expansion of your aerodromes, the installation of schools and services, the numerous trips to America of our personnel for training, and the reorganization of our services'.[53] In the case of the Air Ministry, those expenses came to several billion pesetas.[54] A favorable American response would have to wait for a while, but finally the joint front composed of the US embassy in Madrid and the MAAG emissary—now USAF General Stanley J. Donovan—would get a concession on that point and in the allocation of Sidewinder missiles in the MAP in mid-1958,

Major-General Arthur W. Kissner, USAF, Chief of the MAAG Spain (1953-1958). (Courtesy of the US National Archives at College Park, Still Pictures, RG 342)

52 'Spanish Request for Additional FY 57 Defense Support Assistance', 23 November 1956, RG 59, CDF, 752.5-MSP/11-2356.
53 'Ayuda económica,' 1958, CDMH-AFNFF, doc. 21842, AHEA, N953/72.
54 'Repercusión económica que tiene en este ministerio la aplicación de las ayudas americanas', June 1957, and 'Repercusión económica de la aplicación de los convenios firmados con Norteamérica', 9 October 1957, AHEA, N953/72.

Major-General Stanley J. Donovan, USAF, Chief of the MAAG Spain (1958-1960). (Courtesy of the US National Archives at College Park, Still Pictures, RG 342)

in both cases as a conciliatory gesture in the wake of disagreements caused by the decolonization crisis of Ifni-Sahara (October 1957–June 1958).[55]

Bilateral relations, especially between the two militaries, were clouded by the war between Spain and Moroccan militia groups in the tiny colonial enclave of Ifni and the large territory of Western Sahara in northwest Africa. In the course of that crisis, the US government showed its reluctance to allow the use of MDAP material outside mainland Spain, which increased tension in the convulsive setting of decolonizing North Africa in the 1950s.[56] Likewise, Washington prohibited MAAG personnel

55 'Weekly', 27 May, 10 June, and 18 September 1958, NACP, RG 334, MAAG Spain, SCC, 1952–1962, Box 5.

56 The Ifni-Sahara War has not hitherto attracted the attention of US diplomatic and military historians. An example of its invisibility among the former is the nonetheless magnificent Mathew J. Connelly, *A Diplomatic Revolution. Algeria's Fight for Independence and the Origins of the Post-Cold War Era* (New York: Oxford University Press, 2002). Spanish and Moroccan historians have themselves neglected the scholarly study of the

from giving any type of advice in the theater of operations.[57] As a consequence, during the initial phases of the conflict the SAF had to content itself with using versions of old German models manufactured in Spain (Junkers JU-52-T2Bs, Heinkel HE-111-B21s, and Messerschmitt Bf-109 G2-HA-1112s), emphasizing 'the complete lack of preparation of the units, lacking apparatus, without arming the few available, without reserves of bombs and ammunition.' From the air fleet ceded by the United States, the SAF were only allowed to use the T-3 Douglas C-47 and the Sikorsky SH-19B helicopters in air transport and radar missions, respectively. It was only at the beginning of 1957 that more modern fighter planes, in particular the T-6 Texan equipped with Oerlikon rockets, began to be available. Most of these were transferred at reduced prices to Spain by France (which had obtained them through the Franco-American MDAP). The same happened concerning the most relevant armored vehicles used by the Spanish Army in the conflict, making Paris emerge as the ally that would allow the Spanish to shift the military balance in its own favor. The Ifni-Sahara lesson profoundly affected the Spanish military's perception of the commitment of the US —and of France—to the modernization of the Spanish military.[58]

The Spanish military became increasingly conscious of the risks inherent in the presence of the American bases in their territory at a time when they also felt a growing unease at having placed themselves in a strategic design that was so unequally weighted to the interests of the United States. The assistance and advice from that country was essential for continuing the modernization process that was underway, but it also had serious limitations and drawbacks. Nor were things made easier by the cold American reception to the Spanish proposals for their contribution to the European defense apparatus and for the relocation of bases close to cities such as Madrid and Zaragoza, which would be most exposed to the effects of Soviet nuclear attacks. The Americans made it clear that the contribution of the Spanish armed forces consisted of safeguarding its national territory and the American bases installed there, in addition to minimizing the possible danger from atomic weapons for the populations of two of the largest Spanish metropolitan areas.[59]

conflict. A recent exception is Juan Pastrana, *Arde el desierto. 1957: la guerra de Ifni-Sáhara y la lucha por el poder en Marruecos* (Madrid: Nowtilus, 2017).

57 'Weekly', 3 December 1957, 'Discussions with Spanish Army Minister', 2 January 1958, 'Utilization of MAP Equipment in Africa (Secret)', 7 January 1958, 'Meeting between Chief Navy Section, MAAG and Spanish Navy Officers', 10 January 1958, NACP, RG 334, MAAG Spain, SCC, 1952–1962, Boxes 5 and 7.

58 *Historia de la Aviación*, pp. 295–300; 'Weekly', 22 and 29 January 1958, NACP, RG 334, MAAG Spain, SCC, 1952–1962, Box 5. On Franco-Spanish military cooperation during the conflict, see Pastrana, *Arde el desierto* and Baptiste Colom-y-Canals, 'El papel de los agregados militares en la cooperación franco-española en el Sáhara', in *La historia militar hoy. Investigaciones y tendencias* (Madrid: Instituto Universitario Gutiérrez Mellado-UNED, 2014), pp. 413–415.

59 'Convenios con Norteamérica' and 'Conferencias sobre efectos de las armas nucleares', February 1958; 'Reunión del Jefe del Estado español con los Ministros de Asuntos

Cover of *Noticias de Actualidad*, February 17, 1958. This weekly, the mouthpiece of the US Information Service in Spain, dedicated two special issues and several articles to explain US military assistance and the advisory contribution to the FAS as a way to counter criticism of Spain in the aftermath of the Ifni-Sahara War. (Author's collection)

But beyond bilateral disagreements, and despite the coexistence between the old propeller aviation and the new fighter jets that inevitably gave the SAF a somewhat new image, the transformation driven by US aid and the assimilation of its organizational, logistical, and educational methods would have lasting effects. In the report issued by General Kissner at the end of his prolonged stay in Spain, he concluded that the 'Spanish Air Force possesses the potential for developing and maintaining a modern air force.'[60] Here was an affirmation that symbolized a notable

Exteriores, Ejército, Marina y Aire, junto a otros altos cargos militares', 7 April 1958, CDMH-AFNFF, docs. 21840, 21841, 23918 y 23920.

60 'End of Tour Report of Chief, MAAG Spain, for period 1-july-1956–30-june-1958', 6 August 1958, NACP, RG 334, MAAG Spain, SCC, 1952–1962, Box 6.

step forward after previous assessments. Notwithstanding, it was pointed out that to smooth that process efforts would have to be stepped up in a number of areas: support to the units receiving assistance under the MAP, general reorganization of the armed forces (reducing obsolete units and bases that were not serving any tactical purpose, while applying new personnel policies, especially in terms of management and productivity), and improvement in the efficiency of the supply system (especially fuel and spare parts). Any increase in forces would require additional training and more staff in charge of logistics and maintenance, something the Spanish government was not in a position to undertake on its own. The lack of internal or external financing to acquire new equipment outside of American aid was exacerbated by the expenses incurred in the operations in Ifni-Sahara. Spanish industry was not in a position to produce the electronic and communications equipment required by the program. Spare parts depended on US supplies, and training of specialists was still insufficient in a number of fields (communications, electronics, fire fighting, etc.). In spite of all this, the MAP-supported units had made considerable progress in terms of personnel, supply, and maintenance with the collaboration of the MAAG training advisors. Flight schools had also been substantially upgraded thanks to the training of pilots in American schools and the work of the MAAG tactical advisor. The impact on technical training had mixed results, but significant progress had been made. Instruction in electronics, communications, meteorology, pilot training, and maintenance of flight equipment had been, in that order, the areas where the greatest number of instructional training visits had been carried out in the United States by that time.

In April 1958, the forces of the Air Defense Command, whose operational units were composed of the First, Second, and Third Wings (the Third would disappear months later), Squadrons 41, 51, and 61, and Alert and Control had been fully built up. Before the end of the decade, work was completed to improve the runways of the bases where the new Spanish fighter jets would be housed, namely the Fourth Fighter Wing in Son San Juan, the Fifth in Morón de la Frontera, and the Sixth in Torrejón de Ardoz. Simultaneously, the facilities of the Alert and Control Network were operated, in principle, mainly by American troops, with whom Spanish personnel trained for this purpose would be integrated (one part at Keesler, Missisippi, and another at the headquarters of the 65th Air Division of the USAF in Spain). The first base that came into service was at Villatobas in July of 1958; over the next two years, the other six that had been planned were incorporated. The combat operations center was established in Torrejón de Ardoz, where the Spanish command posts and the 65th Air Division were located.[61] A similar dynamic played out in the founding of the School of Helicopters in 1960 at Cuatro Vientos aerodrome, whose instructors

61 In 1962, the first fully Spanish teams were up and running, though still under the supervision of the USAF, and in December 1964 the Defense Command took over all of the installations. See *Historia de la Aviación*, pp. 300-303.

were pilots who had also taken rotary-wing flight courses at American bases (Gary in San Marcos, Texas, and in Fort Rucker, Alabama). Alongside these reforms and improvements of knowledge and systems in several areas came the creation of the Industrial Vocational Training School (in Agoncillo-Logroño) and the training of SAF personnel in antisubmarine warfare in San Diego, California.

At the end of 1959, the major facilities of the Spanish base program were 97.6 percent complete and virtually 100 percent operational.[62] Their construction had been the priority undertaking. The cornerstone of this deployment was the base of Torrejón de Ardoz, whose runway became the longest in Europe and would continue to be until the construction of the Ulyanovsk Vostochny Airport in 1983. The base hosted the 16th AF as well as 65th Air Division of the Strategic Air Command (SAC), where it cooperated with Spanish Air Force units in the Air Defense Direction Centers. The 16th AF was activated in 1956 as a Joint Military Group to provide command and control of USAF activities in Spain. In 1957, it was realigned under SAC to provide command and control of SAC bases and B-47 Stratojet rotational units assigned and deployed to Spain and Morocco (then progressively replaced by the B-52 Stratofortress). The 65th Air Division directed construction of the bases as well as the establishment of off-base housing and radar sites. In July 1958, the Air Defense Command's 497th Fighter-Interceptor Squadron arrived at this base equipped with American F-86D Sabres. In April 1960, the 497th FIS transitioned to the F-102 Delta Dagger and operated under SAC control until its transfer to the USAF in Europe (USAFE) 86th Air Division (Defense) at Ramstein Air Base in West Germany in July 1960. This transfer was made in order that all USAF fighter assets in Europe could be concentrated under one command. The bases located in Zaragoza and Morón housed strategic bombers and supported the maintenance of the pipeline that spanned the 768 kilometers between Rota and Zaragoza. The aforementioned network of radar stations was connected to all of this. Of lesser importance to the setup were the bases of San Pablo, conceived to give support to the activities of the POL (Petroleum, Oil, and Lubricants) Squadron and Stratcom, and the one at Reus that had the status of a fighter aircraft recovery base. In July 1959, JUSMG-Spain as well as MAAG-Spain were placed directly under CINCEUR, ending the Executive Agent responsibilities of the Secretary of the USAF. In July 1959, JUSMG-Spain and MAAG-Spain were placed directly under CINCEUR, terminating the Executive Agent responsibilities of the Secretary of the USAF.

62 'Material Submitted by JUSMG to Senator Dennis Chavez, Chairman Defense Appropriations Subcommittee', 24/30 November 1959, NACP, RG 59, LF-OWEA 1953–62, Spain, Box 3.

## A Balance Not Free From Controversy

US military officials' assessment of the evolution of the SAF was on the whole positive, and as might be expected, congratulatory regarding their own contribution:

> Considering the posture of the SAF prior to the Military Assistance Program, the SAF has made outstanding progress toward attaining a modern air force. The SAF has discarded many of their traditional methods and procedures in favor of US policies and practices. Progress along these lines is continuing in the field of operations, supply and maintenance, personnel, and management.[63]

A vital part of the MDAP/MAP had been the personnel training programs. Through it Spanish personnel had received courses of instruction at US military schools on aeronautics as well as on equipment, systems, logistics, and other operational functions. To this was added the role played by the numerous Mobile Training Teams and the USAF Training Mission for instruction in the operation and maintenance of modern equipment. The results of all of this were appreciable at the end of that decade in the instruction that was given 'in the flying school system, in the Aircraft and Engine Mechanics Schools, and in the Communications and Electronics Schools of the Spanish Air Force.'[64] Around 4,000 Spanish officers, enlisted men, and civilians had received training outside of Spain or had been sent as observers to US operational units.

In the face of Spanish officials' demands for more material and more modern equipment, their American counterparts told them that they should first show signs of making better use of the equipment already provided by the United States. The biggest problem lay in the weaknesses still present in the 'maintenance of forces.' Effective logistical support was essential to increased efficiency because where the greatest difficulties were observed was in areas where there were no means to 'plan, replace and effectively schedule the procurement, transportation, and maintenance of supplies and equipment.'[65] With regard to the SAF, it was pointed out that the United States had provided enough F-86F fighter planes to outfit nine squadrons, but only seven had been formed—one of which was still in the process of organization—while another was dedicated to a combat training center. The problems of review and maintenance had led to the implementation of a method of standardization of supply and control systems that was not yet fully operational, while inventories of spare parts had been developed on American initiative. On the other hand, the performance of the

63 'End of Tour Report'. Notice of this gradual change for the better was also taken by military observers from other nearby countries interested in the Spanish situation. See 'Relations et conventions hispano-américains', March 1959, SHD-MD, GR 14 S 435.

64 'Material Submitted by JUSMG'.

65 General Caldara, Chief of MAAG, to General Muñoz Grandes, Chief of the Joint Staff, 15 May 1961, CDMH-AFNFF, doc. 3947.

facilities built under the armaments production program for repair and manufacture had gone from being good to not being used at all, resulting in a waste of the $6 million that had been granted for that purpose. A similar concern was being voiced in Washington in interviews between the Spanish ambassador and senior Defense Department officials: if all the available F-86s could not be used, 'we could hardly fly the new types of aircraft that were much more expensive to service and much more complicated'. The lack of Spanish technical resources was also blamed for the incomplete operation of radar installations.[66]

On the Spanish side, the US contribution in armaments and equipment was questioned on the grounds that it was composed of material that was outdated in many cases. The Spanish officials insisted on the need for more modern weaponry to guarantee the defense of the national territory. A report from the Center for the Study of National Defense (CESEDEN) prepared a few years later provided a comprehensive inventory showing the state of use of the supplies delivered and the aid received between 1953 and 1963:

- 270 F86s (40 new, the rest used);
- 24 C47s (DC-3, at half-life);
- 12 C54s (DC-4, at half-life);
- 48 T33s (training jets);
- 16 T34s (training aircraft);
- 120 T6s (training aircraft, antiquated, and equipped with arms by Spain for use in the Sahara);
- 7 SA16As (Gruman rescue planes, at half-life);
- 5 H19Bs (rescue helicopters, at half-life);
- 6 H19As (training helicopters, with no practical use);
- 7 SA16Bs (in good condition);
- navigation networks and communications and electronics equipment;
- equipment for construction of bases;
- munitions, gasoline, etc.;
- network alert, installed by the Americans and maintained by them until 31 December 1964—upon retirement, the 65th Division was to be handed over to the Air Force;
- schools for training of pilots and specialists; and
- microwave network, initially conceived as a control network, now also used as a warning network and therefore saturated.[67]

66 Ambassador in Spain in the United States to the Minister of Foreign Affairs, 17 July 1961, CDMH-AFNFF, doc. 3949.

67 CESEDEN, 'Estudios de los acuerdos con los Estados Unidos ante su posible prórroga en 1968. 2ª fase analítica. Conclusiones de la Comisión Militar', 1968, CDMH-AFNFF, doc. 5299.

To this was added that the deployment of these resources that had been designed to meet American needs, so that the general line of interception of the SAF covered 'approximately three quarters of the territory of the Peninsula where, of course, joint forces are embedded...but...the whole coast of the Cantabrian and the Northwest of Spain has been left without protection.'[68] That observation was in line with the widespread view that the aid and expertise provided to Spain had been scarce in relation to the risks that country was incurring, and much less than that offered to other European countries. In fact, only Portugal had received less, while Yugoslavia, which was not even in NATO and was a Communist regime, had gotten almost twice as much aid.[69] The pacts with the United States had made Spain a potential belligerent against the USSR but had not afforded it the necessary means to guarantee the defense of its territory. Franco's chief adviser, Admiral Luis Carrero Blanco, surmised that the United States had fulfilled its own objectives but not those of Spain, which had to be content with material that was 'practically scraps' and that could not even 'deal with a war of aggression in our outposts and provinces in Africa'.[70]

Despite this widespread recognition of the insufficiency of American aid, it was also acknowledged that these materials ultimately made up 'the bulk of the armaments of our armed forces.'[71] Moreover, even in the Army, usually the most conservative and most resistant to American influence, it was pointed out that the aid had been 'great, compared to what we have contributed economically to the reconstruction of the Army.' Likewise, some of the criticisms raised by the MAAG were not denied:

> Militarily, it can be argued against us, and it is to some extent true, that our absorption capacity has been poor. The arrival of a large amount of material implies serious problems of personnel, mainly of specialists, of logistics and instruction that have not been entirely solved by the Spanish Army; we realize that.[72]

If there was a palpable sense of dissatisfaction with the quantity and quality of American supplies, this was not the case with staff training. The Spanish military

68 Admiral Luis Carrero Blanco, 'Consideraciones sobre los convenios entre España y los Estados Unidos y la situación de nuestra defensa nacional', 1961, CDMH-AFNFF, doc. 4399.

69 According to those estimates, the aid allocated to Spain up until that time barely exceeded $407 million, while the aid delivered to Yugoslavia was upwards of $724 million.

70 The contents of this report were restated, in amplified form, in another document later brought to the Delegate Commission of the Government for the development of the agreements with the US: 'Informe sobre la revisión de los convenios suscritos entre España y los Estados Unidos el 26 de septiembre de 1953', 5 April 1962, CDMH-AFNFF, doc. 3953.

71 'Estudios de los acuerdos'.

72 'Impresiones de la ayuda americana y previsiones militares para el futuro', 1 December 1961, CDMH-AFNFF, doc. 3928.

reports, which were quite critical of the contribution of material, stood out in contrast for the absence of any complaints about American assistance in improving the technical and operational training of the Spanish military:

> American aid has allowed us, for sure, a great advance in the technical order of professional knowledge. Our officers of the three armies are today second to none in their knowledge of use of modern weapons.... Our military capability, in terms of modern armaments, had lagged behind, and this lacuna, which would have been very difficult to overcome by ourselves, has been saved thanks to US aid.[73]
>
> The participation of a significant number of officers, NCOs and specialists in training courses in the USA, joint exercises between Spanish naval and air forces and those of the US and other NATO countries (made possible by the conventions), and the readjustment of our logistics system to handle the maintenance of weapons and equipment received have undoubtedly increased the preparation and effectiveness of our cadres.[74]

Appraisals both during the time and after recognized the modernizing impact of the contacts established in the Spanish armed forces and the SAF in particular, without which would otherwise have prevented the spectacular technological and organizational transformations experienced since the Second World War. Overall, there was a fundamental transformation in the level of instruction being given in the Spanish schools and training centers thanks to the material, the articulations of military doctrine, the tactical knowledge, and the systems of organization that came from the Americans.[75] Being connected to the leading Western power made possible a substantial improvement in procedure and organization, armaments, and training, implying that since then 'the United States [armed forces] has become the doctrinal, organic and operative frame of reference'.[76] The extended visits to the United States provided technical and operational training similar to that received by NATO-affiliated countries, together with improvements in doctrine and methods of organization and training. That immersion in the US military complex eased

73 'Consideraciones sobre los convenios'.

74 'Estudios de los Acuerdos'.

75 Numerous statements to this effect appear in the documents of the military organizations. See aslo General Serrano de Pablo, 'Estudio de los acuerdos con EEUU ante su posible prórroga en 1968. Situación española y razones por las cuales se firmaron los convenios de los EEUU en 1953', in *IV Ciclo de Conferencias sobre Defensa Nacional* (Madrid: CESEDEN, 1968), pp. 15–16; Ángel Liberal Lucini, 'Cuarenta años después (1953-1993)', *Revista de Política Exterior*, 35 (1993), p. 185; Carles Barrachina Lisón, *El retorno de los militares a los cuarteles: militares y cambio político en España (1976–1981)* (Thesis, Universitat de Barcelona, 2002), pp. 20–21.

76 Gabriel Cardona, *El poder militar en el Franquismo* (Barcelona: Flor del Viento, 2008), p. 189.

the relationship of the future allies.[77] On the other hand, the arrival of US military equipment, much more modern in spite of the aforementioned criticisms mentioned than what the Spanish military had had at its disposal up until then, made necessary the training of those in charge of its handling. A part of the armed forces had to catch up with the new techniques, tactics, and maintenance systems, even if they did not travel to the United States.

The training effort had a profound impact in the initial decade of the bilateral military relationship, with priority given to the training of pilots, flight crews, and technical personnel of the SAF. From being almost irrelevant at the start of the 1950s, jet aircraft (training and combat aircraft) equipped with weapons systems, doctrine for how it was to be used, and training equivalent to the NATO countries became priorities. SAF instruction was impregnated with the North American matrix, adopting the methods of the USAF in terms of use, organization, and tactics.[78]

According to SAF figures, in the training sessions held in the United States during that period there were 1,544 people in attendance for 164 courses. Of these 543 were officers (mostly lieutenants and captains, 238 and 201, respectively), 921 non-commissioned officers and troops (including 374 sergeants and 1,258 corporals), and 80 civilians. The variety of courses was considerable. Among those with the largest attendance, the most relevant were those related to fighter jet training: jet piloting (90), anti-submarine warfare (59), advanced F-86 flight training (47), comprehensive piloting (24), helicopter flight training (19), and T-33 and F-86 combat crew (18). Also well attended were those courses geared towards personnel in charge of aircraft maintenance and repair: airplanes and jet fighters (146), jet engines (56), jet aircraft maintenance (39), hydraulic airplane systems (36), aircraft electricians (33), aircraft instruments (30), aircraft maintenance officer (30), operator of electric power generator sets (18), repair of pneumatic systems (18), and aircraft structures and sheet metal repair (17). Priority was also given to the training of those responsible for flight control systems and power plants and their maintenance: radar repairs and on-board and ground-based radio equipment (134), air traffic control operators (86), and aircraft alert and control (30). Other courses that provided important assistance were devoted to logistics: specialists in organization and registration of supplies (72), and official supplies (30). In addition to the training visits to the US, courses were held in several European countries involving a total of 250 people, almost all of them military personnel, with US bases in West Germany the main destination (206), and in smaller numbers France (29) and Italy (15). Many of the courses in West Germany

77 Miguel Platón, *Hablan los militares. Testimonios para la historia (1939–1996)* (Barcelona: Planeta, 2001), p. 109.

78 Colonel Dolz de Espejo y González de la Riva, 'Estudio de los acuerdos con EEUU ante su posible prórroga en 1968. Cantidad y Calidad de la Ayuda recibida. Fuerzas Aéreas', in *IV Ciclo de Conferencias*, pp. 5–6.

were devoted to the transition and training of personnel on jet trainers (84) and avionics (48).[79]

All in all, within the SAF that first period of US aid garnered a 'frankly favorable general opinion.' The agreement for the the joint military bases had allowed the SAF to make the leap to jet aviation, acquire modern equipment, revitalize their methods and procedures, and get out of their previous trap of obsolescence. However, perceptions soured in the 1960s as Spanish requests for further assistance were systematically rejected, placing SAF opinion on 'unfavorable terrain for the continuation of the American bases in Spain.'[80]

Some of these disputes were a consequence of the uneven nature of the bilateral agreements, their limitations on the modernization of the Spanish armed forces, and the shortcomings of Spain's own military structure. They were also affected by the reduction of US facilities abroad, motivated by both a desire to reduce costs and the new advances in ballistic missiles. In Spain, these new circumstances led to the withdrawal of large numbers of strategic bombing and air defense units in 1964 and 1965, including personnel stationed at radar stations. The bases of Torrejón, Morón, and Zaragoza no longer housed SAC bombers; their new role was to serve as bases for tankers that refueled the bombers in-flight. The US base at Rota, now anchoring a Polaris submarine squadron, became the cornerstone of the US deployment in Spain. SAF personnel now had to assume greater responsibility for defense roles and for maintenance and logistics, which in the opinion of those responsible was not in proportion to the level of assistance received at that point from the United States.[81]

In the course of the 1960s, Spanish military aviation began to be augmented by supersonic aircraft, the Lockheed F-104 Starfighter, which would augment the aging fleet of F-86 aircraft and lead to further restructuring within the SAF. But the limited economic resources at Spain's disposal continued to retard its modernization process and perpetuate its dependence on the supplies and equipment promised by the United States. The US continued to provide material, training, advice, and strategic ideas, with the Spanish recognizing that 'even in the aspect of the doctrine of tactical employment, we limited ourselves to copying and copying. Successive generations of

79 'Relación de cursos y visitas de orientación efectuados en el extranjero desde 1954–1963'. AHEA, A10869. The data on the course subjects have been extracted from a quick analysis of the list drawn up by the Air Ministry. A more detailed examination would be required to refine the results given the wide casuistry of denominations, sometimes on related subjects.

80 This commentary and the aforementioned extract are in José Lacalle Larraga–Minister of the Air–to Fernando Mª. Castiella–Minister of Foreign Affairs, 27 September 1966, AHEA, A10913.

81 'Armée de l'Air espagnole. Historique', 28 October 1965, and 'Bases Américaines en Espagne', 25 January 1966, SHD-MD, GR 12 S 110 and 244; 'Memorandum sobre necesidades de la Defensa Nacional española en relación con los acuerdos hispano-norteamericanos', 6 May 1968, CDMH-AFNFF, doc. 5301.

pilots have flown to the USA to update that doctrine but we have never bothered to conserve it, to experience it and to improve it.'[82] That commentary was bittersweet, as was the bilateral relationship in many ways.

82 *Historia de la Aviación*, p. 334.

6

# From Honeymoon to Divorce: Russian Advisors and the Chinese Air Force, 1949-1962

*Xiaobing Li*

## Introduction

In 2009, China and Russia established a new military alliance, and by 2014 the two nations announced a new era of military collaboration as part of an enhanced strategic partnership. This raises serious questions over the future of American security and whether the United States has anything to fear from a potential military superpower of Communist China. The air force of the People's Liberation Army (PLA, China's armed forces, which include the army, navy, air force, and strategic missile force) has been receiving more Russian advisory assistance and new technology than other services. The latest Chinese purchase included Su-35 fighters, accounting for over $1 billion annually from 2014 to 2016.[1] The Chinese and Russian air forces are getting back together after their messy divorce 57 years ago.

The history of Russian advisory assistance to the air force of the People's Republic of China (PRC) in 1949-1959 offers a compelling example of cooperation and confrontation between the two Communist air forces. It provides new and penetrating insight into their engagement and cooperation in the Cold War by answering some important questions concerning why China needed Russian advisors in 1949 and how the Russians conducted their air war in Korea (1950-1953). The war, however, tested the limits of the Sino-Soviet military alliance, and the debates over Russianization or modernization continued in the PLA Air Force (PLAAF). Before the end of

1 Dave Majumdar, 'China to Get Russia's Lethal Su-35 fighter This Year', *The National Interest*, <http://nationalinterest.org/blog/the-buzz/china-get-russias-lethal-su-35-fighter-year-14968> (accessed on 4 July 2016).

the 1950s, international politics and domestic factors had killed the Sino-Soviet friendship and led to their rivalry in Vietnam (1965-1968). Eventually, a Sino-Soviet armed conflict broke-out along their borders in 1969. Newly available historical documents on the shift of the Chinese attitude toward the Soviet advisors include the Chinese Communist Party (CCP) records, PLA briefings, field records, and combat assessments. Through Chinese leaders' writings and papers, and interviews with PLAAF veterans, one may gain a better understanding of the ups and downs of the Soviet advisory experience in the 1950s-1960s.

Although there are several works on Sino-Russian relations in the Cold War, few detail Soviet advisory assistance to the PLAAF.[2] There are many reasons for this, including the lack of access to military sources and the lack of academic freedom in both countries. Several former Soviet military historians have commented on the issue, but for political reasons did not offer any new discussion differing from the official conclusions. Similarly, Chinese historians still have a long way to go before they can present and publish objective accounts of their military relations with Russia.

## Moscow-Beijing Engagement, 1949-1950

The Chinese documents indicate that after his founding of the PRC on 1 October 1949, CCP leader Mao Zedong's (Mao Tse-tung) first priority was to consolidate the new state by finishing-off the remnants of Jiang Jieshi's (Chiang Kai-shek) Nationalist (Guomindang, GMD; or Kuomintang, KMT) forces on Taiwan and other offshore islands.[3] In late 1949, Jiang moved the seat of his government of the Republic of China (ROC) from mainland China to Taiwan. Although the GMD lost the civil war to the CCP, the GMD air force still had more than 200 fighters and bombers at that time.[4] To successfully conduct an amphibious landing campaign, Mao needed an air force,

2 Among the recent books, see: Lorenz M. Lüthi (ed.), *The Regional Cold Wars in Europe, East Asia, and the Middle East: Crucial Periods and Turning Points* (Stanford, CA: Stanford University Press, 2015); Shen Zhihua and Yafeng Xia, *Mao and the Sino-Soviet Partnership, 1945-1959: A New History* (Lanham, MD: Lexington Books, 2015); Nicholas Khoo, *Collateral Damage: Sino-Soviet Rivalry and the Termination of the Sino-Vietnamese Alliance* (New York: Columbia University Press, 2011); Thomas P. Bernstein and Hua-Yu Li (eds), *China Learns from the Soviet Union, 1949-Present* (Lanham, MD: Lexington Books, 2011); and, Lorenz M. Lüthi, *The Sino-Soviet Split: Cold War in the Communist World* (Princeton, NJ: Princeton University Press, 2008).

3 Mao Zedong's Telegram to Lin Biao on 31 October 1949, in Mao, *Jianguo yilai Mao Zedong wengao, 1949-1976* [Mao Zedong's Manuscripts Since the Founding of the State, 1949-1976] (Beijing: Zhongyang wenxian chubanshe [CCP Central Archival and Manuscript Press], 1989), Vol. 1, p. 107, (hereafter *Mao's Manuscripts Since 1949).* Marshal Lin was then the commander of the PLA Fourth Field Army, totaling 1.2 million troops.

4 Taiwan Defense Ministry, Republic of China (ROC), *Guojun houqin shi* [Logistics History of the GMD Armed Forces] (Taipei, Taiwan: Guofangbu shizheng bianyiju [Bureau of History and Political Records, Defense Ministry], 1992), Vol. 6, pp. 199-200.

which the PLA did not have. At that time, the PLA had a few dozen obsolescent Japanese aircraft. The Chinese studied aviation mechanics from Japanese engineers who had not returned to Japan after the war. By 1947, there were only 16 student pilots in flight training programs. Soviet aviation aid and assistance became necessary to prepare the PLA's invasion of Taiwan.

In July-August 1949, the CCP sent two delegations to Moscow and signed an aviation deal with the Soviet Union, which agreed to sell 434 military aircraft to the PLA over the next two years. In mid-October, the first shipment, which included 20 Yak-12 airplanes, arrived in China. The Chinese also proposed that the Soviets help establish four fighter and six bomber training schools in China. Each aviation school was forecast to have at least 120 Soviet advisors, experts, and instructors. Eventually both countries agreed on the establishment of six air force academies as a first step. According to the agreement, Moscow also sent 878 Russian air force advisors and aviation experts to China, helping the PLA to establish its air force.[5]

In late August 1949, the first group of Russian air force advisors arrived.[6] They worked with the PLA General Staff to design China's air force, organizing its headquarters and chain of command, and planning airfield construction. On 19 October, the first group of Russian military aviation training personnel arrived. This included the academy principals, administrators, and instructors. They were divided into two groups: one traveled to North China looking for campus sites for fighter pilot and engineer training, the other to the Northeast (or Manchuria) to prepare bomber training schools. By 30 October the Russians had selected the campus sites for six air force academies and outlined their entire construction plans, curriculum, and training manuals.[7] On 1 December all of the six aviation academies began their classes. Even though some Western historians refer to the Russian advisors as 'Cold War brides', the Chinese air force historians describe them as the 'midwives' of the Chinese air force.[8]

5 Grand-General Xiao Jinguang (PLA, ret.), *Xiao Jinguang huiyilu* [Memoirs of Xiao Jinguang] (Beijing: Jiefangjun chubanshe [PLA Press], 1988), pp. 44-45; Rear-Admiral Yang Guoyu (PLAN, ret.), *Dangdai Zhongguo haijun* [Contemporary Chinese Navy] (Beijing: Zhongguo shehui kexue [China's Social Science Press], 1987), pp. 48-49.

6 The first group of Soviet experts and advisors totaled 220, including three generals, arrived at Shenyang on 26 August 1949. See Liu Shaoqi's telegram to the CCP Central Committee, 'Prepare and Welcome Soviet Experts' Arrival at Beijing', in Liu, *Jianguo yilai Liu Shaoqi wengao, 1949-1952* [Liu Shaoqi's Manuscripts Since the Founding of the State, 1949-1952] (Beijing: Zhongyang wenxian chubanshe [CCP Central Archival and Manuscript Press], 2005), Vol. 1, p. 58. Hereafter as *Liu's Manuscripts Since 1949*. As the vice chairman of the CCP Central Committee, Liu headed the CCP's delegation to Moscow in July 1949.

7 Chen Xi and Li Dongliu, 'Everything for a Successful Air Academy', in PLA Committee for Historical Records Collection and Compilation, *Kongjun huiyi shiliao* [Historical Records of the Chinese Air Force] (Beijing: Jiefangjun chubanshe [PLA Press], 1992), pp. 146, 164.

8 For example, see Wang Suhong and Wang Yubin (PLAAF, ret.), *Kongzhan zai chaoxian* [The Air War in Korea] (Beijing: Jiefangjun wenyi chubanshe [PLA Literature Press],

With the initial Soviet deliveries arriving on 11 November 1949, the PLA established its air force, the PLAAF, with 202 aircraft, including 30 fighters, 11 bombers, and 119 training aircraft. The PLAAF had 139 pilots, 10 engineers and technicians, and 361 ground crew.[9] It also had some former GMD air force personnel, including 63 pilots, 90 engineers and technicians, and 2,042 ground crew. By the end of the year, although China had received 185 Russian-made aircraft, all of them went to the six academies.[10] Despite this growth in capability, the new PLAAF did not have enough aircraft to use against the GMD air force to support an invasion of Taiwan.

Mao paid a state visit to the Soviet Union on 16 December 1949, hoping to get what the new China desperately needed through an alliance treaty between the PRC and the Union of Soviet Socialist Republics (USSR). Soviet leader Joseph Stalin, however, was never easy to deal with, not even for his next-door communist comrade. Mao was frustrated after the two fruitless meetings in December, and became even angrier when he wasn't able to meet with Stalin for more than three weeks in January 1950.[11] Nevertheless, during his long stay in Moscow, a total of 65 days, Mao gained a better understanding of Stalin's intentions. Among other things, the Soviet leader wanted to convince Mao that the Soviet Union had its own difficulties. There would be no 'free ride' for China, and China should share responsibility for the activities of the worldwide Communist movement. Stalin made it clear that China should support international Communist movements in Asian countries.[12]

Stalin engaged Mao in the Cold War. Whether it was the symbolic significance of the Communist group that ideologically bound China to show its duty, or simple nationalistic interest, China was required to make at least some commitment to support the Soviets in the Cold War. Even though Mao was unhappy with Stalin's demand, he understood the Soviet leader's intention and agreed to share 'the international responsibility'. In February 1950, Mao and Zhou Enlai, China's premier and

1992), p. 88.

9 Major-General Wang Dinglie (PLAAF, ret.), *Dongdai Zhongguo kongjun* [Contemporary China's Air Force] (Beijing: Zhongguo shehui kexue chubanshe [China Social Sciences Press], 1989), Tables 1 and 2, pp. 37-38. Wang served as the PLAAF chief staff in 1975-1982 and deputy commander in 1982-1985.

10 Lieutenant-General Han Huaizhi (PLA, ret.), *Dangdai zhongguo jundui de junshi gongzuo* [Military Affairs of Contemporary China's Armed Forces] (Beijing: Zhongguo shehui kexue chubanshe [China's Social Science Press], 1989), Vol. 2, p. 161.

11 For Mao's 'anger' over their 'ill-treatments' of him and his time as a 'half prisoner', see: Luthi, *The Sino-Soviet Split*, pp. 31-33; Jung Chang and Jon Halliday, *Mao: The Unknown Story* (New York: Knopf, 2005), pp. 351-353; and, Philip Short, *Mao: A Life* (New York: Henry Holt, 1999), p. 424.

12 During their second meeting on 24 December, for example, 'Stalin did not mention the treaty at all', but, instead, mainly discussed with Mao 'the activities of the Communist Parties in Asian countries'. The quotation is from Jianzhang Pei, *Zhonghua renmin gongheguo waijiaoshi, 1949-1956* [Diplomatic History of the PRC, 1949-1956] (Beijing: Shijie zhishi chubanshe [World Knowledge Publishing], 1994), p. 18.

foreign minister, signed the Sino-Soviet Treaty of Friendship, Alliance, and Mutual Assistance with Stalin in Moscow.[13] Then, Mao signed a huge military order (1.2 billion rubles, about $220 million at that time) with Stalin, including the purchase of an additional 340 military aircraft.[14] Happy with the engagement with Moscow, Mao wrote to Stalin on 11 February, ordering 628 more airplanes from the Soviet Union; and wrote to Stalin again on the 25th asking for 217 more Russian air force advisors.[15]

On his way back from Moscow, Mao stopped his train in at Shenyang, Manchuria (never trusting flights, Mao always traveled by train and only flew once in his entire life). Among other military officers, Mao met Lu Liping, superintendent of the Northeast Aviation Academy, the largest air force school in the country, and asked about the Soviet advisory assistance. Lu told the chairman that 'the Soviet advisors work hard and train the Chinese pilots very well at the academy'. Then, Mao asked how many combat pilots these six academies could graduate within one year, and how many air force divisions could be established by the first group of graduates. Lu estimated that 'It is possible for the academies to train enough pilots, technicians, and ground crew for seven air force divisions in one year'.[16]

After his return to Beijing, Mao called a meeting of the PLA high command. During the discussions, Mao instructed Nie Rongzhen, acting chief of the General Staff, along with Su Yu, to plan for attacks on Taiwan in 1950, with an emphasis on training airborne forces.[17] The first combat unit of the PLAAF, the Air Force 4th Brigade, was formed in Nanjing on 19 June 1950. It included four regiments and moved to Shanghai on 8 August. This same month, as Stalin suggested, Soviet Air Force General Pavlovich Belov, arrived in Northeast China with one Soviet air force division. Starting in September, more Soviet Air Force divisions began arriving in China under Belov's command. Unfortunately for Mao, the Korean War broke out, altering his plan for invading Taiwan.[18]

13 Zhou Enlai Military Record Compilation Team, *Zhou Enlai junshi huodong jishi* [Zhou Enlai Military Affairs Record] (Beijing: Zhongyang wenxian chubanshe [CCP Central Archival and Manuscript Press], 2000), Vol. 2, pp. 117-118.

14 Han, *Dangdai zhongguo jundui de junshi gongzuo* [Military Affairs of Contemporary China's Armed Forces], Vol. 2, p. 161.

15 Mao's telegrams to Stalin on 11, 15, and 25 February 1950, were quoted in Feng Chu, 'The Sino-Soviet Military Relations in the 1950s' (PhD Dissertation, the Party University of the CCP Central Committee, Beijing, 2006), pp. 45, 59.

16 Then, each PLAAF fighter division had three to four regiments, including 40-50 fighters. Each regiment had four wing commands (*dadui*, battalion); and each wing command had eight to 10 fighters. Wang and Wang, *Kongzhan zai chaoxian* [The Air War in Korea], pp. 91-92.

17 Mao's telegram to Liu Shaoqi, 'Approval of Disposing Four Divisions for Landing Campaign, 10 February 1950'; Mao to Liu, 'Mao's Comments on the Proposal of Attacking Dinghai First, Jinmen Second, 28 March 1950'; Mao to Su Yu, 'Instructions on Paratroops Training', *Mao's Manuscripts Since 1949*, Vol. 1, pp. 256-257, 282.

18 General Ye Fei (PLA, ret.), interviews by the author in Hangzhou, Zhejiang, in July 1996. Ye served as the commander of the Tenth Army Group, Third Field Army of the PLA in

On 25 June 1950, North Korea, or the Democratic People's Republic of Korea (DPRK), launched a surprise attack on South Korea, which signaled the beginning of the Korean War. US President Harry S. Truman immediately responded by sending in armed forces under a UN resolution adopted on 7 July calling for all possible means to aid the Republic of Korea (ROK or South Korea). On 27 June, Truman announced that the Seventh Fleet would be deployed in the Taiwan Strait to prevent a Chinese Communist attack on GMD-held Taiwan. The US naval presence in the Taiwan Strait marked a turning point in the cross-strait situation. What really shocked Mao and the Chinese leaders was not the civil war in Korea, but the subsequent US policy shift from a 'hands-off' policy to a 'hands-on' commitment toward the safety of Taiwan. With Washington's direct involvement in the Taiwan Strait, the PLA now faced a serious challenge.[19] Mao had to put off all offshore offensive operations thereafter.

## The Honeymoon in Korea, 1950-1953

On 5 October 1950, Mao and the Politburo (Political Bureau) of the CCP Central Committee decided to send Chinese troops, known as the Chinese People's Volunteer Force (CPVF), to help the North Korean People's Army (NKPA) against the UN Forces (UNF) in Korea. After 19 October, when the CPVF crossed the Yalu River, the conflict in Korea became a war between China and the United States. By November, 12 Soviet Air Force divisions had arrived in China under Belov's command. According to Stalin's order, their mission was to protect the Yalu bridges, power plants, railroads, and airports 50 miles south of the Chinese-North Korean borders.

To assist in the fight against the UNF, Mao sent Zhou on an emergency trip to Moscow on 8 October to request air support for the Chinese troops within North Korea. Stalin, however, promised only to provide for the air defense of Manchuria, including the air space above the Yalu, but Stalin refused to provide air cover for the Chinese divisions fighting within Korea itself.[20] Nevertheless, Stalin promised to accelerate the creation of the PLA air force. The training of Chinese pilots to fly

1949-1951.

19 Xiaobing Li, 'Truman and Taiwan: A US Policy Change from Face to Faith', in James I. Matray (ed.), *Northeast Asia and the Legacy of Harry S. Truman: Japan, China, and the Two Koreas* (Kirksville, MO: Truman State University, 2012), pp. 127-128; Chief General Hao Bocun (Hau Pei-stun) (GMD Army, ret.), interviews by the author in Taipei, Taiwan, on 23-24 May 1994. Hao served as the commander of the GMD front artillery force on Jinmen (Quemoy) Island in 1950, the chief of the Joint Staff of the GMD Army in 1981-1989, and the defense minister of the ROC in 1989-1990.

20 CCP Central Archival and Manuscript Research Division, *Zhou Enlai nianpu, 1949-1976* [A Chronological Record of Zhou Enlai, 1949-1976] (Beijing: Zhongyang wenxian chubanshe [CCP Central Archival and Manuscript Press], 1997), Vol. 1, pp. 85-87; General Hong Xuezhi (PLA ret.), *Hong Xuezhi Huiyilu* [Memoirs of Hong Xuezhi] (Beijing: Jiefangjun chubanshe [PLA Press], 2007), pp. 373-374.

Russian jet fighters such as MiG-15s, and Soviet jet light bombers, was already under way.[21]

Stalin's commitment to the Chinese air force jump-started the PLAAF. The development of the Chinese Air Force sped-up thereafter. Its first division, the Air Force 4th Division, was formed from the 4th Brigade in Shanghai in September 1950, the 3rd in Shenyang in October, and the 2nd in Shanghai in November.[22] As the Soviet advisors planned, the PLAAF also established its air forces in East China, Northwest, and North China Regional Commands in August-October. By mid-1951, the PLA had 20 air force divisions, including 16 fighter divisions, two bomber divisions, and two fighter-bomber divisions.

Since August 1949, the Russian advisors had worked at the PLAAF HQs, divisional commands, and air force bases across the country. The Russian air force generals planned the operations and provided assessment of the Chinese progress. Unlike civilian advisors, who were under the supervision and management of the Soviet Embassy in Beijing, the Russian air force advisors were under the direct command of the Soviet high command in Moscow. General Vasilievich Zahalov, deputy chief of the Soviet General Staff, served as head of the Soviet Military Advisory Group (SMAG) in 1950-1951. He was followed by General Mikhail Kalasovski in 1951-1953.[23]

The Russian advisors were the planners and caretakers of the Chinese Air Force during the Korean War (1950-1953). In March 1951, the CPVF-North Korean Joint Air Force Command was established under the command of the CPVF General Command with Liu Zhen as the commander and Chang Qiankun and Wang Lian

21 For Mao's confirmation orders and telegrams to his officials and generals, see Mao's telegrams to Chen Yi, 'Order the Ninth Army Group to Move North Ahead of Schedule, October 12 and 14'; Mao to Zhou, 'We Believe that We Should and Must Enter the War, October 13'; and Mao to Zhou, 'The Guidelines and Deployment for the CPVF to Enter Korea and Participate in the War, October 14, 1950', in *Mao's Military Manuscripts Since 1949*, Vol. 1, pp. 246, 248, 252-235, 256-259. See also Shuguang Zhang and Chen Jian (trans. and eds), *Chinese Communist Foreign Policy and the Cold War in Asia: New Documentary Evidence, 1944-1950* (Chicago: Imprint Publications, 1996), pp. 168-171.

22 General Zhang Aiping (PLA, ret.), *Zhongguo renmin jiefangjun* [The Chinese People's Liberation Army] (Beijing: Dangdai zhongguo chubanshe [Contemporary China Press], 1994), Vol. 2, pp. 65, 67-68; Han, *Dangdai Zhongguo jundui de junshi gongzuo* [Military Affairs of Contemporary China's Armed Forces], Vol. 2, pp. 72-73; Wang and Wang, *Kongzhan zai chaoxian* [The Air War in Korea], pp. 98, 104; Xiaoming Zhang, *Red Wings over the Yalu: China, the Soviet Union, and the Air War in Korea* (College Station: Texas A&M University Press, 2002), pp. 224-226; Dennis D. Showalter, 'The First Jet War', in Robert Cowley (ed.), *The Cold War: A Military History* (New York: Random House, 2005), p. 128.

23 Shen Zhihua, *Mao Zedong, Sidalin he chaoxian zhanzheng* [Mao Zedong, Stalin, and the Korean War] (Guangzhou: Guangdong renmin chubanshe [Guangdong People's Press], 2004), p. 372.

(NKPA Air Force) as deputy commanders.[24] The Soviet advisors then coordinated the Chinese and North Korean air cooperation. In the fall, the CPVF began committing its new air force to the war in Korea.[25] The 4th Division, composed of Mig-15 fighters, was the first Chinese air force division deployed on the front under the Joint Command in September 1951.[26] The 2nd, 3rd, 8th, and 10th Divisions joined the 4th shortly thereafter. By October, the Joint Air Command had a total of 450 fighters and bombers for air operations and engagement in Korea.[27] Soviet advisors were assigned to all the Chinese air force divisional and regimental commands.

Although the Chinese air force had few disagreements with their Russian advisors since the Chinese did not have any air war experience before Korea, they often had problems with the Russian decisions. For example, the Russians only trusted the intelligence information from their own sources, mainly the Russian radar. Nevertheless, these ground-based medium range radars deployed along the Chinese

24 Air Force General Liu Zhen was appointed as the commander of the Northeast Air Force and commander of the CPVF Air Force in 1950-1953. After the Korean War, Liu was appointed the commander of the Northeast and Shenyang Air Force Commands, deputy commander of the PLAAF, and commander of the Xinjiang Regional Command. He was promoted to air force general in 1955. For more details, see Tan Zheng, *Zhongguo renmin zhiyuanjun renwulu* [Veterans Profile of the Chinese People's Volunteer Force] (Beijing: Zhonggong dangshi chubanshe [CCP Party History Press], 1992), pp. 134-135; *Xinghuo liaoyuan* Composition Department, *Zhongguo renmin jiefangjun jiangshuai minglu* [Marshals and Generals of the PLA] (Beijing: Jiefangjun chubanshe [PLA Press], 1992), Vol. 1, pp. 66-67. Air Force Lieutenant-General Chang Qiankun was appointed as deputy commander of the CPVF Air Force in 1950-1953. After the Korean War, Chang became deputy commander of the PLAAF. He was promoted to lieutenant-general of the PLAAF in 1955. For more details, see Tan, *Zhongguo renmin zhiyuanjun renwulu* [Veterans Profile of the CPVF], pp. 586-587; *Xinghuo liaoyuan* Composition Department, *Zhongguo renmin jiefangjun jiangshuai minglu* [Marshals and Generals of the PLA], Vol. 1, pp. 442-443.

25 Wang, *Dongdai Zhongguo kongjun* [Contemporary Chinese Air Force], p. 129.

26 Yang Feng'an and Wang Tiancheng, *Beiwei 38 duxian; Peng Dehuai yu chaoxian zhanzheng* [The North Latitude 38th Parallel; Peng Dehuai and the Korean War] (Beijing: Zhongyang wenxian chubanshe [CCP Central Archival and Manuscript Press], 2009), p. 386; Li Qingshan, *Zhiyuanjun yuanchao jishi* [The CPVF Records of Aiding Korea] (Beijing: Zhonggong dangshi chubanshe [CCP Party History Press], 2008), p. 477.

27 Since December 1950, the Soviet Union had provided the Chinese Air Force with 582 MiG-15 jet fighters in three groups. These jet fighters went to the 2nd, 3rd, 4th, 6th, 7th, 9th, 12th, and 14th Air Force Divisions in 1951. See Military History Research Division, China Academy of Military Science (CAMS), *Zhongguo renmin zhiyuanjun kangmei yuanchao zhanshi* [Combat Experience of the CPVF in the War to Resist the US and Aid Korea] (Beijing: Junshi kexue chubanshe [Military Science Press], 1990), p. 159; Shuang Shi, *Kaiguo diyi zhan: kangmei yuanchao zhanzheng quanjing jishi* [The First War since the Founding of the State: The Complete Story of the War to Resist the US and Aid Korea] (Beijing: Zhonggong dangshi chubanshe [CCP Party History Press], 2004), Vol. 2, p. 517.

border as part of Manchuria's air defense only had a range of 100-160 miles.[28] In many cases, the signals detected by these radar units did not give the Joint Air Command enough warning to react or make timely operational decisions. Having missed some combat opportunities, the Joint Air Command asked the Russian advisors to consider using the Chinese intelligence, including early warning reports sent by ground observers serving as air raid 'outposts' and 'air-watchers' on the front.[29] But the Russians continued to ignore the information forwarded by the CPVF General Command because the advisors questioned the accuracy of the Chinese human intelligence.

More importantly, the Chinese strongly disagreed with the Russian belief that the Chinese pilots were no match for US pilots, many of whom were World War II veterans. With a Chinese aircraft loss rate of 5:1, the Russian generals maintained their protective advisory position and opposed any major air engagement with the UNF. The CPVF General Command's complaints about the Russian advisors soon reached Beijing. Mao read the report and supported the Soviet advisors by instructing the CPVF General Command and the Joint Air Command that 'It is better to adopt a reliable method' for the employment of the air force.[30] In 1951, Mao wrote to Liu Yalou, the PLAAF chief, that the Chinese air force bases 'don't have to move into [North Korea]'.[31]

Russian advisors continued to protect the Chinese air force from any major air combat disaster against the US F-86 Sabre fighter. First of all, the Russians insisted that the Chinese air force divisions be based at sites in China proper such as Andong (Antung or Dantung), from where Chinese pilots could fly sorties into Korea. Since the MiG-15 had a maximum range of only 700 miles, the Chinese aircraft could not even reach the 38th parallel, fly over UN-controlled areas, or be engaged over the front. The CPVF General Command was not happy with the Russian advisors, who refused to support the Chinese ground troops down to the 37th and 38th parallels, but instead only conducted air operations above the 39th parallel. Therefore, the Russian decision created the so-called 'MiG Alley', an air space from the Chinese border south only about 100 miles into North Korea between the 39th and 41st parallels for

28 During Zhou Enlai's emergency trip to Moscow on 8-18 October 1950, Stalin promised to provide interceptors and a ground-based air intercept radar system for the defense of Manchuria, including the air space above the Yalu River. But he did not intend to provide radar detection systems to all of North Korea and the 38th Parallel.

29 Wang and Wang, *Kongzhan zai chaoxian* [The Air War in Korea], p. 244.

30 Mao's words are quoted from Wang, *Dongdai Zhongguo kongjun* [Contemporary China's Air Force], p. 129.

31 Mao's instruction to Liu Yalou, Wu Faxian, and Wang Bingzhang on 7 July 1951, in Mao, *Jianguo yilai Mao Zedong junshi wengao* [Mao Zedong's Military Manuscripts Since the Founding of the PRC] (Beijing: Junshi kexue chubanshe [Military Science Press] and Zhongyang wenxian chubanshe [CCP Central Archival and Manuscript Press], 2010), Vol. 1, p. 527. Hereafter as *Mao's Military Manuscripts Since 1949.*

MiG operations, which was about 150-200 miles behind the front line.[32] Among the Russian excuses was the lack of airfields for the PLAAF in North Korea. From the spring of 1951, the CPVF General Command employed ten infantry and engineering divisions of the 23rd Army Group to construct 17 airfields in North Korea. But the construction progressed slowly due to heavy UNF air raids.[33] Thus, all of the PLAAF fighter and bomber divisions operated from their bases in China throughout the war. Peng told the PLAAF officers that the air force should be engaged like the Chinese ground force, which had been fighting heavily and effectively deep within Korea.

Secondly, the Russian advisors did what the Chinese officers never could: refuse frequent requests from the CPVF General Command for air coverage, bombing, and close support for their ground operations. The Russians might have saved the Chinese Air Force since they knew that the PLAAF was no match for the UNF air power and antiaircraft defenses. A large scale bombing or air raid could be a disaster for the newly established Chinese air force. On 30 November 1951, for example, Chinese ground forces requested air support to their landing on the Dahoo Island. With Russian advisors' approval, the 24th and 28th Regiments of the 10th Air Force Division sent 10 Tu (Tupolev)-2 bombers to attack the UNF warships in the Dahoo harbors and UNF defensive positions on the island. During the 10 minute air raid, the Chinese lost five of 10 bombers and four of the eight fighters that flying escort.[34]

Last but not the least, the Russian advisors greatly assisted the Chinese pilots by assigning them to joint missions with seasoned Russian pilots. From November 1950 to July 1953, 12 Soviet Air Force divisions engaged in the air war in Korea, including 72,000 Russian pilots, technicians, ground service members, and anti-air defense troops. In 1952, at its peak, 26,000 Russian air force personnel were sent into North Korea under the command of the Soviet 64th Air Force Army. According to Russian official statistics, the 64th Air Force Army launched 63,000 sorties, including 818 large-scale sorties (regimental and above). More than 2,820 Russian fighter pilots engaged in some 1,400 battles.[35]

32 Conrad C. Crane, *American Airpower Strategy in Korea, 1950-1953* (Lawrence: University Press of Kansas, 2000), pp. 50, 68-69, 85.

33 Zhou Enlai's telegrams to Kim Il-sung and Peng Dehuai on the construction of the airfields in North Korea on 15 and 22 March 1951, Zhou, *Zhou Enlai junshi wenxun* [Selected Military Works of Zhou Enlai] (Beijing: Renmin chubanshe [People's Press], 1997), Vol. 4, pp. 171-173, 175-180.

34 General Hong Xuezhi (PLA, ret.), *Hong Xuezhi Huiyilu* [Memoirs of Hong Xuezhi] (Beijing: Jiefangjun chubanshe [PLA Press], 2007), p. 511; Chen Zhonglong (ed.), *Kangmei yuanchao zhanzheng lun* [On the War to Resist the US and Aid Korea] (Beijing: Junshi wenyi chubanshe [Military Literature Press), 2001), p. 301; Xiaobing Li, 'Chinese Army in the Korean War, 1950-53', in *The New England Journal of History*, 60:1-3 (2004), p. 286.

35 Xiaobing Li, *China's Battle for Korea: The 1951 Spring Offensive* (Bloomington: Indiana University Press, 2014), p. 229.

Future Chinese General Wang Hai gained his combat experience in Korea by following the Russian pilots into air combat against the UN fighters. As a wing (battalion) commander of the PLAAF 3rd Division, Wang recalled the considerable advice the Russian advisors offered in the Korean War. On 20 October 1951, 50 MiG-15 fighters of the 3rd Division, including six MiG-15s in Wang's wing, moved into the front airport along the Yalu. Wang had his first victory on 18 November when his 9th Regiment joined 88 Soviet fighters flown by World War II veterans and attacked 20 US F-84s over Sukchon. The Chinese pilots followed the Russians closely move by move through the battle. After their return, the Russian pilots also shared their combat records, photos, and assessments with the Chinese.[36]

Before pulling out of the front on 14 January 1952, the 3rd Division engaged in 21 air-to-air battles and conducted 2,318 sorties. According to the Joint Air Command's reports, the division shot down or damaged 64 enemy aircraft.[37] Mao was delighted by these combat results and wrote: 'Congratulate the Air Force 3rd Division!'[38] The division's second tour, from 1 May 1952 to 26 January 1953, saw a record 31 battles and 1,147 sorties. During the two tours, the 3rd Division had 44 fighters shot down and 19 damaged. The division lost 18 pilots, including one regimental commander and six wing commanders.[39]

Wang Hai was shot down once in 1953 but was rescued by peasants after parachuting into Manchuria. He was promoted to 3rd Division's deputy commander in 1953, and made its commander in 1956. Wang became a colonel in 1959 and an Air Force general in 1988. He served as both the PLAAF's deputy commander and commander from

36 General Wang Hai (PLAAF, ret.), *Wode zhandou shengya* [My Military Career] (Beijing: Zhongyang wenxian chubanshe [CCP Central Archival and Manuscript Press], 2000), pp. 77-78.

37 Wang, *Dongdai Zhongguo kongjun* [Contemporary China's Air Force], pp. 112-113; Wang and Wang, *Kongzhan zai chaoxian* [The Air War in Korea], pp. 137-141; Li, *Zhiyuanjun yuanchao jishi* [The CPVF Records of Aiding Korea], pp. 483-484; PLA Composition Committee (ed.), *38 xian shang de jiaofeng: kangmei yuanchao zhanzheng jishi* [The Fight Over the 38th Parallel: The Recorded Truth of the War to Resist the US and Aid Korea] (Beijing: Jiefangjun wenyi chubanshe [PLA Literature Press], 2010), pp. 410-411; China National Military Museum (ed.), *Kangmei yuanchao zhanzheng fengyunlu* [The Operational Files of the War to Resist the US and Aid Korea] (Beijing: Huacheng chubanshe [Huacheng Publishing House], 1999), pp. 359-360.

38 Mao's writing on the PLAAF 3rd Division's briefing of its first tour on 1 February 1952, in *Mao's Military Manuscripts Since 1949*, Vol. 2, p. 8.

39 Because of the heavy losses of their jet fighters and wing commanders, the Chinese air force divisions began their rotation in Korea in early 1952. Their wing commanders were always the first ones who got shot at and ran out of ammo since they had to lead the attacks. See Tan Jingjiao, *Kangmei yuanchao zhanzheng* [The War to Resist the US and Aid Korea] (Beijing: Zhongguo shehui kexue chubanshe [China Social Science Press], 1990), pp. 198, 208; Wang, *Dongdai Zhongguo kongjun* [Contemporary China's Air Force], pp. 130-131; Wang and Wang, *Kongzhan zai chaoxian* [The Air War in Korea], pp. 134-137.

1982-1992.[40] In June 1984, General Wang visited the United States and was surprised when at the meeting General Charles A. Gabriel, the USAF chief of staff, told Wang that he had served as an F-86 Sabre pilot in the Korean War in 1951-1952. They had actually met over the Yalu in an air battle on 29 August 1952.[41] Gabriel visited Beijing and met Wang again in October 1985. He later wrote to Wang, and in a letter dated 10 June 1992, said that 'My favorite quote is still your Chinese expression: "From exchange of blows come good friends."'[42]

Throughout its participation in the Korean War from September 1951 to July 1953, the Chinese Air Force launched 26,491 sorties but only engaged in 366 battles.[43] The PLAAF lost 339 warplanes, including 231 MiG-15 and MiG-15bis fighters, another 151 warplanes were damaged. They also lost 116 pilots during the air war.[44] The NKPA had several air force divisions with 240 warplanes that participated in air battles from 1951 to 1953. North Korea lost about 150 aircraft. The Soviet 64th Air Force Army lost 345 fighters and more than 299 pilots.[45] In the 'Soviet Red Army Cemetery' in Lushun (or Port Arthur), among the 2,030 Soviet graves are those of 142 Russian pilots from the Korean War. Marshal Nie Rongzhen concluded: 'At any

40 Air Force General Wang Hai became deputy commander and commander of the 9th Regiment, 3rd Air Force Division in 1952, and deputy commander of the 3rd Division in 1953. After his return to China, he was ranked lieutenant-colonel of the PLAAF in 1955. Wang was promoted to the division commander in 1956, air force colonel in 1959, and to the deputy commander of the 2nd Air Force Army in 1965. He served as the chief of the Training Department in the PLA Air Force Headquarters in 1969. Wang was appointed as the air force commander of the Guangzhou Regional Command in 1975. He became the deputy commander of the PLA Air Force in November 1982, and the commander of the PLA Air Force in 1985-1992. Wang was promoted to air force general in 1988. See Tan, *Zhongguo renmin zhiyuanjun renwulu* [Veterans Profile of the CPVF], pp. 27-28.

41 PLAAF General Wang and USAF General Gabriel were happy with some uncertainty when they were told by their own interpreters that 'you shot down your counterpart during that battle'. Obviously, the interpreters translated it in opposite ways, <www.nytimes.com/1988/01/11/us>. See also Li, *Zhiyuanjun yuanchao jishi* [The CPVF Records of Aiding Korea], pp. 487-488.

42 A photocopy of General Charles Gabriel's letter was included in Wang, *Wode zhandou shengya* [My Military Career], pp. 310-311.

43 For the Chinese statistics on UNF losses of the warplanes, see Wang and Wang, *Kongzhan zai chaoxian* [The Air War in Korea], pp. 249-250; PLA Composition Committee (ed.), *38 xian shang de jiaofeng* [The Fight over the 38th Parallel], pp. 415-416; Wang, *Wode zhandou shengya* [My Military Career], pp. 149-150. UNF statistics shows that US Air Force, Navy, and Marine Corps lost a total of 2,998 warplanes during the Korean War, including 1,644 lost in operations and 1,354 in combat. For more on the UNF statistics, see 'Korean War Aircraft Loss Database' (KORWALD), <www.dtic.mil/dpmo/pmkor/korwald.htm>.

44 Zhang, *Zhongguo renmin jiefangjun* [The PLA], Vol. 2, pp. 101-103; Shuang, *Kaiguo diyi zhan* [The First War Since the Founding of the State], Vol. 2, p. 819.

45 Shen Zhihua, 'The Soviet Air Force in the Korean War,' in *Zhonggong dangshi yanjiu* [Studies on CCP History], no. 2 (2000), pp. 27-29; Zhang, ibid., pp. 219-221; Shuang, ibid., Vol. 2, p. 820.

rate, the Soviets played an important role in the air war in cooperation with Chinese and Korean air forces'.[46]

## Same Bed, Different Dreams: The Departure from Dependency, 1954-1959

By the end of the Korean War, the PLAAF had 3,000 fighters and bombers, making China's Air Force the third largest in the world.[47] It had 33 divisions outfitted with Soviet equipment and technology and relied almost exclusively on Soviet-designed aircraft. From 1951 to 1955, China purchased 5,000 Russian aircraft.[48] Jeanne L. Wilson points out that the Soviet Union sought to keep China reliant upon the Soviets to prohibit any connection with the West.[49] For example, the Soviet leaders offered fighter and bombers to the PLAAF, but did not allow schematics or any type of production information to be passed to their Communist brethren. This forced the Chinese military leaders to continuously turn toward their northern neighbors for military supplies. Throughout the 1950s, China spent about $2 billion on arms purchases. For Marshal Peng Dehuai, who became China's first defense minister in 1954, there was no other option for supplying his navy and air force.[50]

From 1954 to 1957, China's armed forces became Russianized institutionally and from a technological perspective because the CCP carried out Soviet-style political, economic, and social reforms. Mao told the PLA that the Chinese military 'must learn all of the Soviet experience and really master all of their advanced technology in order to change our army's backward condition'.[51] In 1954, Peng ordered all ranks to cooperate and maintain close working relationships with their Russian advisors.[52]

46 Marshal Nie Rongzhen (PLA, ret.), 'Beijing's Decision to Intervene', in Xiaobing Li, Allan R. Millett, and Bin Yu (eds and trans.), *Mao's Generals Remember Korea* (Lawrence: University Press of Kansas, 2001), p. 58.

47 Major-General Xu Yan (PLA), *Mao Zedong yu kangmei yuanchao zhanzheng* [Mao Zedong and the War to Resist the US and Aid Korea] (2nd edition, Beijing: Jiefangjun chubanshe [PLA Press], 2006), p. 397; Xiaoming Zhang, 'Air Combat for the People's Republic', in Mark A. Ryan, David M. Finkelstein, and Michael A. McDevitt (eds), *Chinese Warfighting: The PLA Experience since 1949* (New York: ME Sharpe, 2003), p. 278.

48 Wang, *Dongdai Zhongguo kongjun* [Contemporary China's Air Force], pp. 68, 82; Military History Research Division, CAMS, *Zhongguo renmin zhiyuanjun kangmei yuanchao zhanshi* [Combat Experience of the CPVF in the War to Resist the US and Aid Korea], p. 461.

49 Jeanne L. Wilson, *Strategic Partners: Russian-Chinese Relations in the Post-Soviet Era* (Armonk, NY: ME Sharpe, 2004), p. 70.

50 Ming-Yen Tsai, *From Adversaries to Partners: Chinese and Russian Military Cooperation after the Cold War* (Westport, CT: Praeger, 2003), pp. 25-27.

51 Mao's instruction on General Xiao Xiangrong's report on the PLA officers' relations with the Soviet advisors, Tsai, ibid., pp. 1-2.

52 There were heated debates in the high command about whether the PLA should learn from the Soviet Union and how to learn from the Soviet Union through the 1950s. There was no consensus in the military. Peng issued several instructions and said many times at the CMC and other high command meetings that 'We must learn from the Soviet Union'.

Therefore, after the Korean War Soviet advisors continued to work at all the levels of the air force commands. During the 1950s, among the 80,000 Soviet advisors sent to China, the majority were military advisors.[53] In Beijing, for instance, among 442 chief advisors were 310 chief military advisors, 72 economic and technology, 47 government and foreign policy, and 13 intelligence and national security chief advisors. The SMAG General HQs in Beijing assigned its advisors to all of the PLA headquarters in the capital city, and sent many others down to the PLA regional, army, and divisional commands across the country.[54] General Peterlusovski served as the head of the SMAG to China in 1953-1957. The last chief of the SMAG was General Dulufanov, who served from July 1957 to July 1960.[55]

Many of the Russian air force advisors worked side by side with Chinese officers on operational planning, air force base construction, and airplane repair and manufacturing. Following the Soviet model, the PLAAF experienced some major institutional developments, including building a centralized command system, multiple levels of administration, and various air defense forces. By the end of 1955, the PLAAF established 11 first-level departments in its administrative command structure and had 4,400 aircraft. In 1957, the Air Force merged with the surface-based air defense force and included 11 anti-aircraft artillery (AAA) divisions. In July 1958, the Air Force established three surface-to-air missile battalions. By the late 1960s, the Air Force had created 50 air divisions in 13 air force armies.[56] Of all the services the Air Force most closely followed Soviet technology, doctrine, tactics, and training.[57] Technology increasingly took a larger part of the forces and defense budget through the 1950s. While the infantry troops decreased from 61.1 percent of its total

The quotation and meeting minutes of 5 June 1953, 26 January 1954, and 16 August 1955 are from the footnotes in Wang Yan, et al., *Peng Dehuai zhuan* [Biography of Peng Dehuai] (Beijing: Dangdai zhongguo chubanshe [Contemporary China Press], 1993), pp. 523, 541, 552.

53 Shen, *Mao Zedong, Sidalin he chaoxian zhanzheng* [Mao Zedong, Stalin, and the Korean War], p. 371. Shen found the information in the archives of the Second Division, ROC Defense Ministry, defense intelligence agency in Taiwan. He believes that the numbers collected by the intelligence agents in the 1950s were incomplete.

54 Yang Guoyu, *Dangdai Zhongguo haijun* [Contemporary China's Navy] (Beijing: Zhongguo shehui kexue chubanshe [China Social Science Press], 1987), pp. 48-49.

55 Shen, *Mao Zedong, Sidalin he chaoxian zhanzheng* [Mao Zedong, Stalin, and the Korean War], p. 372.

56 Military History Research Division, CAMS, *Zhongguo renmin jiefangjun de qishinian, 1927-1997* [Seventy Years of the PLA, 1927-1997] (Beijing: Junshi kexue chubanshe [Military Science Press], 1997), p. 462.

57 Deng Lifeng, 'A Historic Meeting of the PLA', in Military History Research Division, CAMS, *Junqi piaopiao; xinzhongguo 50 nian junshi dashi shushi, 1949-1999* [PLA Flag Fluttering; Facts of China's Major Military Events in the Past Fifty Years, 1949-1999] (Beijing: Jiefangjun chubanshe [PLA Press], 1999), Vol. 1, p. 179.

in 1950 to 42.3 percent in 1958, the air force had increased from 4.5 percent to 12.2 percent of the PLA total forces by 1958.[58]

From 1954 to 1958, the PLAAF systematically introduced Soviet organization and doctrine as a model for Chinese air force modernization. It translated Soviet Red Army regulations, manuals, curriculum, handbooks, and research into Chinese and distributed them to all units. The Soviets trained the first generation of Chinese air force officers. Lieutenant-General Qiao Qingchen joined the PLAAF in 1956. As a result of the speedy development of the air force, promotion and advancement occurred faster than in other services. Qiao became commander of an aviation division in the 1960s, and then deputy political commissar of the Fourth Air Force Army. He rose to major general in 1988 and was promoted to lieutenant-general in 1996. By May 2002, he became the chief of the Chinese Air Force.[59]

After the mid-1950s, Mao stopped the emphasis on 'learning from the Soviet Union', and instead made a new call for 'learning from the Soviet lessons'.[60] This was intended to demonstrate that the Soviets were not always correct, and China should avoid their mistakes. Soon, Soviet and Chinese leaders split on strategic issues, nuclear policy, and military relations because of international politics and domestic factors. Marshal Liu Bocheng, for instance, questioned the copying of the Soviet model and suggested that the PLA treasure the Chinese experience and not lose sight of the 'people's war' doctrine.[61] In the late 1950s, Liu stressed Chinese experience, proposed Chinese ways of building a modern conventional army, and opposed entirely copying the Soviet model.

The PLAAF also tried to depart from its dependency on the Soviet Union and began to emphasize self-strengthening. Initially, the Soviets delivered the aircraft directly to China. After the mid-1950s, the Chinese began to co-produce Soviet models of weapons and aircraft with Russians in China. The Chinese also learned how to reengineer, modify, and produce their own variations of these weapon systems in China starting in the late 1950s. After 1955, for instance, the PLA copied the Russian 37mm gun and later made its own double-barreled version. In the same year, the Chinese produced copies of Russian 57mm and 100mm anti-aircraft guns, but they were all equipped with Chinese anti-aircraft fire control radar.[62] In 1956, the

58 CAMS, *Zhongguo renmin jiefangjun de qishinian* [Seventy Years of the PLA], pp. 457-458.
59 Major-General Qin Chaoying (PLA), interviews by the author at the China Society of Strategic and Management Research, Beijing, in July 2000.
60 Shen Zhihua, *Sulian zhuanjia zai zhongguo, 1948-1960* [Soviet experts in China, 1948-1960] (Beijing: Zhongguo guoji guangbo chubanshe [China International Broadcasting Publishing House], 2003), p. 253.
61 *Xinghuo Liaoyuan* Composition Department, *Zhongguo renmin jiefangjun jiangshuai minglu* [Marshals and Generals of the PLA], Vol. 1, p. 6.
62 Lt. Wang Xiangcai (PLAAF, ret.), interviews by the author, Harbin, Heilongjiang, in August 2003.

PLAAF tested the Qian-5 fighter (a Chinese version of the Russian MiG-17 fighter). By 1959, the nation manufactured the Qian-6, a modified MiG-19 fighter.[63]

It was apparent that the Chinese air force needed modernization rather than Russianization. It made sense to the PLAAF officers that since China's air force had grown, it was ready to take on new challenges, and to operate independently with or without Russian advisory assistance. The air operations against the GMD-held offshore islands during the 1954-1955 Taiwan Strait crisis became a key test for the Chinese Air Force.

It was the first attempt in PLA history at joint operations between air, naval, and land forces in a single campaign. In early 1954, the PLA front command, or the Zhejiang Front Command (ZFC), planned a bombing campaign against the Dachen Islands, a group of islands situated east of Zhejiang province in the East China Sea. At the command meetings, Lieutenant-General Nie Fengzhi, ZFC air force commander, disagreed with the Russian advisors' bombing plan. Nie recalled that the Russian plan, copied from their World War II concentrated bombing strategy, did not work on the scattered targets on the small islands. What really upset him was that after their plan was rejected at the ZFC, the Russian advisors ran to the bombing division and asked the Chinese wing commanders to use their plan. Nie had to call all the division commanders himself and order them to execute the ZFC plan.[64]

The Chinese air operation went well without Russian advisors' assistance or interference. From 18 March to 20 May 1954, the 2nd Division of the PLAAF engaged the GMD Air Force over the Dachen Islands. The combat-experienced division had just returned from Korea, and was equipped with MiG-15s, while the GMD lacked jet fighters, although American F-84 fighters had just arrived in Taiwan.[65] In six air engagements, six GMD fighters were shot down while the PLAAF lost only two. From 1 November ZFC bombers and fighters raided the Dachens, flying more than one hundred sorties and dropping over one thousand bombs.[66] Between 21 December and 10 January 1955, the ZFC Air Force conducted bombing raids against the Dachens five times, mounting 28 bomber and 116 fighter sorties. On 10 January the bombers raided Dachen Harbor, sinking one GMD LST and damaging four other

63 Deng, 'A Historic Meeting of the PLA', Vol. 1, p. 180.

64 General Nie Fengzhi (PLAAF, ret.), 'Join Forces with the Army and Navy to Liberate the Yijiangshan Island', in PLA Committee for Historical Records Collection and Compilation, *Kongjun huiyi shiliao* [Historical Records of the Chinese Air Force], pp. 447-448.

65 The air force bases in east coast cities like Shanghai, Hangzhou, and Ningbo were also used by Nie's jets in the air campaigns.

66 Ma Guansan, deputy commander of the ZFC naval force, 'Remember the Combat Years in the East China Sea', in General Nie Fengzhi (PLAAF, ret.) (ed.), *Sunjun huige zhan donghai* [Three Services Wield Weapons in East China Sea Combat] (Beijing: Jiefangjun chubanshe [PLA Press], 1985), p. 29.

ships.[67] In January, after the ZFC dominated both the air and the sea around the Dachens, it selected the landing site at Yijiangshan, a small islet seven miles north of the major Dachen Islands.[68]

Nevertheless, there was a disagreement over the bombing of Yijiangshan between Colonel Shayek, the Russian advisor to the 1st PLAAF Division, and Ji Tingxie, the division commander. Ji insisted on his plan and opposed Shayek's advice by saying that he was the commander and should make the final decision. Shayek reported the disagreement to SMAG in Beijing and explained why his plan was best. He even threatened to resign if the Chinese did not accept his bombing plan. After an emergency meeting, the PLAAF and SMAG HQs agreed to dismiss both the Chinese commander and the Russian advisor at the same time before the landing campaign.[69]

The attack began at 0800 hours on 18 January as 54 bombers and 18 fighters raided key GMD positions, headquarters, and defense works at both Yijiangshan and Dachen. Over six hours the bombers dropped 127 tons of bombs on the islands. The ZFC then launched the landings using 10,000 men. By 0200 hours the next day, the PLA had annihilated all remaining GMD pockets of resistance. The GMD lost its entire garrison of 1,086 men, including 567 dead and 519 prisoners. The landing force suffered 1,592 total casualties, including 393 dead; the naval forces had 23 dead and 139 wounded. The air force had no losses except eight bombers and fighters damaged.[70] The controversy over the bombing and air support marked the beginning of the Chinese Air Force officers saying 'No' to their Russian advisors.

## A Bloody Divorce: The Sino-Soviet Split and Rivalry, 1958-1962

In 1958-1959, the great Sino-Soviet polemic debate further undermined the ideological foundation of the Sino-Soviet alliance. In a deeper sense, Beijing's confrontation with Moscow in 1960 fundamentally changed the essence of the Cold War.[71] The Sino-

67 Han, *Dangdai Zhongguo jundui de junshi gongzuo* [Military Affairs of Contemporary China's Armed Forces], Vol. 1, pp. 215-216.

68 Fanghe Dong, *Zhang Aiping zhuan* [Biography of Zhang Aiping] (Beijing: Renmin chubanshe [People's Press], 2000), Vol. 2, pp. 674-675; Han, ibid., Vol. 1, pp. 216-217; Xiaobing Li, 'PLA Attacks and Amphibious Operations during the Taiwan Straits Crises of 1954-55 and 1958', in Ryan, Finkelstein, and McDevitt (eds), *Chinese Warfighting*, p. 152.

69 Shen, *Sulian zhuanjia zai zhongguo, 1948-1960* [Soviet Experts in China, 1948-1960], p. 243.

70 Di Jiu and Ke Feng, *Chaozhang chaoluo; guogong jiaozhu Taiwan haixia jishi* [Record of the CCP-GMD Confrontation in the Taiwan Straits] (Beijing: Zhongguo gongshang chubanshe [China Industrial and Commercial Press], 1996), pp. 210-212; Han, *Dangdai Zhongguo jundui de junshi gongzuo* [Military Affairs of Contemporary China's Armed Forces], Vol. 1, pp. 220-221.

71 Yang Kuisong, 'Origins of the US-Soviet Cold War and Its Impact on China's Revolution', in Zhang Baijia and Niu Jun (eds), *Lengzhan yu zhongguo* [The Cold War and China]

Soviet split buried the shared consciousness and assumption among Communists and Communist sympathizers all over the world that communism was a solution to the problems created by the worldwide process of modernization. The hostility between China and the Soviet Union reached a new height in 1969-1972, when bloody clashes occurred along the Sino-Soviet borders. Reportedly, Moscow's leaders even considered a 'preemptive nuclear strike' against China.[72]

The conflict between the two Communist parties extended to strategic issues. From 31 July to 3 August 1958, Soviet leader Nikita Khrushchev visited Beijing and proposed a Russo-Chinese joint fleet, a permanent naval force including both the PLA and Soviet navies, and a long wave radio system between the two countries. Mao declined the Soviet offer by denouncing them as an attempt to control the Chinese military.[73]

In July Beijing prepared a large-scale bombing and shelling campaign against the GMD-held islands in the Taiwan Straits off the coast of Fujian province without informing Moscow or Khrushchev during his visit. After the PLAAF deployed its air force in the two southern provinces at the end of July, its fighters challenged the GMD Air Force over the Taiwan Strait. Between 29 July and 22 August PLA fighters downed four GMD fighters and damaged five, while the PLA lost only one fighter.[74] Meanwhile, US planes began escorting GMD shipments to Jinmen, and equipped GMD F-86 fighters with new air-to-air missiles, their first use in combat. The PLAAF only discovered that the GMD had air-to-air missiles on 24 September when PLA fighters were shot down by the missiles in an engagement with GMD fighters.[75] On 23 August 1958 the PLA began an intensive artillery bombardment

(Beijing: Shijie zhishi chubanshe [World Knowledge Publishing], 2002), pp. 51-88; Chen Jian and Xiaobing Li, 'China and the End of the Cold War', conference paper at the Fifth Cold War Conference Series: From Détente to the Soviet Collapse at the First Division Museum of Cantigny, Wheaton, IL, 12 October 2005.

72 Yang Kuisong, 'From the Zhenbao Island Incident to Sino-American Rapprochement', in *Dangshi yanjiu ziliao* (Party History Research Materials), no. 12 (1997), pp. 7-8; Xu Yan, 'The Sino-Soviet Border Clashes of 1969', in *Dangshi yanjiu ziliao* (Party History Research Materials), no. 6 (1994), pp. 6-10; Thomas Robinson, 'The Sino-Soviet Border Conflicts of 1969: New Evidence Three Decades Later', in Ryan, Finkelstein, and McDevitt (eds), *Chinese Warfighting*, pp. 198-216.

73 Chu, 'The Sino-Soviet Military Relations in the 1950s', pp. 117-121.

74 Wang, *Dongdai Zhongguo kongjun* [Contemporary China's Air Force], pp. 338-343; Major-General Xu Yan (PLA), *Jinmen zhizhan* [Battle of Jinmen] (Beijing: Zhongguo guangbo dianshi chubanshe [China Broadcasting and Television Publishing House], 1992), pp. 212-214; Shen Weiping, *8-23 paoji Jinmen* [Bombardment of Jinmen on 8/23] (Beijing: Huayi chubanshe (Huayi Publishers), 1999), Vol. 1, pp. 128-145.

75 Wang, *Dongdai Zhongguo kongjun* [Contemporary China's Air Force], p. 345; History Compilation and Translation Bureau, ROC Defense Ministry, *8-23 Paozhan shengli 30 zhounian jinian wenji* [Recollection for the 30th Anniversary of the Victorious 23 August Artillery Battle] (Taibei, Taiwan: Guofangbu yinzhichang [Defense Ministry Printing Office], 1989), pp. 33-34.

of the GMD-held Jinmen Island. In the following two months, several hundred thousand artillery shells rained down on Jinmen. At one point, a PLA invasion of the island seemed imminent.

In response to the rapidly escalating PLA threat, the Eisenhower Administration reinforced US naval forces in East Asia and directed US warships to help the GMD protect Jinmen's supply lines. Khrushchev wrote twice to Mao in October 1958 offering Russian C-75 bombers with surface-to-air (SAM) missiles and Soviet advisors. In his replies, Mao only accepted Russian bombers and SAM missiles, but did not want any Soviet advisors. The Russian aid and new technology never came.[76]

The problems between China and the Soviet Union reached new heights when supporters of the Dalai Lama launched an armed rebellion in Tibet against the Chinese central government in March 1959. His independence movement received official support from the Indian government, suddenly raising tensions between India and China. Ignoring the information and suggestions from Beijing, Moscow issued an official statement on 9 September condemning the Chinese and defending India's policy toward Tibet.[77] Mao criticized Khrushchev as a 'new revisionist' who had 'betrayed the international communist movement' with his 'socialist imperialist' aggressive policy.[78] In 1960, the Soviet Union unilaterally ended 600 bilateral contracts and withdrew all the Soviet experts from China. On 16 July 1960, the Soviet government informed the Chinese government that it would withdraw all of its advisors. By 13 August, all of the 12,000 Soviet advisors had left China, taking with them their blueprints and designs. The Soviets also stopped shipments of equipment and materials that the Chinese aviation program desperately needed.[79] In 1961, the Soviets canceled all projects of scientific and technical cooperation, including joint nuclear programs. Obviously, the Soviet Union did not want to see a strong, nuclear-capable, and unfriendly neighbor. In 1962, Soviet agents instigated the migration of tens of thousands of Chinese citizens in Yili Prefecture to the Soviet Union.

76 Xiaobing Li, *A History of the Modern Chinese Army* (Lexington: University Press of Kentucky, 2007), pp. 188-189.

77 Marshal Nie Rongzhen (PLA, ret.), *Nie Rongzhen huiyilu* [Memoir of Nie Rongzhen] (Beijing: Jiefangjun chubanshe [PLA Press], 1984), Vol. 2, p. 804; Yang, *Zouxiang polie* [Road to the Split], p. 454.

78 For example, Premier Zhou said on 29 April 1968 that the Soviet Union [like America] was apparently encircling and containing China. Li Danhui, 'Conflicts between China and the Soviet Union in Their Efforts to Aid Vietnam and Resist America', in Zhang Baijia and Niu Jun (eds), *Lengzhan yu zhongguo* [The Cold War and China] (Beijing: Shijie zhishi chubanshe [World Knowledge Publishing], 2002), p. 373, n. 1.

79 Nie, *Nie Rongzhen huiyilu* [Memoir of Nie Rongzhen], Vol. 2, p. 806; Tang Xiuying, 'A Sword Thrusting the Sky', in Political Department, PLA General Armaments Department (ed.), *Liangdan yixing; zhongguo hewuqi daodan weixing yu feichuan quanjishi* [Two Bombs and One Star: A Complete Record of China's Nuclear Bombs, Missiles, Satellites, and Space Programs] (Beijing: Jiuzhou chubanshe [Jiuzhou Press], 2001), p. 366.

The Sino-Soviet split had a negative impact on the PLA leaders, who were divided between pro-Soviet professionals and Mao's loyalists. Mao labelled the former as the 'rightists'. Peng's military career ended when Mao accused him of forming a 'right opportunist clique' and conducting 'unprincipled factional activity' in the party and army, charges that often reflected pro-Soviet political positions, and removed him from his post as minister of defense in the summer of 1959. Marshal Lin Biao, as the new defense minister, terminated most of the programs upon which Peng had embarked. A top-down purge went through the PLA. In less than six months, 1,848 high and middle ranking commanders and officers were dismissed, criticized, or jailed for either questioning the Great Leap Forward and People's Communes, or allegations they provided supported for or sympathized with Peng.[80] That same year, Lin abolished the Soviet-style system of military ranks established by Peng in 1955. Lin blamed this system for having changed the PLA tradition of equality among soldiers and commanders.[81]

After the Sino-Soviet split in 1960, the Chinese lost their only source of equipment for air force modernization. Their participation in the Vietnam War in 1965-1968 opened up a new window of opportunity to learn from the US Air Force, the world's most advanced air service.[82] Obviously, there was a huge technological gap between the American and Chinese forces, much larger than that in the Korean War. Major-General Xu Changyou pointed out during an interview that 'when the Americans developed the post-World War II jet fighters in 1950, we used Russian made World War II weapons. We had a five-year technology gap in Korea. Then, when the Americans had the most advanced aircraft in the world by the end of the 1960s, we still used the same air defense systems. There was a 20 year technology gap in Vietnam'.[83]

Although the military alliance between Beijing and Moscow did not last long (less than 10 years), Soviet air advisory assistance had successfully turned Chinese peasant flying squads into a modern air force within five years. The active role that Russian advisors played in the early 1950s not only developed communist military cooperation, but also created a strong air force capable of fighting against technologically advanced

80 China Academy of Military Science (CAMS), *Zhongguo gongchandang zhengzhi gongzuo 70 nian* [The Seventy Years of the CCP Political Tasks] (Beijing: Jiefangjun chubanshe [PLA Press], 1992), Vol. 5, p. 238.

81 Xiaobing Li, 'Chinese Military Ranking and Promotion,' in Jing Luo (ed.), *China Today* (Westport, CT: Greenwood Press, 2005), Vol. 2, pp. 402-405.

82 Lieutenant Wang Xiangcai, interview by the author in Harbin, Heilongjiang, on 20-21 August 2003. Lieutenant Wang served in the 1st Battalion, 3rd Regiment, 61st AAA Division. See also Marshal Xu Xiangqian (PLA, ret.), 'The Purchase of Arms from Moscow', in Li, Millett, and Yu (trans. and eds), *Mao's Generals Remember Korea*, pp. 143-146.

83 Major-General Xu Changyou (PLAAF, ret.), interviews by the author in Shanghai in April 2000. He served as the secretary of General Zhang Aiping, former defense minister of the PRC.

Western forces, including the US Air Force. The advisory assistance to the PLAAF transformed the PLA into a professional force with new capacities. Ironically, as Soviet advisory assistance made the PLAAF more professional or Soviet-like, Mao and the CCP became more ideological and radicalized toward the end of the 1950s. To continue their revolution, the Chinese leaders emphasized ideological elements, human spirit, and independence in the PLA's development. The Soviet advisors favored technological improvements, institutional control, and dependence on Soviet aid. This same political gap also divided the PLA leadership and resulted in disagreements about Chinese military modernization. The Soviet advisory assistance mission to the PLAAF in the Cold War still serves as a history lesson to the Chinese military leaders today.

7

# US Air Force Military Civic Action in Thailand, 1964-1976: Flawed Doctrine–Poor Execution

*Eric D. Roehrkasse*

---

## Introduction[1]

In 2013, former Supreme Allied Commander, Europe, Admiral James Stavridis, told *US News and World Report*, 'You can't kill your way to success in a counterinsurgency effort. You have to protect the people, get the civil military balance right, train the locals, and practice effective strategic communications'.[2] Many would argue with Admiral Stavridis, but certainly, killing the 'bad guys' and using strategic communications (sometimes called psychological operations) have a place in both conventional and unconventional warfare, but the other pieces—actively protecting the people (versus simply not killing them), civil-military relations, and training the locals—rarely play

1 This chapter is a significant rewriting of my MA thesis, submitted to Temple University in 2012. Special thanks to Dr. Petra Goedde, whose seminar on international history in the spring of 2011 led me to the subject of this chapter. Thanks also to Dr. Benjamin Talton, the second reader for my thesis, whose course on Third World history encouraged me to look deeper into the Thai context of Military Civic Action. My advisor, Dr. Richard Immerman, deserves credit for teaching me to think, speak, and write like a historian. I am grateful to Tom Lauria, the archivist at AFHRA, for collecting, declassifying, and mailing the material I requested. Thanks to Lieutenant-Colonel Grant Weller from the USAF Academy History Department who made me aware of the opportunity to contribute to this volume, and to Colonel Ed Kaplan for providing feedback. Finally, special thanks to Donald Stoker and Edward Westermann for their input, edits, flexibility, and most of all encouragement.

2 Oliver Barrett, 'Talking 'Smart Power' With Admiral Stavridis', *World Report* (blog), *US News & World Report*, 25 July 2013, <http://www.usnews.com/opinion/blogs/world-report/2013/07/25/recently-retired-nato-commander-james-stavridis-on-conflict-resolution> (accessed 21 November 2015).

a central role (if any role) in a conventional conflict. Scholar and French army officer David Galula writes: 'The population...becomes the objective for the counterinsurgent as it was for his enemy'.[3] This direct engagement with the civilian population is a significant factor that separates counterinsurgency from conventional warfare, and it is arguably the source of the greatest difficulty.

Military Civic Action (MCA) is an element of counterinsurgency doctrine (COIN) where US service members apply their combat skills—such as engineering or medical care—to help the indigenous (or host nation) military contribute 'to the social and economic development of a society'.[4] It is an idea that was born in the White House during the administration of President John F. Kennedy, a period in which academics and businessmen (later dubbed Kennedy's 'whiz kids') influenced and led policymaking.[5] On 18 December 1961, National Security Advisor McGeorge Bundy sent National Security Action Memorandum 119 (NSAM 119) to Secretary of State Dean Rusk and Secretary of Defense Robert McNamara, with the remark, 'By civic action we [President Kennedy and Bundy] mean using military forces on projects useful to the populace at all levels in such fields as training, public works, agriculture, transportation, communication, health, sanitation, and others helpful to economic development…establishing a link between army and populace'.[6] Over fifty years later, the US Defense Department's Joint Publication 3-57 still defines MCA in similar terms: 'These programs use predominantly indigenous military forces in such fields as education, training, public works, agriculture, transportation, communications, health, sanitation, and other areas to improve HN [host nation] economic and social development…showing the people that their government is capable of meeting the population's basic needs'.[7] From a memo circulated among the Cabinet in 1961 down to the latest revisions of Joint Doctrine, MCA has remained largely unchanged.

This chapter explores the inception of MCA in 1961 as part of President Kennedy's foreign policy and follows the process of integrating it into military doctrine and applying it during the US Air Force's (USAF) presence in Thailand between 1964 and 1976. The Kennedy administration directed the US military to execute MCA as part of a larger effort to modernize the so-called Third World in an effort to

3 David Galula, *Counterinsurgency Warfare, Theory and Practice* (1963; repr., New York: Greenwood Publishing Group, 2006), p. 52.

4 John W. DePauw and George A. Luz (eds), *Winning the Peace: The Strategic Implications of Military Civic Action* (New York: Greenwood Publishing Group, 1992), p. 1.

5 For the origin of this term, see David Halberstam, *The Best and the Brightest* (New York: Random House, 1972).

6 United States, Department of State, Office of the Historian, 'National Security Action Memorandum No. 119', 18 December 1961, *Foreign Relations of the United States* (hereafter *FRUS*), *1961-1963,* Vol. 8, National Security Policy, Document 65, <http://history.state.gov/historicaldocuments/> (accessed 30 October 2015).

7 *Civil-Military Operations*, Joint Publication 3-57 (Washington, DC: Joint Chiefs of Staff, 2013), pp. 1-11, <www.dtic.mil/doctrine/new_pubs/jp3_57.pdf> (accessed 30 October 2015).

protect these nations from the 'false modernity' of communism.[8] The USAF, having MCA forced into its doctrine rather than conceiving it through examination of past experience, sought to reverse-engineer the policy, retroactively incorporating military experience to legitimize MCA as part of military doctrine. This effort to legitimize MCA did not involve, however, the necessary language and cultural training for those assigned to perform MCA. Despite the rhetoric, USAF leaders fundamentally believed that 'the capability to defeat an enemy's forces is the only rational objective of military preparedness'.[9] This belief caused a flawed doctrine to be applied poorly to an incompatible situation in Thailand.

Despite realities on the ground in Thailand and shifts in foreign policy from the Kennedy and Johnson administrations to those of Presidents Richard M. Nixon and Gerald Ford, the core guidance regarding MCA remained unchanged. Because the White House dictated the definition of MCA, the Pentagon had little room to critique or revise it. Once the administration that developed the policy of MCA left Washington, those military members assigned to perform the mission became confused as to its goal. In the end, USAF MCA in Thailand failed to prevent a communist insurgency or to improve the Thai military's image because the doctrine was flawed from its inception, failed to adequately align with the situation in Thailand, and could not be successfully implemented due to inadequate training.[10]

## Military Civic Action and Modernization Theory

The flaws in MCA as military doctrine have their origins in modernization theory. The advent of military civic action as an element of US foreign and military policy began even before Bundy's memorandum with President Kennedy's foreign aid address to Congress in March 1961. In this speech he stated that 'military assistance will in the future more heavily emphasize the internal security, civil works and economic growth

8 For more on modernization theory and the Cold War, see Michael Latham, *Modernization as Ideology: American Social Science and 'Nation Building' in the Kennedy Era* (Chapel Hill: University of North Carolina Press, 2000).

9 'Testimony of General Frederic H. Smith, Jr., Air Force Vice Chief of Staff before the House Subcommittee on Defense Appropriations in 1963', quoted in Robert F. Futrell, *Ideas, Concepts, Doctrine: Basic Thinking in the United States Air Force, 1961-1984* (Maxwell Air Force Base, AL: Air University Press, 1989), pp. 48-49.

10 A note on sources: nearly all of my unpublished primary source material is from the US Air Force Historical Research Agency (AFHRA) archives at Maxwell Air Force Base, Alabama. The archive is indexed using an IRISNUM. With the help of archivist Tom Lauria the sources were declassified for use in this research. Most of the material consists of weekly reports from various USAF units in Thailand. These provide a look at the day-to-day efforts, frustrations, and perspectives of those engaged in MCA. There are also several unit histories. Reports on military civic action by various commands are the most concentrated record of MCA activities and often make recommendations for improvement in the areas of implementation and training.

of the nations thus aided'.[11] Kennedy rooted this statement, along with the rest of his address on the subject of foreign aid, in the social scientific theory of modernization. Kennedy's concept of modernization can be linked clearly to the ideas put forth by Dr. Walt Rostow in his 1960 book, *The Stages of Economic Growth: A Non-Communist Manifesto*. Rostow was one of Kennedy's 'whiz kids'; during the administration of President Lyndon B. Johnson; he replaced McGeorge Bundy as National Security Advisor. David Milne, Professor of US Foreign Relations at the University of East Anglia suggests what these policymakers understood by 'modernization': 'Rostow believed that it was incumbent upon the United States to push those nations languishing in the first two stages toward greater material progress—blunting the appeal of Marxism-Leninism along the way'.[12] Modernization—bringing underdeveloped nations into the liberal, democratic, capitalist camp—became a new weapon in America's anti-communist foreign policy.

Military civic action, as a product of modernization theory, shared its assumptions and characteristics. These included faith in economic and social uplift as panaceas for insurgency and the practice of basing the policy's validity on the 'proof' of civic action's role in the history of America's development. Just as Rostow claimed modernization theory followed the pattern of American development, US military thinkers began to link military civic action to American military history. For the US Air Force, academic lectures and professional journals identified these antecedents as support for MCA's inclusion in military doctrine.

One of the most prolific USAF historians, Dr. Robert F. Futrell, gave a two-part lecture in December 1963 on the 'Background and Growth of Military Civic Actions'. The first part, entitled 'The Role of Military Civic Action in the Development of the United States', covered the time from American independence until the 1920s. The second part, 'Recent Military Civic Action in the United States Air Force', discussed the interwar years until the early 1960s. In his opening comments, Futrell declared that the Air Force believed, 'that its concept of *building nations* through military civic actions is feasible because it recognizes that military men played just this same sort of role in the development of the United States' [emphasis added].[13] He specifically identified how the military contributed to the progress of the US through Rostow's five stages of economic growth, thus drawing a direct link between modernization theory and the doctrine of military civic action.

11 John F. Kennedy, 'Special Message to the Congress on Foreign Aid', 22 March 1961, Gerhard Peters and John T. Woolley (eds), *The American Presidency Project*, <http://www.presidency.ucsb.edu> (accessed 26 October 2011).

12 David Milne, *America's Rasputin: Walt Rostow and the Vietnam War* (New York: Hill and Wang, 2008), p. 62.

13 AFHRA: IRISNUM 00467848: Robert F. Futrell, 'Background and Growth of Military Civic Action: the Role of Military Civic Action in the Development of the United States', (lecture, Aerospace Studies Institute, Maxwell AFB, AL, December 1963), p. 2.

Futrell made a persuasive but flawed case for the historical example of MCA in US development. He correctly identified Thomas Jefferson as the first president to actively use the military for American social and economic development, highlighting his establishment of West Point as an engineering school and role in dispatching Lewis and Clark to the Pacific Northwest.[14] Futrell further citied the role of the Army Corps of Engineers in developing and maintaining America's waterways and dams, highlighting the 1824 Rivers and Harbors Act as the origin of that responsibility.[15] In the early twentieth century, Army aviation provided airmail service, took part in firefighting efforts, and performed aerial surveys for various government departments.[16] It is clear that the US military did in fact provide technical expertise and infrastructure that was beneficial to civil society. However, this is not the full story.

Futrell's argument identified the fact that the technical competence and discipline inherent in military institutions makes them uniquely suited to push undeveloped nations toward a better quality of life. Omitted from this explanation was the political environment within which the US military operated. During most of the period covered in Futrell's lecture, the military was *not* an influential institution in the United States. According to military historian William Skelton, the US Army suffered from popular mistrust of military power and high personnel turnover prior to 1815.[17] This was also the time of the famed Lewis and Clark Expedition, Lieutenant Zebulon Pike's mission to the western territories, and the establishment of West Point. As the US Army reformed following its dismal showing in the War of 1812, it remained subordinate to government policy. Even after these reforms, West Point was noteworthy for producing more railroad presidents than generals in the years prior to the American Civil War.[18] In *The Railroad and the State,* Robert Angevine writes, 'The army officers surveying early American railroads were skilled civil engineers rather than military professionals', indicating that the US military was less an instrument of war and more an agency for civil development during this period.[19] The *Posse Comitatus* Act of 1878 further restricted the power of the US military within the nation's territory. Above all, the US had a history of peaceful transfers of political power. The political environment behind Futrell's examples was different in vital ways

14 Ibid., p. 4.

15 Ibid.

16 AFHRA: IRISNUM 00467849: Futrell, 'Background and Growth of Military Civic Action: Recent Military Civic Action in the United States Air Force', (lecture, Aerospace Studies Institute, Maxwell AFB, AL, December 1963), p. 5.

17 William B. Skelton, *An American Profession of Arms: The Army Officer Corps, 1784-1861* (Lawrence, KS: University of Kansas Press, 1992), p. xv.

18 Samuel P. Huntington, *The Soldier and the State: The Theory and Politics of Civil-Military Relations* (Cambridge: Harvard University Press: 1957), pp. 197-219.

19 Robert G. Angevine, *The Railroad and the State: War, Politics, and Technology in Nineteenth-Century America* (Stanford, CA: Stanford University Press, 2004), p. 87, <http://books.google.com> (accessed 2 January 2016).

from the underdeveloped and developing nations targeted by the twentieth-century policy of military civic action, particularly in cases such as Thailand.

## Thailand: Politics and Development Policies

Understanding how MCA failed to fit the situation in Thailand requires a brief discussion of its political, social, and economic situation prior to the USAF arrival in 1964. Marshall Sarit Thanarat, head of the Royal Thai Army, came to power in Thailand after staging a coup in 1958. Thailand was an absolute monarchy until 1932, when the military staged a revolution to create a constitutional monarchy. The king remained as a symbol of the Thai nation, but the loss of absolute power did not sit well with the royal family. Tension existed between the king and prime minister until Sarit took power.[20] Recognizing the important role of the monarch in the Thai consciousness, Sarit sought the king's sponsorship of his political power.[21] Having inaugurated his legitimacy through royal patronage, Sarit sought to preserve long-term popular legitimacy through national development.[22]

In 1959 the World Bank published a development plan at the request of Sarit's government, which Thailand's National Economic Development Board then drew from to create the National Economic Development Plan for 1961-1965.[23] The plan called for increased per capita output of goods, government investment in education and infrastructure, government expansion of social services, and government assistance.[24] This was the beginning of Sarit's development policies. By 1962, Prime Minister Sarit became increasingly concerned with the insurgency by the Communist Party of Thailand (CPT) and the Pathet Lao in neighboring Laos. Both movements were also a growing concern for the United States.

The Thai and US governments believed the most vulnerable part of Thailand was the northeast, a poor rural area bordering Laos and populated by ethnic Laotians. Sarit created a new five-year plan that emphasized community development and greater administrative control, with the goal of gaining the loyalty of the populace.[25] The US collaborated with Sarit to focus development in the northeast and provided $300 million to fund it.[26] Drawing back from nation-wide development efforts targeted at securing legitimacy and instead focusing on the northeast indicated a new security focus for Thailand: counterinsurgency. To execute Sarit's plan, the Thai

20 Thak Chaloemtiarana, *Thailand: The Politics of Despotic Paternalism* (Ithaca, NY: Cornell University Press, 2007), p. 3.
21 Ibid., p. 205.
22 Ibid., p. 147.
23 Ibid., p. 151.
24 Ibid., pp. 151-152.
25 Alagappa, Muthiah, *The National Security of Developing States: Lessons from Thailand* (Dover, MA: Auburn House Publishing Co., 1987), pp. 179-180.
26 Ibid., p. 180.

government took three approaches: community development plans; the Accelerated Rural Development (ARD) Plan, established in 1964; and Thailand's own MCA program consisting of Mobile Development Units (MDUs).

The Thai government dispatched the first MDU to Kalasin Province on 15 August 1962.[27] By June 1963, there were seven teams in the field.[28] These teams, although a creation of the Thai government, were heavily financed through US foreign aid funds.[29] The stated objective of these units was to 'demonstrate to the rural people… the RTG's [Royal Thai Government's] interests and capability in improving their living standards and hopefully thereby winning their loyalty'.[30] However, a report by the Joint Thai-US Combat Development and Test Center in June 1963 indicated that these units were ineffective in the first year.[31] According to the report, a team would enter a town, hastily round up the residents, let some officials make speeches, hand out some clothes and pictures of the king, and hurry out of town 'as quickly as possible in order to rush to the next village'.[32] Sometimes MDUs stayed in a province for a more extended period in order to establish various community and social development programs. However, the provincial officials did not have the resources to keep these programs going.[33] The theme of this report foreshadows many future reports on military civic action: MCA efforts failed due to poor execution. This would not change even after the USAF introduced its own program in Thailand in 1964.

## USAF Military Civic Action Begins in Thailand, 1964-1966

In early March 1964, Detachment 6 of the 1st Air Commando Wing from Hurlburt Field, Florida, deployed to Udorn, Thailand, under the code name WATER PUMP. This unit was part of the special operations capability created in support of President Kennedy's new national defense strategy of 'flexible response'. The mission of US

27 Chaiyo Krasin, 'Military Civic Action in Thailand', *Military Review* (January 1968), p. 75, <http://cgsc.contentdm.oclc.org/cdm/singleitem/collection/p124201coll1/id/593/rec/2> (accessed 30 October 2015).

28 Lee W. Huff, *Observations on National Security Organization Mobile Development Unit-2 Operations* (Bangkok, Thailand: Joint Thai-US Military Research and Development Center, 1963), p. ii.

29 'Memorandum for the record', 29 January 1965, *FRUS, 1964-1968,* Vol. 27, Mainland Southeast Asia, Regional Affairs, Document 286.

30 Alagappa, *National Security*, p. 180.

31 The Thai-US Military Research and Development Center was highlighted in Eric Wakin's book *Anthropology Goes to War: Professional Ethics and Counterinsurgency in Thailand* (Madison, Wisconsin: University of Wisconsin Center for Southeast Asian Studies, 1992), p. 82. This organization conducted research on behalf of the Defense Department's Advanced Research Projects Agency (DARPA). Lee Huff, the author of the report cited in this paragraph, was listed by Wakin as a social scientist who compromised professional ethics by offering his services for COIN in Thailand.

32 Huff, *Observations,* p. 2.

33 Thak, *Thailand,* p. 172.

Special Operations Forces was to train foreign militaries in counterinsurgency.[34] Appropriately, then, the Pentagon tasked this detachment with training the Royal Laotian Air Force in airborne counterinsurgency tactics.[35] Thailand shared its eastern border with Laos, and served as a relatively stable location from which to train Laotian and Thai pilots. Since the mission of special operations forces was counterinsurgency, and since military civic action was a counterinsurgency function, MCA was on the mind of those airmen en route to Thailand. However, for all the rhetoric about the importance of MCA, the US government and USAF leadership were far more interested in the kinetic, anti-guerilla element of counterinsurgency.

Although Thailand soon became the primary launch and recovery site for American air missions over Laos and Vietnam, this deployment to Thailand was not intended as the harbinger of a larger presence. That is not to say that the US did not see Thailand as a potential base of operations. In 1964 US and Thai officials frequently discussed possible regional cooperation. The Thai government was receptive to military training but resisted increased American military presence because it might '"act as a magnet" for some Chi[nese]Com[munist] counter-move and...increased pressures on Thailand'.[36] For the foreseeable future, this was supposed to be the only USAF presence in Thailand. However, the situation changed after the 2 August 1964 Gulf of Tonkin Incident. By the end of 1965, there were well over 8,000 USAF personnel in Thailand distributed among five Thai bases.[37] This increased presence, which grew further in the coming years, became an important factor in the conduct of USAF MCA.

As the US conflict in Vietnam escalated, the Communist Party of Thailand also stepped up its efforts. Though it declared armed struggle as its revolutionary strategy in 1961, the party's first confrontation with government forces did not take place until 7 August 1965, a date annually celebrated by the CPT as 'Gun Firing Day'.[38] The Chinese Foreign Minister had already stated in January 1965 that Thailand was to be the site of the next 'war of national liberation'.[39] By the end of 1965, the Thai government organized its counterinsurgency effort by establishing the Communist Suppression Operations Command (CSOC) under the leadership of General Saiyud

34 Warren A. Trest, *Air Commando One: Heinie Aderholt and America's Secret Wars* (Washington, DC: Smithsonian Institute Press, 2000), p. 121.

35 Ibid., p. 140.

36 Paper Prepared by Assistant Secretary of State for Far Eastern Affairs (Bundy), 23 May 1964, *FRUS, 1964-1968,* Vol. 27, Mainland Southeast Asia; Regional Affairs, document 270.

37 Jeffrey Glasser, *The Secret Vietnam War: the United States Air Force in Thailand, 1961-1975* (Jefferson, NC: McFarland & Co., 1995), pp. 58-59. These bases were Don Muang, Korat, Takhli, Udorn, and Nakhon Phanom.

38 Thomas Marks, *Maoist Insurgency Since Vietnam* (London: Frank Cass, 1996), p. 23.

39 Saiyud Kerdphol, *The Struggle for Thailand: Counter-Insurgency, 1965-1985* (Bangkok: S. Research Center, 1986), p. 23.

Kerdphol.[40] The CSOC called for a new way of fighting the insurgents through a combination of civil, police, and military efforts. Though tasked with overseeing the Thai counterinsurgency effort, the CSOC did not have the necessary authority to muster sufficient resources. General Saiyud and the CSOC emphasized the necessity of MCA to address the sources of unrest, but other Thai military leaders disagreed and implemented brutal suppression tactics.[41] Like the US military, the Thai military put more emphasis on killing guerillas than winning the 'hearts and minds' of the people.

Until 1966, USAF MCA remained the domain of the Special Operations personnel of Detachment 6. Shortly after arriving in 1964, the flight surgeon for Detachment 6 began a medical civic action program in the villages surrounding Udorn Royal Thai Air Force Base (RTAFB).[42] At this time, however, there was no provision for a dedicated, full-time MCA program. Detachment 6 medical personnel undertook this effort during off-duty time in addition to their primary responsibilities.[43] Despite this, it took on the appearance of an all-out effort. The flight surgeon spent up to a week at a time in remote villages, leaving behind a skeleton crew to tend to the American clinic on base. Nearly every week from 20 December 1965 to 24 April 1966, a team was out for at least one day, usually more.[44] The Detachment 6 flight surgeon did his best to follow his understanding of MCA policy guidance, despite the lack of real interest by US Air Force leaders.

The program's vigor is impressive considering that the Detachment 6 flight surgeon had only one other doctor and four technicians to staff two MEDCATs (medical civic action teams). His remaining practitioners were frequently parceled out to other locations, and one doctor had to remain at Udorn at all times. The scope of the military civic action program caused the flight surgeon to protest the assignment of his personnel to sites—presumably in neighboring Laos—with code names like CHARLIE and VICTOR.[45] He argued that his primary mission and responsibility was to northeastern Thailand, 'the area of greatest need and potential benefit' due to

40 Marks, *Maoist Insurgency*, p. 35.

41 Saiyud, *Struggle for Thailand,* pp. 5-6, 16.

42 Trest, *Air Commando One,* p. 142.

43 Michael E. Haas, *Apollo's Warriors: US Air Force Special Operations During the Cold War* (Maxwell Air Force Base, AL: Air University Press, 2000), pp. 240-241.

44 AFHRA: IRISNUM 00446512: Detachment 6 (Det 6), 1st Air Commando Wing (Weekly Activity Reports [WAR], 20 December 1965 to 5 June 1966).

45 The identities of these locations are not clear, but if the flight surgeon was arguing that his unit's responsibility was to Thailand, and given the secrecy requiring code names for sites despite the already SECRET classification of these reports, it is likely they were in Laos. This is corroborated by a website containing stories from veteran Air Commandos who trained the Laotian Air Force. On this site, VICTOR was identified as Vientiane, the capital of Laos. Don Moody, 'Nevermore Until Tomorrow', *The Great Adventures of Bob and Don*, <www.ravens.org/Adventures/Episode0000.htm> (accessed 30 October 2015).

the strong communist influence there.[46] This officer's comments, which were endorsed by his commander, Lieutenant-Colonel Benjamin M. Washburn, emphasized his belief that MCA efforts were equally if not more important than other USAF efforts in the region. This argument would be repeated frequently in the coming years and largely fall on deaf ears.

Another complaint, beginning with the Detachment 6 effort and continuing throughout the USAF presence in Thailand, was that the USAF MCA teams were poorly equipped. For several weeks the detachment commander complained of the failure of US Pacific Air Forces headquarters to deliver vehicles, radios, and other required equipment. On 2 January 1966 the commander wrote, '[T]here might soon be some shadow of doubt [within the Thai government] as to what official backing we have back home so long as we continue to operate with such deplorable equipment'.[47] Despite these protests, there is no indication that Detachment 6 ever received additional manpower or equipment for use in the military civic action mission. Even the medical supplies used by the MEDCATs came from a Detroit-based non-profit charity, World Medical Relief, which donated 5,000 pounds of supplies on a bimonthly basis.[48] Despite these frustrations and shortcomings, the MCA efforts persisted.

The Udorn team continued military civic action activities until May 1966 in cooperation with the Thai MDU teams. In the weekly activity reports, the teams identified increased communist insurgent activity, such as assassinations of teachers and village leaders, followed by requests from Thai officials for MDU teams to respond to those areas.[49] Despite the lack of support from headquarters and the increase in communist agitation, the MEDCAT personnel felt their work was making a difference. In his report for the week of 14 through 20 March 1966, the flight surgeon wrote, 'The goodwill generated in the Thai Government by the MEDCAT visits has been credited with a great deal of the information leading to the arrest of [sixty] communist sympathizers'.[50] Three weeks later, communist insurgents offered 30,000 bhat (equivalent to $1,442 at 1960s rates) for the assassination of any American, a princely sum considering that at the time the per capita income in the northeast rural areas was only 818 bhat.[51] The MEDCATs were unconcerned, but not because of their confidence in the success of MCA. Instead, the report for that week argued, 'people in the village know from experience that the money will never be paid'.[52] Such

46 AFHRA: IRISNUM 00446512: Det 6, WAR, 2 January 1966.
47 Ibid.
48 Trest, *Air Commando One,* p. 142.
49 AFHRA: IRISNUM 00446512: Det 6, WAR, 14-20 March 1966.
50 Ibid.
51 Average income listed in Hayao Fukui, *Food and Population in a Northeast Thai Village* (Honolulu: University of Hawaii Press, 1994), p. 293. Currency conversion provided by www.bahtrate.com, which states that the baht to US dollar exchange rate from 1956 to 1973 was 20.8 baht to 1 dollar.
52 AFHRA: IRISNUM 00446512: Det 6, WAR, 4-10 April 1966.

a statement suggests there would be concern if the communists were known to pay as promised.

The MEDCATs may have not been alarmed by the threat to US personnel, but it appears the Thai government linked USAF visits with insurgent attacks on villagers and wished to sever that link. During the second week of May 1966, the flight surgeon reported he was 'quite concerned over the impending finish of our civic action program'.[53] The following week the flight surgeon reported MEDCAT programs had been canceled indefinitely 'at the request of the RTG [Royal Thai Government], because of concern for the safety of the team members'. Although disappointed, the Detachment 6 flight surgeon wrote, 'For two years the mobile teams have been operating full time with the final objective being the absorption of our program by some agency or the RTG....Our only desire at this point is to insure that all future activities continue to prove as successful as past operations'.[54] Unfortunately, it is difficult to measure the so-called success of past operations to which the flight surgeon referred. The Udorn program fizzled out in May 1966, but this was not the end of USAF military civic action in Thailand.

## The USAF Presence Grows: The MCA Effort Resurges, 1966-1968

Between 1 January and 31 December 1966, the USAF presence in Thailand increased from just over 8,000 to 24,783 due to the escalation of air operations over Vietnam.[55] As USAF forces in Thailand surged, US policy emphasis on MCA experienced its own resurgence. In his foreign aid address to Congress on 1 February, President Johnson announced his proposal for the Military Assistance and Sales Act of 1966. In it, he called for '[g]reater emphasis on civic action programs. We shall give new stress to civic action programs through which local troops build schools and roads, and provide literacy training and health services'. He also reemphasized the importance of indigenous military participation to improve their image: 'Through these programs, military personnel are able to play a more constructive role in their society, and to establish better relations with the civilian population'.[56] In its first iteration, MCA had been treated as more of a hobby than a policy. President Johnson intended to reverse this.

General John P. McConnell, US Air Force Chief of Staff after Curtis E. LeMay's retirement in January 1965, translated Johnson's policy into action. Later in 1966, McConnell said, 'Second to combat operations our efforts in the area of civic action are the most valuable contribution we can make to the defeat of communist

53 AFHRA: IRISNUM 00446512: Det 6, WAR, 9-15 May 1966.
54 AFHRA: IRISNUM 00446512: Det 6, WAR, 16-22 May 1966.
55 Glasser, *Secret Vietnam War*, pp. 82-84.
56 Lyndon B. Johnson, 'Special Message to the Congress on the Foreign Aid Program', 1 February 1966, online by Gerhard Peters and John T. Woolley, *The American Presidency Project*, <http://www.presidency.ucsb.edu/> (accessed 1 November 2011).

insurgency, the establishment of solid and progressive governments, and lasting peace in SEA [Southeast Asia]'.[57] A working paper published in August 1970 as part of the USAF CORONA HARVEST program stated, 'in 1966, the Civic Action Program in SEAsia [sic] transformed from a voluntary humanitarian effort into an official program'.[58] In November 1966, the Pentagon published the *Joint Manual for Civil Affairs*, signed by all three service departments. While the definition of MCA remained the same, it received new emphasis: 'military civic action projects are fully as important in promoting security and stability as are conventional tactics, weapons, and roles'.[59] If there was ever a time that MCA had a chance of success, this was it.

In 1965, Lieutenant-Colonel Malcolm S. Bounds arrived at Headquarters Pacific Air Forces (PACAF), the USAF command responsible for operations in Asia. In 1966, he produced official guidance for a PACAF Military Civic Action Program.[60] This guidance stated objectives consistent with those put forth by President Johnson and General McConnell. However, the real change from past MCA efforts was that PACAF created full-time civic action positions and periodic reporting requirements to provide necessary oversight. For Thailand, this program came on line shortly after the Detachment 6 MCA program ceased operations in mid-1966. The 606th Air Commando Squadron (606 ACS) advance team arrived at Nakhon Phanom RTAFB in April 1966, followed on 5 July by a formal Civic Action Section.[61] Unlike the Detachment 6 program, which received donated medical supplies and rehabilitated or broken vehicles for their use, the 606 ACS received a defined allotment of foreign assistance funds. Because those funds came primarily through the State Department, the new program required the USAF to coordinate MCA activities with the US Operational Mission (USOM) at the Embassy in Bangkok. As with the original Detachment 6 effort, the focus of the 606 ACS MCA effort was medical.[62] By fiscal year 1969, their budget was over $800,000, not including military personnel pay or operations and maintenance of vehicles and aircraft.[63]

57 AFHRA: IRISNUM 1007067: 'Report on USAF Logistics Activities in Support of Operations in Southeast Asia, 1 January 1965-31 March 1968' (working paper for CORONA HARVEST, August 1970), pp. III-6-149.
58 AFHRA: IRISNUM 1007067, pp. III-6-149.
59 *Joint Manual for Civil Affairs* (Washington, DC: Joint Chiefs of Staff, 1966), p. 29, <http://www.marines.mil/news/publications/> (accessed 2 November 2011).
60 Malcolm S. Bounds, 'Military Civic Action', *Air University Review* (May-June 1969), <http://www.airpower.au.af.mil/airchronicles/aureview/1969/may-jun/bounds.html> (accessed 7April 2011).
61 AFHRA: IRISNUM 00451168: '606th Air Commando Squadron (Lucky Tiger) Activities', 5 October 1966, p. 5.
62 AFHRA: IRISNUM 00410604: '606 ACS (LUCKY TIGER) Activities', report for 28 March to 30 September 1966.
63 AFHRA: IRISNUM 00470520: 'USAF Military Civic Action', (Semiannual Report, October 1968), p. 93.

Initially, these new USAF MEDCATs had to carve out their own niche. Their primary activities included assistance at Thai clinics and dispensaries. However, this quickly expanded beyond providing training and staff support at these clinics as the teams took an active role by venturing into the remote corners of northeast Thailand to provide medical care and training.[64] Eventually, this included the use of riverboats to reach previously inaccessible areas along the Mekong River.[65]

One activity initiated by the US Air Force that later had significant support and profound impact was veterinary assistance. By November 1966, the USAF veterinarian in Thailand coordinated with Thai Public Health to institute a rabies control program in addition to the livestock program he started in August.[66] Based on the success of these efforts, USOM, the US State Department, and the Thai Department of Technical and Economic Cooperation signed Project Agreement 180-8045 in June 1968, establishing a livestock civic action program to be staffed by four USAF veterinarians and five USAF technicians.[67] By the middle of 1968, USAF MCA activities by the 606 ACS were expansive and robust and the MCA section grew to nearly one hundred personnel.[68]

This new PACAF program also established smaller MCA offices at all seven Thai bases with a USAF presence.[69] Unlike the 606 ACS group, however, this was a more gradual program. By the end of 1968, PACAF was still in the process of shifting from the initial part-time effort to one led by a full-time base civic action officer (BCAO).[70] This increased manpower requirement, not only in Thailand but in Vietnam as well, exceeded the capacity of the 1st Air Commando Wing. To meet the increased demand, the Air Staff drew officers from a variety of Air Force Specialty Codes (AFSCs). These officers were unfamiliar with military civic action and lacked requisite language and cultural training. To prepare them to act as BCAOs, they received a brief two-week training course before going 'down range'.[71] There was a trade-off between quality and

64 AFHRA: IRISNUM 00451168: 'Medical Training for Royal Thai Government Health Workers in remote site operations', 26 December 1969.

65 AFHRA: IRISNUM 00451169: 'Medical Training for Royal Thai Government Health Workers, Riverboat Medical Operations', 27 December 1969.

66 AFHRA: IRISNUM 00410604: '606 ACS (LUCKY TIGER) Activities', report for 15-22 October 1966.

67 AFHRA: IRISNUM 00451167: 'Veterinary Assistance to Royal Thai Government Livestock and Rabies Programs', 25 December 1969.

68 AFHRA: IRISNUM 00451168: 'Medical Training for Royal Thai Government Health Workers in remote site operations', 26 December 1969.

69 AFHRA: IRISNUM 00470520: 'USAF Military Civic Action'. The seven bases listed in this report included the five already mentioned above (Udorn, Takhli, Korat, Don Muang, and Nakhon Phanom) and two others that opened between 1965 and 1968 (U-Tapao and Ubon).

70 Ibid., p. 127.

71 Betty Barton Christiansen, *The United States in Southeast Asia: Military Civic Action* (unpublished manuscript, Air Force History and Museums Program, 1998), p. 189, <http://www.au.af.mil/au/awc/awcgate/af/usaf_sea_civic_action.pdf> (accessed 6

quantity. Though the 606 ACS program was strong during this time, poorly trained BCAOs at the other air bases would add to the confusion over the objectives and conduct of MCA in Thailand in the years to come.

The PACAF MCA program remained essentially unchanged while Colonel Bounds was in charge. In one of the final reports during his tenure, which ended in late 1968, PACAF informed Headquarters Air Force about the status of the program after two years. The primary concern was the lack of Royal Thai Air Force (RTAF) participation. USAF MCA personnel frequently tried to encourage RTAF personnel to go along on MCA projects, but to no avail. The October 1968 report cited three reasons for the lack of RTAF participation: fear of impinging on the responsibilities of other Thai agencies, insufficient resources to divert from other RTAF missions, and 'reluctance on the part of military men to get involved in programs that they consider civilian in nature'.[72] A memorandum dated Christmas Day 1968 to the chief of the Civic Action Center reinforced this difficulty. The USAF advisor to the RTAF Surgeon General, Air Marshall Tragool Thavaravej, reported, 'Marshall Tragool has no interest whatsoever in civic action activities.…Tragool senses the US desire that he take an interest in civic action, but intends to do nothing about it'.[73] Without the cooperation of such an influential Thai officer, USAF MCA appeared destined to fail.

The end of 1968 witnessed a major setback to USAF MCA. Guidance from the US Embassy in Bangkok prompted the creation of 7th/13th Air Force Operations Plan (7/13 AF OPLAN) 451-68, 'Orient Express', on 16 October 1968. This plan limited MCA efforts to within a 16-kilometer radius of each base and gave the 606 ACS approximately 12 months to phase out their work in rural areas outside this radius.[74] The restricted movement of the well-trained and supplied 606 ACS to within 16 kilometers of Nakhon Phanom RTAFB made the seven BCAOs the best means for reaching other parts of Thailand. Unfortunately, BCAO training remained 'hardly adequate to prepare them for the social, economic, political and military problems that [would] frustrate them during their one year sojourn in Thailand'.[75] Restrictions on the movement of those conducting MCA activities, reliance on poorly trained BCAOs, and RTAF intransigence led to adaptations that undermined the purpose of military civic action. These factors were compounded by changes in US and Thai foreign policy in 1969.

September 2011). Despite the title, Captain Christiansen's focus was on MCA in Vietnam. Nonetheless, her analysis of the MCA training program is relevant Air Force-wide for this period.

72 AFHRA: IRISNUM 00470520: 'USAF Military Civic Action', p. 127.

73 AFHRA: IRISNUM 00517096: Memorandum from Major Grant H. Wagner to Chief, CAC, 'RTAF Interest in Civic Action Activities', 25 December 1968.

74 AFHRA: IRISNUM 00451166: 'Medical Training for Royal Thai Government Health Workers in Mobile Medical Team Operations', (Semi-Annual Civic Action Report, 28 December 1969).

75 AFHRA: IRISNUM 00470520: 'USAF Military Civic Action', p. 127.

## The Shift from Nation-Building to Air Base Defense, 1969-1972

A February 1969 memorandum by the Acting Director of USAF Civic Action provided an account of a meeting with the US Embassy in Bangkok on the subject of MCA. In the meeting, the Embassy conveyed that General Kriangsak Chomanan, chief of Thai Supreme Command, opposed 'the remote operations of the 606 CAC [Civic Action Center] primarily on the basis of the high exposure of US troops in a person-to-person medical care situation with Thai citizens...General Kriangsak feels that Thai counterinsurgency efforts <u>must</u> be manned by Thais'.[76] Accordingly, the Thai Supreme Command organized a 40-man tri-service mobile medical team in December 1968, 'entirely separate from the military input to Mobile Development Units'.[77] Based on these comments, it seems clear that the Thai military wanted to take complete control of MCA efforts within their country. This sentiment was reinforced by General Saiyud Kerdphol: 'We must make it clear that this counter-insurgency effort is being directed and fought by Thais and not our allies whose role must be an indirect, supporting one'.[78] These sentiments combined with several events in 1969 to signal a significant change in the nature of US-Thai relations that influenced the conduct of USAF MCA in Thailand.

Many Thai people had long resented the American military presence. The US military in Thailand was associated with undesirable changes such as prostitution, increased crime, biracial children, and the erosion of culture, particularly in the smaller towns.[79] Additionally, the massive flow of money into the Thai economy by nearly 47,000 American servicemen led to wild inflation and deep economic dependence.[80] Thai officials and businessmen enjoyed the benefits of increased American investment, but the July 1969 Nixon Doctrine threatened this growth. Efforts emanating from this doctrine, such as Vietnamization, would reduce the role and presence of the US military personnel in Southeast Asia and put more of the responsibility on those nations to fight their own wars. This meant the days of a large US military presence in Thailand were numbered.

Previously, the objections of the Thai population to America's negative influence were subordinated to the close military and economic relationship between Thai elites and the US government. However, facing the eventual US withdrawal from Southeast Asia under Nixon's initiative, these elites began to explore other options. Additionally, the CPT, largely absent from this discussion since the beginning of armed insurgency

76 AFHRA: IRISNUM 00517096: Major Grant H. Wagner, Memorandum for Record, 19 February 1969.
77 Ibid.
78 Saiyud, *Struggle for Thailand*, p. 93.
79 Glasser, *Secret Vietnam War*, pp. 102-3.
80 Suchita Ghosh, 'Thailand's Relations with the US and China: The Search for an Independent Foreign Policy', *China Report* (1976), p. 51, SAGE Journals, <online.sagepub.com> doi: 10.1177/000944557601200405 (accessed 3 November 2011).

in 1965, seized on the growing political consciousness of the Thai people and the declining influence of the United States to regroup.[81] Thailand was approaching a domestic crisis with the start of a new decade.

The Nixon Doctrine signaled an about-face in US foreign policy toward the Vietnam War, and this would have significant impacts on MCA activities. Johnson and his Vietnam strategy had been discredited by the Tet Offensive and this led him to announce he would not run for reelection. Many in Congress believed it was the focus on modernization, the cornerstone of both Kennedy's and Johnson's foreign policy, that 'eventually produced the political and military commitments that ended in mire like Vietnam'.[82] Criticism of modernization came from left-wing voices that highlighted the damaging effects of capitalism (economic development) on poor nations and from right-wing critics of social engineering (social development).[83] In concrete terms, the US failure to transform South Vietnam into a stable country exposed the flaws of modernization theory. This critique of modernization theory left military civic action without a stable foundation.

By 1969, the critical elements of the USAF MCA effort—Thai government support and the US emphasis on modernization in counterinsurgency—were exhausted. Additionally, the lack of RTAF participation and the restriction to a 16-kilometer radius around the seven Thai air bases prevented USAF BCAOs from accomplishing the stated objectives of the MCA program. Despite these crushing blows, the idea of abandoning MCA in Thailand was never considered. Instead, those tasked with MCA sought a new mission.

By the end of 1969, the proscription of USAF MCA activities to within 16 kilometers of each base was complete. The 606 ACS was limited to providing medical training in and around Nakhon Phanom RTAFB. The BCAOs, now the best means of reaching the widest Thai population, were 'primarily concerned with community relations, humanitarian, and good will projects designed to enhance the image of the US in the eyes of the Thai people', despite the fact that the image of the US was never previously a goal of MCA.[84] The following year, 7th Air Force Regulation (7AFR) 55-8, *Operations: Military Civic Action*, dated 28 August 1970, explicitly stated, 'MCA must not be confused with community relations or humanitarian programs', yet that is exactly what was happening in Thailand.[85] The BCAOs were responding

81 Thomas Marks, *Making Revolution: The Insurgency of the Communist Party of Thailand in Structural Perspective* (Bangkok: White Lotus, 1994), p. 121.

82 David Ekbladh, *The Great American Mission: Modernization and the Construction of an American World Order* (Princeton, NJ: Princeton University Press, 2010), p. 222.

83 Latham, Michael E., *The Right Kind of Revolution* (Ithaca, NY: Cornell University Press, 2011), p. 157.

84 AFHRA: IRISNUM 00451166: 'Medical Training for Royal Thai Government Health Workers in Mobile Medical Team operations', p. 8.

85 AFHRA: IRISNUM 00524873: *Operations: Military Civic Action* (7th Air Force Regulation 55-8, 28 August 1970), p. 4.

to present realities in contradiction to doctrine. Despite changing conditions both politically and on the ground, MCA doctrine was not subjected to a comprehensive reappraisal. The goals of MCA remained social and economic development—elements of modernization theory—and improvement of the indigenous military's image. The fundamental assumptions of modernization still existed in MCA doctrine at a time when modernization had been discredited and the Thai military was keeping its distance from USAF MCA. These factors created a fundamental crisis in the purpose and practice of USAF MCA.

Despite the lack of a complete review of MCA in USAF doctrine, one small change took on major significance in its concept and execution. In July 1969, the same month President Nixon declared his intent to gradually withdraw from Southeast Asia, the USAF added airbase security as a goal of MCA.[86] It was the last priority of MCA below all the previous objectives: improving socio-economic status, improving the host nation military's image, and encouraging the host nation air force to participate. However, being unable to participate in activities aimed at the first three objectives, the lowest priority quickly became dominant in USAF MCA. It gave renewed purpose to a program that was rapidly losing meaning amid policy changes in the US and Thailand. It was also a purpose in which BCAO's had a vested interest as America's influence in the region receded. Dissatisfaction with American presence and policy in Thailand increased the need to ensure the safety of US forces. However, this objective, combined with inadequate training stateside, also changed the methods of conducting MCA. These factors created so much confusion within the USAF that individual BCAOs, tasked with a job and hell-bent on doing it, began interpreting both the purpose of MCA and its methods of execution as they saw fit.

One officer's account is particularly illustrative of the frustration and confusion over USAF MCA in the early 1970s. Captain Charles Murphy Jr., was the BCAO at Korat RTAFB from July 1971 to December 1972.[87] In both his end-of-tour report and an oral interview in 1973, Murphy addressed the lack of adequate training, a lack of support from their leaders, the frustrations of working with the Thai military, and his personal interpretation of the proper purpose and execution of MCA. Murphy considered his training insufficient, although he professed to be better prepared for MCA than most. His experience included voluntary MCA work in Vietnam in 1968 and some graduate work in cultural anthropology.[88] In 1969, Murphy began teaching at the Special Air Warfare School at Eglin AFB, Florida, on the subject of civic action. There is no indication, however, that he received formal training on military

86 AFHRA: IRISNUM 00524870: *War Planning: Civic Action Program* (7AFR 28-1, 5 July 1969), p. 6.

87 While it may be tenuous to assume that Murphy's experience reflected that of all USAF BCAOs in Thailand during this time, his account of MCA efforts contain a level of detail and honesty missing from other available sources.

88 AFHRA: IRISNUM 00904782: Charles G. Murphy Jr., interview by Lyn R. Officer and Hugh N. Ahnmann, 4 June 1973, interview #675, transcript.

civic action before he began instructing others. Instead, he claims to have walked into the commanding general's office and told the general 'I wanted to instruct because I thought I knew something about what was going on'.[89] Though he may have had some idea of the complex nature of cultural factors (and practical experience in Vietnam), he never received training in the context of Thai culture. In his end of tour report, he states that his lack of language training was a 'serious limitation to my effectiveness in this program'.[90] His recommendations for enhanced training for future BCAOs indicates that inadequate training and preparation remained a critical issue into the 1970s.

The concept of operations suggested in Murphy's end-of-tour report reveal vestiges of the original modernization and development assumptions. He identified the need to 'eliminat[e] sources of discontent which could be used by an insurgent to get support for his own cause'.[91] However, the object was no longer nation-building. Instead, he identified the goal as 'keeping the base safe from hostile action'.[92] In his oral history, Captain Murphy asserted that he came to this conclusion following his tour in Vietnam: 'I get back to the states…and suddenly I find out that the purpose for the civic action program, the whole basis of the thing, is not just development or 'do gooder' or anything like that. It is…creating an environment around an installation [and] you deny it to the enemy'.[93] Since MCA as defined in USAF doctrine was no longer part of the US government's foreign policy strategy, airmen like Captain Murphy adapted it to a more limited—but in their minds more relevant—purpose.

Captain Murphy may have departed from the script to a greater extent than other officers (it is difficult to compare since there are few if any similar exit interviews), but his reasons for doing so reflect the situation already described in Thailand. When asked where he received operational guidance, he answered, 'Me'.[94] He asserted that the USAF policy guidance, Air Force Regulation 55-7, was useless and that the base commander 'doesn't even know why he's got you'.[95] In his end-of-tour report, Murphy indicated additional reasons for pursuing his own course with the MCA program. Most significant was the elimination of the civic action program manager position at 7/13th Air Force headquarters and that 'PACAF had for all practical purposes lost all interest in the programs'.[96] As the war in Vietnam drew to a close, there was little interest at all levels in the official goals of MCA. Yet as the USAF presence declined in Thailand, MCA was assigned one last mission.

89 Ibid.
90 AFHRA: IRISNUM 00517604: Charles G. Murphy Jr., 'Base Civic Action Program' (End of Tour Report, July 1971-December 1972), p. 16.
91 AFHRA: IRISNUM 00517604: Murphy, End of Tour Report, p. 8.
92 Ibid.
93 AFHRA: IRISNUM 00904782, Murphy, interview, p. 13.
94 AFHRA: IRISNUM 00904782, Murphy, interview, p. 55.
95 AFHRA: IRISNUM 00904782, Murphy, interview, p. 54.
96 AFHRA: IRISNUM 00517604: Murphy, End of Tour Report, p. 16.

## Thai Instability and the USAF Withdrawal, 1973-1976

Nineteen seventy-three was a landmark year in Southeast Asia. For the United States, that year meant the Paris Peace Accords in January, withdrawal of American forces from Vietnam by the end of March, and the beginning of the drawdown in Thailand. With the end of US involvement in Vietnam, there was no longer a need for the huge presence of American combat aircraft and their associated support personnel. Air operations continued over Laos and Cambodia, which were not signatories to the Paris Peace Accords, until the Congressionally mandated termination date of 15 August 1973.[97] On 1 January 1973, before the signing of the accords, the USAF presence was nearly 36,000 (83 percent of the total US military presence of 43,550).[98] By 1 January 1974, USAF presence was down to 30,646, and by 1 January 1975 it was 20,576.[99] At this time there was still an expectation on the part of both US and Thai officials that the USAF would retain a presence in Thailand to protect Southeast Asian and Indian Ocean interests.[100]

As late as July 1974, the US was negotiating to retain a permanent presence at U-Tapao RTAFB with minimum forces necessary for intelligence, the Military Assistance Program, search and rescue, US Embassy support, and Diego Garcia operations.[101] Since MCA was now concerned with airbase defense, 13th Air Force leaders saw a need to continue the program for the foreseeable future, albeit with limited aims.[102] The 13th Air Force's second semiannual report for 1974 stated that its MCA objective was to, 'assist the Royal Thai Government in strengthening the country's overall economic posture, thus building the confidence of the local villagers in both the RTG and the American forces [to]...encourage these individuals to report any suspicious activity'.[103] At first, it appears there was still a modernization element in the program. Later in the report, however, discussion of MCA activities dropped all references to nation-building and mentioned only 'goodwill projects' done in hopes that 'villagers would provide defense related intelligence information with regard to planned insurgent attacks on US tenanted military bases'.[104] Beyond that, BCAOs

97 Glasser, *Secret Vietnam War*, pp. 196-197.
98 AFHRA, IRISNUM 1006524: Harold J. Smarkola Jr., *History of Thirteenth Air Force Advanced Echelon, 1 July-31 December 1974* (Office of History, 13AF Advanced Echelon, June 20, 1975, portions declassified 2 August 2011), p. 134.
99 Ibid.
100 Ibid., p. 135.
101 Ibid.
102 The command element in Thailand was no longer 7/13th Air Force. The 7th Air Force was responsible for Vietnam operations, including air operations from Thailand. When that conflict ended, only the 13th Air Force remained in Thailand.
103 AFHRA: IRISNUM 1006524: Smarkola, p. 25.
104 Ibid., p. 168.

hoped MCA efforts would help the Thai people view US personnel as 'a friendly partner…apart from the larger political issues concerning US units in Thailand'.[105]

The domestic environment in Thailand reached its most volatile point in 1973. The repressive military government of Thanom Kittikachon collapsed amid student and labor protests demanding a new constitution and greater democracy.[106] Over the next several years, Thailand struggled to develop a stable government as forces from the right and left attempted to seize political influence.[107] In September 1974, a meeting between Thai Ambassador Anand Panyarachun and US Secretary of State Henry Kissinger indicated that the fall of the military regime would require a significant reevaluation of the Thai relationship with the US.[108] Less than a year later, relations between the US and Thailand became strained nearly to the breaking point. In May 1975, the Khmer Rouge from Cambodia boarded the US cargo ship SS *Mayaguez*. Without consultation with the Thai government or notification of the US Ambassador to Thailand, American aircraft launched from Thai bases and successfully secured the release of the ship.[109] The Thai government felt its sovereignty was violated and demanded all US forces withdraw within one year.

With the end of the USAF presence in Thailand in sight, so-called MCA efforts actually increased while other efforts were winding down. At this point, however, military civic action barely resembled its original purpose. Rather than the once lofty goal of NSAM 119 to 'undertake civic action projects as [an] indispensable means of strengthening their society's economic base', the program now sought to 'minimize

105 Ibid., p. 169.

106 Thak, *Thailand*, p. 230.

107 Thomas A. Marks, 'Anatomy of a Counterinsurgency Victory', *Military Review* (January-February 2007), p. 43, <http://cgsc.cdmhost.com/cdm/landingpage/collection/p124201coll1> (accessed March 20, 2011).

108 Memorandum of Conversation, 12 September 1974, *FRUS, 1969-1976*, Vol. E-12, *Documents on East and Southeast Asia, 1973-1976*, Document 388. The exchange between Anand and Kissinger was very frank, as this excerpt shows (the State Department historian incorrectly used Anand's second name rather than the Thai convention of using the first name):
PANYARACHUN: We think that the relationship needs a new basis. You have cooperated with the military faction. This was understandable since the military ran the government. Now that image needs to be rectified. There are some irritants in the relationship that need to be removed.
KISSINGER: Like what?
PANYARACHUN: Your military presence. Not the military presence itself, but the number and the way they came in. It gave the impression that Thailand is not master in its own house. We need to adjust to the new realities of the situation.

109 Telegram 8690 from the Embassy in Thailand to the Department of State, 13 May 1975, 'MEASURES TO OBTAIN RELEASE OF THE MAYAGUEZ', *FRUS, 1969-1976*, Vol. E-12, *Documents on East and Southeast Asia, 1973-1976*, Document 399. In this telegram, Ambassador Masters writes, 'I cannot stress to [sic] strongly the damage to US-Thai interests which is likely to result from this unilateral action'. He finishes the telegram with this statement: 'May I know what is going on?'

the social and economic impact of base closure on the local community'.[110] At Nakhon Phanom, the BCAO continued supporting 'humanitarian projects', long forgetting that humanitarian and community relations work was not MCA. At Udorn, the MCA office worked to 'leave the civilian and military community with a lasting impression of beneficial and friendly US involvement'.[111] It is interesting to note that military civic action, one of the first functions of the USAF in Thailand, 'continued at a high level… until the final moments of base closure'.[112] Compared to the initial program in 1964, however, this effort was almost unrecognizable.

## Thailand After the US Withdrawal

By July 1976, American forces completed their withdrawal and American counterinsurgency aid dropped precipitously.[113] In October 1976, a violent assault by the Thai government on Thammasat University drove thousands of students and other activists into the jungle.[114] With the Americans gone and the Thai government in a fragile state, the CPT had its most promising opportunity to mount a communist revolution. As in South Vietnam, USAF MCA in Thailand had failed to curtail the rising insurgency. Thai development efforts failed to address the sources of discontent and suppression created more insurgents than it eliminated. Unlike their South Vietnamese counterparts, however, the Thai government eventually recognized the political nature of the insurgency and made meaningful changes.

General Kriangsak Chomanan, installed as Prime Minister after 1977, recognized the need to react differently to the communist insurgency and ease the political disenfranchisement of the populace. His main action was to distinguish between true communist subversives and those who simply wanted greater democracy. To the latter he granted amnesty. He also eased press censorship and extended recognition to moderate trade unions.[115] This took the pressure off those who were not true communists but associated with the CPT as their best chance for political change.

Thailand's fight against the CPT received some unexpected assistance with the outbreak of the Sino-Vietnamese War in 1979. The CPT, with loyalties to both Vietnamese and Chinese communist parties, lost their external support.[116] Many of those who fled to the jungle in the aftermath of the 1976 assault on Thammasat University were reintegrated into Thai society, and those who were students resumed

110 AFHRA: IRISNUM 1009402: *History of 656th Special Operations Wing* (Nakhon Phanom RTAFB, 1 July—31 October 1975), p. 5.
111 AFHRA: IRISNUM 1011581: *Terminal History of the 432d Combat Support Group* (Udorn RTAFB, 24 December 1975-15 March 1976), p. 1.
112 Ibid., p. 6.
113 Alagappa, *National Security*, p. 189.
114 Marks, 'Anatomy of a Counterinsurgency Victory', pp. 43-44.
115 Alagappa, *National Security*, p. 190.
116 Marks, 'Anatomy of a Counterinsurgency Victory', p. 44.

their education.[117] With the loss of foreign communist support and receding disaffection with the Thai government, the CPT began to lose influence.

It was not until the Thai government abandoned the idea that economic and social progress was the answer for political problems that Thailand could effectively defeat the communist insurgents. It is possible that the decade of US presence and assistance helped forestall a communist spillover from Laos and that the war in Vietnam helped ensure the independence of Thailand. But at the end of the day, it was the Thai people themselves who demanded greater political liberalization and the Thai leadership that recognized the need to change the political environment to separate the communists from the disaffected. It was not USAF military civic action that ended the insurgency; it was Thai political reform.

## Conclusion

Given the checkered history of USAF military civic action in Thailand, it is remarkable that MCA remains part of US military doctrine. Perhaps like modernization theory and all its underlying assumptions, MCA went dormant in the late 1960s but never died.[118] Perhaps like counterinsurgency, MCA fell out of favor only to reemerge following 9/11. In 1992, members of the US Army War College's Strategic Studies Institute edited a volume of essays entitled *Winning the Peace: The Strategic Implications of Military Civic Action*. The question posed by the volume, which the essays contained within attempted to answer, is whether military civic action has any relevance in the post-Cold War environment.

Colonel Richard L. Sutter, then a civil affairs officer in the US Army Reserve, wrote an essay for *Winning the Peace* entitled 'The Strategic Implications of Military Civic Action' in which he argued the fallacy behind military civic action policy and doctrine was economic determinism.[119] According to Sutter this fallacy—which is also a significant criticism of modernization theory—oversimplifies insurgency and 'permits the least-informed and experienced…to provide ready solutions to insurgency'.[120] He rejected the non-military objectives and ad hoc employment of civic action, saying 'every military capability has some particular target as its object and the corollary assumptions of economic determinism and American liberalism do not describe this target'.[121] This describes one of the main failures of MCA during the 1960s and 1970s:

117 Alagappa, *National Security*, p. 190.
118 Michael Latham claims modernization was recast as 'globalization' which celebrated the potential for meeting rising expectations with free market capitalism, see *The Right Kind of Revolution*, p. 191.
119 Sutter, Richard L., 'The Strategic Implications of Military Civic Action', in John W. DePauw and George A. Luz (eds), *Winning the Peace: The Strategic Implications of Military Civic Action* (New York: Greenwood Publishing Group, 1992), p. 167.
120 Ibid.
121 Ibid., p. 169.

MCA was focused on a form of American liberalism—modernization theory—as its target, and when policies and ideologies shifted in the late 1960s with the Nixon Doctrine, MCA lost its focus and became something else altogether.

This examination of USAF MCA in Thailand during the 1960s and 1970s points to several larger issues that transcend that time and place. One issue is the proper employment of military forces to achieve foreign policy goals. The military unquestionably exists to help achieve policy objectives, but there is a tendency to use the military even when another instrument of power is needed (economic, diplomatic, or information). Often this is the result of convenience. Though not perfect, when compared to many other bureaucratic agencies the US military is organized, efficient, fast, and obedient. President Theodore Roosevelt put it well when he transferred the building of the Panama Canal from civil agencies to the US Army: 'the great thing about an Army officer is that he does what you tell him to do'.[122] Perhaps the reason the military seems suitable for nearly every foreign policy problem is the overwhelming focus on military capability compared to other instruments of power. Budget numbers do not reveal the whole story, but it is telling to note that in fiscal year 2011 the State Department was allocated over $50 billion for its entire budget, including the Peace Corps and USAID, whereas the Defense Department received $718 billion.[123] When your best tool is a hammer, everything looks like a nail.

Another subject that arises when examining the origins of MCA is the proper role of political policy in the development of military doctrine. When doctrine is created from the top down, it becomes dogma and is more resistant to change than doctrine shaped by military theory and experience.[124] Policy determines *what* the military will do while doctrine explains *how* it should be done. *Air Force Doctrine Document 1* states, 'Military doctrine is authoritative, but unlike policy, is not directive'.[125] Doctrine provides guidance to be applied flexibly. When policymakers create doctrine, the

122 Quote in Rudolph C. Barnes, *Military Legitimacy: Might and Right in the New Millennium* (London: Routledge, 1996), p. 147.

123 US Government Printing Office, 'Budget of the United States Government: Browse Fiscal Year 2011', <http://www.gpoaccess.gov/usbudget/fy11/index.html> (accessed 21 November 2011). The military obviously requires more money to operate than the State Department, particularly given the expense of caring for military families, base infrastructure, and top-end military equipment. However, to put it into perspective, 10 percent of the State budget went to Foreign Military Financing, meaning State funded the Department of Defense's foreign military assistance mission. The Department of Defense provides a ready pool of manpower that receives funding to accomplish projects for other departments. Military research and development alone exceeded the entire State Department budget by nearly $20 billion.

124 Andrew Birtle's *US Army Counterinsurgency and Contingency Operations Doctrine, 1942-1976* (Washington, DC: US Government Printing Office, 2006), addresses the politicization of doctrine during the Kennedy administration and how that changed COIN doctrine from flexible guidance to inflexible dogma (chapter 6 and p. 490).

125 *Air Force Doctrine Document 1* (Washington DC: Air Force Departmental Publishing Office, 2015), p. 13.

military is unable to use the doctrine flexibly or apply experience to change the doctrine. What happens then is either the military follows a doctrine unsuited to the situation or the military abandons the doctrine and thus loses direction. Both occurred with USAF MCA in Thailand.

Turning the microscope from the politicians to the military, this work points to the problem of inadequately preparing US service members for the conflict at hand. The Pentagon spends years training and equipping service members in core specialties. The belief that developing a quality airman, soldier, sailor, or marine can overcome a lack of culture, language, and diplomatic skills when advising foreign militaries or conducting MCA leaves service members frustrated and grasping to demonstrate performance. This was true in 1961 and remains true in 2016. Because of the US involvement in Afghanistan and Iraq, the USAF decided to renew a focus these core specialties. In December 2013, Chief of Staff of the Air Force, General Mark A. Welsh III, verified this shift: 'The assumption we are using is that you have an Air Force to fight and win the full-spectrum, high-end fight. If you lose the counterinsurgency action, it'll be embarrassing.... If you lose the full-spectrum conflict, it could be catastrophic'.[126] After Vietnam, the US had no taste for counterinsurgency, but it reemerged as a US problem after 9/11. It appears the USAF again has no taste for counterinsurgency after Operations ENDURING FREEDOM and IRAQI FREEDOM. The question is: What will the USAF do when the necessity of conducting counterinsurgency resurfaces? Will it attempt MCA again, misapplying it to the target population and deploying airmen with a two-week crash course on culture, or will there be a true reevaluation of the doctrine? This reevaluation must occur now, before it is needed again.

126 Amaani Lyle, 'Air Force's Top Officer Outlines Tough Budget Decisions', *DoD News*, 11 December 2013, <http://archive.defense.gov/news/newsarticle.aspx?id=121328> (accessed 10 October 2015).

# 8

# Relegated to the Backseat: Farm Gate and the Failure of the Air Advisory Effort in South Vietnam, 1961-1963[1]

*Edward B. Westermann*

## Introduction

In describing the problems that he faced in conducting revolutionary war in China, Mao Tse-tung remarked, 'The only way to study the laws governing a war situation as a whole is to do some hard thinking. For what pertains to the situation as a whole is not visible to the eye, and we can understand it only by hard thinking; there is no other way'.[2] Without doubt, the prosecution of counterinsurgency operations requires a great deal of 'hard thinking' as the American experience in the Republic of Vietnam (RVN) between 1961 and 1963 so aptly demonstrates. The nature of peoples' war as a political, social, economic, and military struggle illustrates the profound complexity associated in combating insurgencies whether clad in the armor of communism, nationalism, or religious ideology.

The American air advisory experience in South Vietnam offers a number of insights into the strengths and weaknesses of military power in the insurgency environment. First, it highlights the specific roles and missions that airpower offers against guerrilla or insurgent forces. Second, it also exposes the limits of third party support to a country involved in this type of warfare. Third, it warns against an over reliance on military technology when faced with 'war in the shadows'. Finally, and perhaps most importantly, it demonstrates the critical importance of cultural awareness and linguistic abilities among advisory forces.

1 The author would like to thank Routledge for the permission to reprint this chapter.
2 Mao Tse-tung, *Six Essays on Military Affairs* (Peking: Foreign Language Press, 1972), p. 12.

## Establishing a Capability

In an attempt to expand service capability in the counterinsurgency role, General Curtis E. LeMay, Chief of Staff of the US Air Force, ordered the establishment of a small Special Air Warfare Command (SAWC) in early 1961.[3] Although several leading participants in the SAWC later attributed the support of the services as mere 'lip service' and a 'passing fad', LeMay apparently established the fledgling command for several reasons.[4] Despite his oft-stated predilection for 'strategic airpower', he recognized the need for an air force capability to support Third World governments in the counterinsurgency role.[5] Likewise, a conviction took root within the Air Staff that 'if the Air Force failed to provide adequate air support to the Army, the Army would furnish its own [air force]'; a belief heightened by the Army's development of helicopter and light aircraft assets.[6]

The first step in building an Air Force counterinsurgency capability occurred with the selection of Colonel Benjamin H. King to head the new 4400th Combat Crew Training Squadron (CCTS) at Eglin Air Force Base, Florida. It was from the ranks of the 4400th CCTS that the initial cadre of the USAF Farm Gate advisory effort to South Vietnam would be drawn. One indication of the rush to establish the unit involved King's interview for the position in the early hours of a Saturday morning and the almost total lack of guidance he received on the unit's mission after assuming command.[7] Officially established on 14 April 1961, the 4400th (code-named Jungle Jim) included 124 officers and 228 airmen and an assortment of vintage aircraft. According to LeMay, the unit was created in order to 'jump-start the Air Force's special air warfare program'.[8] In his testimony to Congress, he described the mission of the 4400th as involving 'counterinsurgency and unconventional and psychological warfare operations'.[9]

The unit's aircraft consisted of an array of World War II era and propeller-driven aircraft, including 16 C-47s, eight B-26s, and eight T-28s. In one respect, the advanced age of the aircraft proved a problem. King recalled, 'We had no training program. We

3 Monro MacCloskey, *Alert the Fifth Air Force: Counterinsurgency, Unconventional Warfare, and Psychological Operations of the United States Air Force in Special Air Warfare* (New York: Richards Rosen Press, 1969), p. 148.
4 USAF Historical Research Agency (hereafter AFHRA), K239.0512-218, USAF Oral History Interview (hereafter ORI) #218, Major-General Gilbert Pritchard, 21 August 1969.
5 AFHRA, K239.0512-592, USAF ORI #592, General Curtis LeMay, 8 June 1972.
6 James Corum and Wray Johnson, *Airpower in Small Wars: Fighting Insurgents and Terrorists* (Lawrence: University Press of Kansas, 2003), pp. 244-245.
7 AFHRA, K239.0512-219, USAF ORI #219, Brigadier-General Benjamin King, 4 September 1969.
8 Warren Trest, *Air Commando One: Heine Aderholt and America's Secret Air Wars* (Washington, DC: Smithsonian Institution Press, 2000), p. 121.
9 MacCloskey, *Fifth Air Force*, pp. 148-149.

had no one . . . that at the time he arrived was fully qualified in the type airplane that we had assigned'.[10] However, these propeller driven aircraft constituted the perfect platforms for supporting Third World countries as they could operate from austere locations with little supporting infrastructure. Their ability to operate 'low and slow' provided a major advantage for spotting and attacking insurgents operating in areas of heavy ground cover as did their capability to land and take off from short, unimproved runways.

Ostensibly, the mission involved training indigenous forces to fly these aircraft in preparation for counterinsurgency operations. In truth, the training and advisory mission was from the start a 'cover' for the unit's real mission. LeMay told King that the unit's primary job involved the ability 'to conduct combat operations . . . under extremely austere operating conditions anywhere in the world, and to be a responsive force, either overtly or covertly, to support United States policy'.[11] The pilots that joined the unit were all volunteers and under the impression that they would be conducting 'cloak and dagger' operations by infiltrating and exfiltrating agents and supplies from denied areas.[12]

From its inception the 4400th enjoyed a special status made outwardly visible by the unit's distinctive uniform consisting of an Australian bush hat, fatigues, scarf, and combat boots personally selected by LeMay.[13] A more substantive manifestation of the unit's unique mission included the routine practice of taking aircrews from their post flight debriefings and placing them in the swamps of the Florida panhandle for a three-day escape and survival trek.[14] The distinctive aircraft, uniform, and training of the 'air commandos' reinforced the perception of an elite unit preparing for special missions. Certainly, King interpreted the unit's charter in this light. In fact, LeMay later admitted, 'They [4400th CCTS] went over there [Southeast Asia] to fight right from the start. We knew it, nobody ever said that though'. He also disclosed that this information was common knowledge among the Joint Chiefs of Staff (JCS) and that it was merely policy considerations that prevented 'the announcement that this outfit was going over to go into combat'.[15]

The formation of the 4400th under the pretext of providing an advisory capability proved important in several respects. First, it showed that despite the Kennedy administration's stated objectives and Secretary of Defense Robert McNamara's subsequent statements, the USAF created the Farm Gate program with the intention

10 AFHRA, K239.0512-219, USAF ORI #219, King.

11 Ibid.

12 AFHRA, K239.0512-415, USAF ORI #415, Major-General Rollen Anthis, 30 August 1963.

13 Robert Futrell, *The Advisory Years to 1965* (Washington, DC: Office of Air Force History, 1981), p. 79.

14 Michael Haas, *Apollo's Warriors: United States Air Force Special Operations during the Cold War* (Maxwell AFB, AL: Air University Press, 1997), p. 223.

15 AFHRA, K239.0512-415, USAF ORI #592, LeMay.

of capitalizing on US capabilities and employing US pilots in a direct combat role.[16] Second, the unstated assumption that combat operations constituted the real goal of the unit certainly influenced the way in which the men approached their 'advisory' duties with their South Vietnamese counterparts. For example, upon their arrival in Vietnam, Farm Gate pilots 'were not happy to discover that training the Vietnamese Air Force (VNAF) was their primary mission'.[17] Third, the actual charter established for the Farm Gate program demonstrated an expanded US commitment to the Diem regime.

In response to a recommendation by the JCS to strengthen the American air commitment and South Vietnam's President Ngo Dinh Diem's agreement to accept combat units, President John F. Kennedy authorized the deployment of a detachment of the 4400th on 11 October 1961 'to serve under the MAAG [Military Assistance Advisory Group] as a training mission and not for combat at the present time'.[18] Two days later, King departed with two other USAF officers to brief Admiral Harry D. Felt, the Commander in Chief Pacific Command (CINCPAC) on the unit's capabilities. Felt initially appeared skeptical of the 4400th's ability to conduct counterinsurgency missions, especially with its assigned aircraft. King's team, however, convinced Felt of the soundness of their approach and the team left for Vietnam to meet with the commander of the Air Force MAAG section. Upon arrival, King evaluated several potential airfields, eventually selecting the airstrip at Bien Hoa near Saigon based on its accessibility to the capital and its central location for air operations. During his trip to Pacific Command headquarters (PACOM) and Vietnam, King recalled 'It was never mentioned that we would have the responsibility of training VNAF [the Vietnamese Air Force]'.[19]

The first aircraft that reached Bien Hoa in November with their USAF markings replaced by VNAF insignia 'found a rundown French air base with a flight surface consisting of a single pierced-steel-plank runway 5,800 by 150 feet'.[20] From the beginning of operations, King's unit, Detachment 2 Alpha, 4400th CCTS, operating under the classified designation of Farm Gate, suffered from a confused command relationship. Orders and directives emanated from a plethora of organizations including PACOM and Pacific Air Force headquarters (PACAF) through 13th Air

16 Robert McNamara, *In Retrospect: The Tragedy and Lessons of Vietnam* (New York: Times Books, 1995) pp. 29, 62.
17 Haas, *Apollo's Warriors*, p. 228.
18 Futrell, *Advisory Years*, p. 80. See also AFHRA, K239.0512-489, USAF ORI #489, Ambassador Frederick E. Nolting Jr., 9 November 1971. Ambassador Nolting remarked, 'President Diem on many occasions told me that he, as much as he was tempted from time to time to ask for American combat forces in difficult situations—he didn't think that a struggle won with foreign troops would be viable out there [in Vietnam]'.
19 AFHRA, K239.0512-219, USAF ORI #219, King.
20 Futrell, *Advisory Years*, p. 81.

Force and the 2nd Advanced Echelon (ADVON) as well as the MAAG and Tactical Air Command headquarters.

For his part, King, operating on personal instructions from LeMay, believed that he worked for the Country Team Chief, Ambassador Frederick E. Nolting Jr. and the Central Intelligence Agency's chief of station in Saigon. As a result, King repeatedly ran afoul of Brigadier-General Rollen H. Anthis, 2nd ADVON commander, during discussions of the 4400th's primary mission. Based on his conversations with LeMay, King continued to maintain that the 'training of the [Vietnamese] nationals was a cover story' while Anthis 'was very emphatic . . . that our mission over there was to assist the VNAF in establishing a capability'.[21]

A message of 6 December 1961 from Major-General Thomas S. Moorman Jr., vice commander in chief of PACAF, appeared to resolve the issue concerning the nature and objectives of the Farm Gate program. The message described Farm Gate as a 'covert operation' that utilized the 'training function as cover . . . in support of RVNAF actions against the Viet Cong within the borders of SVN [South Vietnam]'. Moorman continued, 'This [mission] will include all feasible operational activity, overt and covert, and will be in addition to advisory and training functions'. Addressing the command relationships, Moorman's message vested command authority with CINCPAC for the 'operational control of all Farm Gate operational missions flown with USAF crew-members [sic]'.[22] In practice, the commander of PACAF exercised operational control over Farm Gate aircrews through his subordinate commanders at 13th Air Force and the 2nd ADVON. In other words, Moorman's message should have resolved the issue of daily control of Farm Gate in favor of Anthis; however, among the air commandos, the issue of Anthis' authority remained a point of contention until the summer of 1963.[23]

In addition to describing the nature of the Farm Gate program, Moorman's message also outlined the following objectives:

1. Deny Viet Cong supply routes and concentrations in South Vietnam.
2. Establish armed air patrols of SVN borders and shorelines, to include river, highways, rail and trail traffic suppression, day and night.
3. Seek out and destroy/disrupt Viet Cong Command/Control organization.
4. Seek out and destroy any Communist airlift effort into SVN.
5. Develop and implement an aggressive program of offensive air operations, to complement and to set the pattern for VNAF operations, to neutralize all manifestations of communist actions and strengths in SVN.[24]

21 AFHRA, K239.0512-219, USAF ORI #219, King.
22 AFHRA, K717.1623, Message signed by Major-General Thomas S. Moorman Jr., Subject: Concept of Employment of Farm Gate, 6 December 1961.
23 Trest, *Air Commando One*, p. 127.
24 AFHRA, K717.1623, Message signed by Major-General Thomas S. Moorman Jr., Subject: Concept of Employment of Farm Gate, 6 December 1961.

On the one hand, the objectives established an ambitious charter for a relatively small unit operating a limited number of vintage aircraft. On the other hand, these objectives also underlined the primary focus of the 4400th on direct combat operations to counter the Viet Cong insurgency, a point underlined by the glaring omission of a *specific* objective concerning the training of VNAF personnel.

Despite the omission of the training aspect of the program, Moorman did address the relationship between US and Vietnamese forces. For example, US operations and intelligence personnel were to augment their Vietnamese counterparts at the VNAF Operations Center at Tan Son Nhut airbase on the outskirts of the capital. Furthermore, USAF personnel received instructions to 'conduct coordinated planning with the ARVN and VNAF'. Finally, Moorman ordered that VNAF personnel accompany Farm Gate crews during operational missions in order to utilize the "training through operations' technique', a point again moderated by the remark that the unit's training and advisory mission with VNAF constituted a 'cover story' for the employment of American forces in operational missions within South Vietnam.[25]

The JCS also weighed in on the issue of training versus operations in a message designed to 'insure no misunderstanding in the authority granted for the use of Jungle Jim [Farm Gate] aircraft'.[26] The JCS message emphasized the program's 'principal purpose' involved the *training* of VNAF personnel. Despite this pronouncement, Admiral Felt, the commander of Pacific Command, maintained the position that Farm Gate aircraft could conduct 'all kinds of conventional combat and combat support flights' contingent upon the presence of a VNAF observer on board.[27] This example highlighted two major issues facing the program from its inception. First, the tortured chain of command and lines of authority resulted in competing and conflicting statements on the unit's mission. Second, this conflicting guidance essentially relegated the training and advisory role to a subordinate role in the eyes of the unit's leadership and its pilots.

## Flawed by Design

The secondary role assigned to the training and advisory missions by senior USAF leaders profoundly influenced the way Farm Gate pilots approached their duties. In several respects, the 4400th was ill-prepared to undertake an advisory mission. For example, it was only after King and his men arrived in Vietnam that the unit 'began to think seriously about setting up a training program for foreign nations'.[28] While the unit's aircrews proved to be expert operators, they had little understanding of the culture or the history of their Vietnamese hosts and this lack of cultural awareness

25 Ibid.
26 Futrell, *Advisory Years*, p. 83.
27 Ibid.
28 AFHRA, K239.0512-219, USAF ORI #219, King.

significantly handicapped the advising effort. Likewise, the inability of advisors to speak Vietnamese, or even French, provided a major obstacle to any planned advisory and training mission. One army advisor later observed that during the war 'thousands of Vietnamese learned English . . . but only a handful of the many thousands of Americans who received language training ever learned to really speak Vietnamese'.[29] In fact, one senior Vietnamese general could not recall a single instance 'in which a US advisor effectively discussed professional matters with his counterpart in Vietnamese'.[30]

In addition to acting as a bar to communication, the language barrier also contributed to the *de facto* isolation of the 4400th from their VNAF counterparts at Bien Hoa. Colonel Robert L. Gleason, a former Farm Gate commander, later remarked, 'We [US personnel] went to one side of the base, sat there with our own cantonment, maintenance and operations, VNAF down on that side of the base . . . and so forth and so on'.[31] Another pilot recalled 'we really didn't have a great deal to do with the Vietnamese' and he could not recall a single instance of a joint gathering or party between USAF and VNAF personnel at Bien Hoa during his entire tour in 1963.[32] Likewise, the fact that Farm Gate personnel were sent on temporary duty to Vietnam for periods of six months provided an added obstacle to establishing close relationships with their VNAF counterparts or building continuity in any training program.[33] General Anthis recognized the need for continuity in working with the South Vietnamese Air Force and went so far as to recommend tour lengths of 18 to 24 months instead of the initial 179-day temporary duty and later one-year assignments in country.[34]

## Training the VNAF

By the end of 1961, the VNAF certainly required US assistance in a number of areas, including equipment, training, infrastructure, logistics support, and maintenance. One of the most pressing needs involved increasing the size of the air force and the number of trained aircrew and mechanics. In November, the South Vietnamese Air Force consisted of approximately 100 fixed-wing aircraft, including a propeller driven ground attack version of the A-1H (AD-6), TO-1D observation aircraft, C-47

29 Stuart A Herrington, *Stalking the Vietcong: Inside Operation Phoenix: A Personal Account* (New York: Ballantine Books, 1982), p. 253.
30 Ronald Spector, *Advice and Support: The Early Years* (Washington, DC: Center of Military History, 1983), p. 286.
31 AFHRA, K239.0512-218, USAF ORI #218, Pritchard.
32 AFHRA, K239.0512-357, USAF ORI #357, Major Roy Lynn, 9 September 1970.
33 AFHRA, K239.0512-219, USAF ORI #219, King.
34 AFHRA, K239.0512-240, USAF ORI #240, Major-General Rollen Anthis, 17 November 1969.

transports, and an additional 17 helicopters.[35] In order to augment VNAF strike capabilities, the US Navy (USN) delivered 15 T-28C's on 11 December 1961, and, by the end of the month, USAF trainers under the aegis of the MAAG began formal training for Vietnamese pilots, and maintenance, electronic, and ordnance personnel. In addition, PACOM supported plans for the creation of a second A-1H squadron in order to increase the VNAF fighter strength to a total three squadrons; however, these plans immediately ran into the problem of finding and training a sufficient number of qualified pilots.[36]

A message from PACOM underscored the '[k]ey to build-up of VNAF . . . is to increase number of qualified pilots AS[A]P, with the objective of replacing USAF pilots flying with VNAF and turning job over to VNAF completely'.[37] USAF and USN Military Training Teams provided the cadre for the initial aircraft qualification programs with Farm Gate personnel slated to provide advanced air-to ground training for VNAF pilots.[38] Despite the evident need for instructors to train VNAF students, Farm Gate pilots only 'grudgingly' embraced this role, but King did send four T-28 pilots to the South Vietnamese air base at Nha Trang to provide flight training.[39]

On 15 January 1962 Anthis briefed Secretary McNamara on the initial progress of the Farm Gate program and optimistically reported that American pilots were training their Vietnamese counterparts in a variety of missions, including night attack and night reconnaissance, flare drops, outpost air support, and aerial resupply. Additionally, Anthis predicted that the VNAF would be an 'Air Force' within a year at which point General Emmett O'Donnell Jr., the PACAF commander, cautioned, 'You can't make an air force overnight'.[40] With respect to training, O'Donnell's pessimism proved well-founded. In order to create an additional VNAF T-28 strike squadron, 30 USAF C-47 pilots moved into VNAF squadrons to allow Vietnamese pilots to transition to the T-28.[41] Although offering a short-term advantage, this program robbed Peter to pay Paul and failed to address the shortage of pilots. It also had an unintended negative consequence, resulting in the VNAF closing down its flying training school at Nha Trang.[42]

35 AFHRA, K 71, 7.0413-30; Carl O. Clever, *Support Activities*, part VI, [Project CHECO (Contemporary Historical Evaluation of Counterinsurgency Operations)], May 1964, p. 20. Corum and Johnson. *Small Wars*, p. 235. By 1965, the A-1 'Skyraider' became the mainstay of the VNAF fighter force with six operational squadrons and a total of 146 aircraft.

36 Clever, *Support Activities*, pp. 20-22.

37 Ibid., p. 23.

38 Ibid., pp. 21, 23.

39 Futrell, *Advisory Years*, p. 127.

40 Clever, *Support Activities*, pp. 17-18.

41 AFHRA, K239.0512-240, USAF ORI #240, Anthis.

42 AFHRA, K239.0512-415, USAF ORI #415, Major-General Rollen Anthis, 30 August 1963.

O'Donnell's comment highlighted another key point in the creation of an air advisory mission. Regardless of the sophistication of the aircraft chosen, the development of an air force requires a number of supporting technological and infrastructure initiatives. For example, communications and air traffic control systems are critical to ensuring flight safety and facilitating operational responsiveness. Likewise, maintenance of aircraft and their associated communications, navigational, and propulsion systems is vital for achieving high sortie rates. Unfortunately, finding and training the specialized maintenance personnel in the Vietnamese armed forces 'required for aviation technology presented an unending challenge to South Vietnamese authorities'.[43] In fact, as late as May 1963, Brigadier-General M.B. Adams, Assistant Chief of Staff, Plans, Military Assistance Command—Vietnam, informed McNamara that a phase-out of USAF flying units was possible; however, he warned 'the RVN Armed Forces would not be able to provide the technical support, maintenance, and communications for the VNAF if USAF support personnel were relieved'.[44]

Problems with communications and air traffic control provided major barriers for effectively controlling and employing VNAF and US aircraft. The state of communications in South Vietnam proved abysmal. Although Bien Hoa was located only 20 miles from Saigon, King recalled that communications were so poor that 'you were a damn sight better off to get in an airplane and fly down there and talk than try to talk over the phone'.[45] In response to this problem, the USAF airlifted the 5th Tactical Control Group into South Vietnam in early January 1962 and the unit set up a tactical air control system within a period of only 14 days.[46] One stopgap measure to improve communications involved using a Farm Gate C-47 as an airborne radio relay connecting the ARVN command post and the Joint Operations Center at Tan Son Nhut with strike aircraft.[47] Despite these efforts, one report noted, 'the root of the entire [communications] deficiency lies in the lack of suitable radio equipment'.[48]

Despite these setbacks, the USAF and VNAF made progress and the establishment of a Joint Air Operations Center at Tan Son Nhut and two auxiliary air operations centers (AOCs) at Da Nang and Pleiku constituted a major step in improving the coordination of aircraft operations. Unfortunately, even in this endeavor some US support personnel displayed a lack of cultural awareness and sensitivity to Vietnamese pride. For example, Americans usurped their Vietnamese counterparts and 'simply

43 Corum and Johnson, *Small Wars*, p. 250.
44 Clever, *Support Activities*, p. 19.
45 AFHRA, K239.0512-219, USAF ORI #219, King.
46 AFHRA, K239.0512-415, USAF ORI #415, Anthis.
47 AFHRA, K526.549-2, Report from Detachment 2 Alpha to Commander, 22d ADVON, 5 June 1962.
48 AFHRA, K526.549-2, Report entitled: 'Development of New Tactics and Techniques', 14 January 1962.

took over the control centers'.[49] Despite the creation of the AOCs and the use of airborne radio relays, 'limited and failure-prone communications between the centers and the airfields' continued to plague operations until the installation of a new communications system in September 1962.[50]

The US penchant to seek increased efficiency at the cost of allowing the Vietnamese to retain control of operations became a hallmark of US participation in Vietnam and constituted a fatal weakness in the advisory effort. General Maxwell Taylor observed, 'It was a natural reaction of many Americans to want to take over for themselves the tasks of the Vietnamese. Many times I have seen a young military officer, arriving for just one year of service attempt to energize a Vietnamese counterpart who had been in the field for the last eleven years'.[51] Even as late as 1971, US advisors fell victim to this mindset as one Lieutenant serving with the ARVN noted, 'As an American military man, schooled in the direct, aggressive approach to problem-solving, I was going to get the job done, with or without the help of the Vietnamese'.[52] Although promoting short-term success, this approach created a 'superior-subordinate' relationship rather than an advisory relationship and eventually sacrificed long-term rapport by alienating South Vietnamese military leaders and creating a dependency relationship.

The primitive communications infrastructure was not the only bar to rapid decision-making. Bureaucratic and domestic political considerations, including the need to receive ARVN approval for missions, often resulted in long delays in striking targets and significantly degraded operational response times. Approval for striking targets often required the concurrence of local and regional Vietnamese political and military leaders and even President Diem himself.[53] In some cases, the authorization for missions came down from the 2nd ADVON two to three days after the initial request while even the fastest approvals required between two and six hours.[54] This cumbersome approval process severely handicapped effective aerial operations and points to a key issue of insurgency warfare. The Viet Cong relied on stealth and speed in their campaign against the RVN. Likewise, agility and responsiveness constituted a major strength of airpower; however, the procedural and physical obstacles to rapid decision-making prevented Farm Gate personnel from taking advantage of the unit's major strength.

Poor infrastructure provided another impediment to effective operations. Aerial operations rely on the use of fixed, improved airfields, aircraft ramps, hangars, petroleum, oil, and lubricants and logistics facilities, air traffic control structures, and

49 John Schlight, *A War too Long: The History of the USAF in Southeast Asia* (Washington, DC: Air Force History and Museums Program, 1996), p. 9.

50 Futrell, *Advisory Years*, p. 107.

51 Maxwell D. Taylor, *Responsibility and Response* (New York: Harper & Row Publishers, 1967), pp. 50-51.

52 Herrington, *Vietcong*, p. 64.

53 AFHRA, K239.0512-415, USAF ORI #415, Anthis.

54 AFHRA, K239.0512-219, USAF ORI #219, King.

meteorological services. For combat aviation units, requirements also include weapons supply points and storage areas, intelligence support, and base security forces. In late 1961, this infrastructure and these types of facilities existed, if they existed at all, in the most rudimentary forms. In fact, the few suitable airfields in South Vietnam quickly became overcrowded by the growing US air presence and by the transfer of aircraft to the VNAF.[55]

**Farm Gate Goes to War**

While Anthis continued to underline the training aspect of the Farm Gate mission, the reality of daily operations combined with the nascent state of VNAF training increasingly led to greater US participation in combat operations. Brigadier-General Heine Aderholt, one of the most flamboyant and successful of the air commandos, complained, 'Either the 2nd Advanced Echelon in Saigon didn't understand or didn't give a damn, the Farm Gate boys started flying close air support for the Vietnamese army . . .[t]hat should have been a job for the VNAF and its A-1s, not the Americans'.[56] This focus on combat operations led to the continued relegation of VNAF pilots and their training to a position of second rank.

Early Farm Gate operations reflected the scope of the problems facing King and his unit upon their arrival at Bien Hoa. While initially focusing on gaining familiarity with the area and the established procedures at Bien Hoa, the unit's first 'mission' involved observing a flight of VNAF attack aircraft make bombing and strafing runs. Although armed, the Farm Gate T-28s did not participate in the attack. As the 4400th under King's command attempted to embark upon combat operations, the tortured command relationship with the 2nd ADVON became apparent. Although willing to accept Anthis' authority on issues concerning administration and support, King rejected 2nd ADVON's attempts to control operational combat missions on the 'covert side of the house'.[57]

Despite back channel communications through the American embassy to LeMay, King and his unit found themselves at the mercy of 2nd ADVON, especially for intelligence and flight authorizations. After speaking with the Director of Operations at 2nd ADVON headquarters in Saigon, King left the meeting with the impression that the headquarters would not grant Farm Gate aircraft permission for any *daylight* strike operations. Consequently, King acquired some parachute flares and began experimenting with using a C-47 as a flare ship to support night operations. Later, after receiving intelligence information on a Viet Cong supply area, a flight of Farm

55 Corum and Johnson, *Small Wars*, p. 250.
56 Trest, *Air Commando One*, p. 123.
57 AFHRA, K239.0512-219, USAF ORI #219, King.

Gate T-28s attacked a group of sampans and 'obliterated the target', proving the unit's ability to serve as a night rapid reaction force.[58]

The ability of Farm Gate pilots to fly combat missions at night proved significant in two respects. First, the VNAF pilots did not fly at night and they remained reluctant to conduct nighttime strike missions even as late as 1963.[59] Second, the unwillingness of VNAF aircrews to fly at night ceded a major advantage to the insurgents as the Viet Cong often used the cover of darkness to launch their attacks against isolated villages and garrisons throughout the South. Therefore, Farm Gate operations at night provided an important increase in available firepower to both ARVN and US Special Forces contingent upon rapid forwarding and approval of air support requests from the field.[60]

Flying nighttime strike missions to isolated hamlets required both skill and courage. Locating the target area alone often proved difficult and placed a premium on map reading and dead reckoning skills for navigation.[61] One technique used by friendly forces to identify Viet Cong troop concentrations involved igniting cans of oil pointed in the direction of the enemy attack. Using the burning markers as an orientation point, the C-47 flare ship would provide illumination for the T-28s to attack.[62] The high standards required of Farm Gate pilots included the expectation that 'pilots should be trained to the extent that their proficiency will enable them to destroy one shack with one bomb', an impossible standard for pilots operating primarily at night.[63] Although important, strike missions proved less critical than aerial supply and transportation in countering the insurgent threat.

## Mule Train

The requirement for airlift to support isolated outposts and hamlets constituted one of the most pressing requirements for supporting ARVN forces and their US army advisors early in the war. Farm Gate, with its complement of C-47s, possessed a limited capability to conduct resupply efforts, but these aircraft could not meet the demand for aerial transport and resupply. As a result, LeMay ordered the deployment of a detachment of Fairchild C-123 transport aircraft to South Vietnam in January 1962.[64] Sixteen C-123s, complete with aircrews, maintenance, medical staff, loadmasters, and

58 Ibid.
59 AFHRA, K239.0512-357, USAF ORI #357, Lynn. Admittedly, some reports cite the support of VNAF C-47 flareships during night missions.
60 AFHRA, K239.0512-219, USAF ORI #219, King.
61 AFHRA, K717.1623, Message from PACAF headquarters to Tactical Air Command, 28 February 1962.
62 AFHRA, K239.0512-240, USAF ORI #240, Anthis.
63 AFHRA, K717.1623, Message from PACAF headquarters to Tactical Air Command, 28 February 1962.
64 Clever, *Support Activities*, p. 5.

air base personnel, began arriving for temporary duty at Tan Son Nhut in early January under the code name Mule Train. Although not technically part of the Farm Gate program, Mule Train operated under the command of 2nd ADVON and constituted an additional pillar of the American air support effort in South Vietnam. In fact, orders and messages from PACAF headquarters routinely treated the missions of both programs as part of a single effort.[65]

A week after arriving in Vietnam, Mule Train aircraft were averaging three airlift missions per day with over 500 sorties flown by the end of February, transporting 3,600 passengers and delivering 695 tons of cargo.[66] The standards expected of the airlift crews proved as stringent as those demanded from their Farm Gate counterparts and called for precision in the delivery of air dropped heavy cargo and airborne forces to 'pinpoint targets', including 'small clearings in the jungle, swamps, or rice paddies'. Furthermore, Mule Train aircrews required the skill to fly into and out of 'short, rough, and marginal airfields' on a routine basis.[67]

With the approach of the rainy season in the spring of 1962, Mule Train became a 'very valuable asset' and missions gained added importance as secondary roads became nearly impassable mud holes.[68] However, it was the ability of the aircraft to allow US and ARVN forces to avoid Viet Cong ambushes along road and waterways throughout the country that constituted a major benefit of the effort. A top secret Air Force historical study in 1964 remarked that 'inland surface transportation in the RVN was extremely limited because of Viet Cong operations. Consequently, airlift operations achieved a relative importance seldom experienced in more conventional environments'.[69] Over 40 years later, US forces relearned the same lesson in Iraq.[70]

The ability of the Viet Minh to conduct ambushes along the paths, waterways, and roadways throughout the country was legendary and made famous by the journalist Bernard Fall in his classic work, *Street Without Joy*.[71] The Viet Cong proved every bit as skilled in the art of the ambush as their predecessors as the following account demonstrates: 'The VC ambush was perfectly placed and timed, hitting my column from the dense bamboo to our right, exploding a captured American Claymore mine and raking the trail with AK-47 fire. Bright green tracers slashed through the shade, cutting leaves and chipping wood. . . .Now I heard the distinctive crack of AK fire

65 AFHRA, K717.1623, Message signed by Major-General Thomas S. Moorman, Jr., Subject: Concept of Employment of Farm Gate, 6 December 1961.

66 Futrell, *Advisory Years*, p. 108.

67 AFHRA, K717.1623, Message from PACAF headquarters to Tactical Air Command, 28 February 1962.

68 AFHRA, K717.1623, Message from PACAF headquarters to Tactical Air Command, 10 March 1962.

69 Clever, *Support Activities*, p. 4.

70 Steven Komarow, 'Pentagon Boosts Number of US Air Missions', *USA Today*, 15 March 2006, http://www.usatoday.com/news/world/iraq/2006-03-15-air-missions_x.htm.

71 Bernard B. Fall, *Street Without Joy: Indochina at War, 1946-54* (Harrisburg, PA: Stackpole, 1961).

from our left front. The VC had just sprung the leg of their L-shaped ambush'.[72] In this case, artillery and air support helped limit casualties to one dead, and two wounded; however, the description of the ambush highlights the important role played by concealment in allowing the Viet Cong force to achieve tactical surprise, a scenario repeated a thousand-fold in the paddies and jungles of Vietnam throughout the war.

Based on the poor physical infrastructure and the geography of South Vietnam, and the threat posed by Viet Cong ambush, the importance of tactical airlift in supporting ARVN forces continued to increase throughout the first two years of the Mule Train program. For example, the airlift force doubled from 16 to 32 C-123s in June 1962 and a third squadron moved into country in April 1963. In recognition of the challenging flying environment and the combat conditions experienced during these missions, General LeMay ordered the re-designation of the units from tactical airlift squadrons to 'assault airlift' squadrons in the spring of 1963.[73]

## Ranch Hand

In addition to their use in a mobility role, transport aircraft proved their value in non-traditional roles. Recognition of the problem posed by the heavy foliage found along many of South Vietnam's road and waterways led to the creation of a Combat Development and Test Center in Vietnam in the summer of 1961. Among other projects, the center began to search for herbicides to destroy Viet Cong food sources and to 'deprive the Viet Cong of assembly and ambush areas'.[74] After early small scale efforts at defoliation using C-47s and H-34s, the USAF settled on C-123 aircraft equipped with aerial spray systems and defoliant agents. The aircraft deployed from Pope Air Force Base in North Carolina and were flown by aircrew who had volunteered but had not been selected for the original Farm Gate mission. In fact, it was only at their en route stop at Clark Air Base in the Philippines that the aircraft and aircrew technically separated from the Farm Gate mission and adopted the code name Ranch Hand.[75]

In mid-January, Ranch Hand aircraft escorted by VNAF fighters and using a VNAF L-19 observation aircraft as a forward air controller (FAC), flew six defoliation missions.[76] The results of the missions, however, proved disappointing as the vegetation failed to die. Based on this inauspicious start, the cancellation of the Ranch Hand program appeared to be 'imminent'.[77] However, an investigation of the

72 Tommy Franks, *American Soldier* (New York: Regan Books, 2004), p. 74.
73 Clever, *Support Activities*, pp. 8-10.
74 Futrell, *Advisory Years*, p. 73.
75 Haas, *Apollo's Warriors*, p. 250.
76 AFHRA, K717.1623, Message from PACAF headquarters to the Chief of Staff of the USAF, 15 January 1962.
77 AFHRA, K717-1623, Report entitled 'Comments on Notes on Secretary of Defense Meeting', 13 March 1962.

missions revealed that 'most of the plants had been dormant, and the herbicide . . . worked only on actively growing plants'.[78]

The results of the investigation provided the program with a reprieve and led to further testing. Later missions in October directed at mangrove forests along the waterways of the Ca Mau peninsula stripped over 90 percent of the foliage in the targeted areas, initiating an expanded effort throughout the country. The success of these defoliation missions resulted in requests from the Vietnamese to use the aircraft against suspected Viet Cong food supplies. President Kennedy subsequently approved a limited program targeting guerrilla food sources, but the State Department insisted on the right to approve targets for each mission.[79]

Early in the program, Ranch Hand aircraft, in addition to their spraying activities, also provided logistics support by moving troops and materiel. By 1967, however, the spray missions dominated the effort with aircraft flying an average of 20 spray missions a day. Between 1965 and 1970, Ranch Hand aircraft sprayed approximately '41 per cent of South Vietnam's mangrove forests, 19 per cent of the uplands forests and 8 per cent of all cultivated land' primarily using the controversial dioxin-based Agent Orange.[80] The tactical and operational success of these missions in stripping away the Viet Cong's advantage of concealment once again highlighted the utility of airpower in an auxiliary role in the counterinsurgency environment, though the aftereffects of the defoliation operations on the physical health of US and Vietnamese citizens alike constituted the effort's most enduring legacy.

## Evaluating Early US Air Support

The decision to create the Farm Gate, Mule Train, and Ranch Hand programs and deploy these units to South Vietnam within a period of only two months provides several important insights into the nature of US military and political objectives in the early stages of the conflict. First, all three programs offered complementary capabilities designed to improve the operational situation in South Vietnam by providing tactical level support to Vietnamese forces. Second, the initial performance of these units provided a significant adjunct to ARVN forces and especially to a South Vietnamese Air Force suffering from limited resources, political restraints, and a lack of operational freedom. Third, the requirement for a fairly robust infrastructure ranging from bases to supply depots to communications and navigational aids highlighted the intrinsic complexity and demands of any air advisory effort, including those employing relatively unsophisticated aircraft. Finally, and perhaps most importantly,

78 Futrell, *Advisory Years*, pp. 113-116.
79 Ibid., pp. 116-117.
80 Haas, *Apollo's Warriors*, pp. 253-254. Based on the health issues for US forces and the indigenous population associated with the spraying program, and North Vietnamese claims of chemical and biological warfare, the Ranch Hand program became one of the most controversial efforts of the war.

the prosecution of these programs demonstrated that the advisory mission took a back seat to the employment of these aircraft under US control.

## Taking a Backseat

The requirement for VNAF observers on-board USAF aircraft served merely as a cover to legitimize US participation in combat operations and served as a political foil to mitigate the US's clear violation of the Geneva Accords.[81] In the early stages of the program, pilots, especially those in the two-seat T-28, protested the requirement for VNAF personnel to accompany them. One Farm Gate commander complained 'The requirement that a VNAF pilot be a member of the T-28 crew, always riding in the back seat, has been unsatisfactory to both VNAF and USAF personnel. . . . Qualified VNAF pilots do not like this duty, and the VNAF crew member is often unqualified. Little training is provided, and the VNAF man often becomes violently ill in flight'.[82] This comment once again highlighted the minimal utility of the training provided under this construct in which the VNAF 'student'/observer essentially served as ballast. An attempt by PACAF headquarters to remove the restriction in July foundered, as did a request that 'USAF crews in Farm Gate aircraft be allowed to lead or act as wingman with VNAF aircraft'.[83] In truth, the requirement for VNAF observers did at times seem to approach the absurd, as was the case during a night mortar attack against the Soc Trang airfield on 10 September 1963 during which the Viet Cong pinned down the VNAF T-28s. Four air commandos, however, made it to their aircraft and drove off the attackers. After the attack, these Americans received commendations for their bravery and reprimands for failing to have a VNAF observer on-board.[84]

If the observer program essentially proved a façade, in one area, at least, USAF air advisors initiated efforts to begin working more closely with their VNAF counterparts. While VNAF pilots on-board USAF aircraft seemed a waste of resources, such was not the case for VNAF Forward Air Controllers (FACs). The program to train VNAF FACs offered one positive example of an effort to train and advise VNAF personnel. A two-day seminar involving USAF and VNAF personnel in February 1962 addressed problems and procedures involved with forward air control and resulted

81 AFHRA, K717.1623, Memorandum for General Martin [PACAF Commander] from Colonel John B. Kidd, 20 February 1963. The Geneva Accords prohibited the participation of third party military forces in combat operations in Vietnam. Although not a signatory power to the accords, the United States agreed in principle to accept the stipulations of the agreement.

82 AFHRA, K526.549-2, Report from Detachment 2 Alpha to Commander, 2nd ADVON, 5 June 1962.

83 AFHRA, K717.1623, Message from PACAF headquarters to Chief of Staff of the USAF, 6 July 1962.

84 Haas, *Apollo's Warriors*, p. 229.

in an agreement 'to develop and jointly conduct a formal FAC course'.[85] In truth, the program was the product of necessity as Farm Gate aircraft required the presence of a Vietnamese forward air controller prior to conducting attacks.[86]

Flying 'low and slow' in L-19s, Vietnamese FACs played a key role in Farm Gate missions based on their intimate knowledge of the local terrain. Still, the ultimate test of their effectiveness rested on their ability to guide strike aircraft onto the target, a skill that required both reliable radios and clear verbal communications. The absence of Vietnamese and French speaking USAF pilots placed the onus on VNAF FACs to learn English, again highlighting the problem caused by the American neglect of linguistic skills in the 'advisory' effort. Likewise, the limited number of VNAF forward air controllers provided an additional obstacle for expanded cooperation.[87]

The renewed emphasis on improved training and coordination between USAF and VNAF crews was not entirely coincidental. On 21 January 1962 Farm Gate aircraft accidentally attacked a village in Cambodia, killing several civilians and raising concerns at the 'highest level' of the US government. In the wake of the attack, PACAF headquarters warned, 'If we are to avoid the imposition of highly limiting controls on the application of Farm Gate, we must take every effort to avoid another incident and, in addition, demonstrate the effectiveness of our control and ability to discriminate in the selection and designation of targets as well as in the conduct of air strikes'.[88] The concerns expressed at PACAF headquarters proved justified as Secretary McNamara tightened guidelines for US aircrews in Vietnam. One reflection of the discrimination exercised by Farm Gate aircraft is apparent in the return of over half of T-28 strike sorties with unused ordnance in 1962.

Despite the increased restrictions on operations, Farm Gate aircraft provided much needed firepower in support of ARVN forces on several occasions. For example, two T-28s supported by a C-47 flareship scrambled during the night of 1 March 1962 in response to the distress call of a Vietnamese outpost 30 miles north of Saigon. Using napalm, rockets, and machineguns, the T-28s played a key role in breaking the assault. Two days later, a B-26 assisted two Vietnamese AD-6s in a strike aimed at a Viet Cong assembly point 105 miles northeast of Saigon. Caught in the open, the Viet Cong suffered 12 killed.[89] The missions not only highlighted the value of rapid responsiveness in counterinsurgency warfare, but they also signaled an expansion of operations, including daytime strikes.

A review of the types of missions flown by Farm Gate aircraft in early 1962 clearly demonstrates that not only VNAF personnel, but the training mission as well, took

85 AFHRA, K717.1623, Message from PACAF headquarters to USAF headquarters, 13 March 1962.
86 Futrell, *Advisory Years*, pp. 144, 174.
87 AFHRA, K717.1623, Message from PACAF headquarters to USAF headquarters, 13 March 1962.
88 Futrell. *Advisory Years*, p. 120.
89 Ibid., p. 121.

a backseat to operational sorties. For example, Farm Gate aircraft, including T-28s, B-26s, and C-47s, flew 254 operational missions but not a single training sortie in January and February. The following table provides an overview of the number of operational and training sorties flown by Farm Gate aircraft between January and November 1962.[90]

| Aircraft Type | Timeframe | Operational Sorties | Training Sorties |
|---|---|---|---|
| T-28 | Jan.-Nov. 1962 | 1,589 | 205 |
| RB-26 | Jan.-Nov. 1962 | 1,042 | 74 |
| SC-47 | Jan.-Nov. 1962 | 699 | 29 |
| Total | | 3,330 | 308 |

Table 1 Overview of the number of operational and training sorties flown by Farm Gate aircraft

Operational missions constituted an astounding 92 percent of Farm Gate sorties, with training sorties comprising only eight percent.

With respect to Farm Gate operational sorties, the types of armaments employed provided an important adjunct to existing capabilities as VNAF aircraft faced a temporary prohibition against carrying bombs in the wake of a failed coup attempt by two disgruntled VNAF pilots against the Diem regime in February 1962.[91] Farm Gate pilots became especially adept at the employment of napalm. The incendiary proved useful in burning through heavy jungle cover. In August alone, crews flew eight missions using napalm, including three day strikes and five night missions. Additionally, C-47 crews conducted flight tests involving the release of napalm in 'fuzed barrels dropped in a string from the C-47 via the roller rail system'. The major weakness in this procedure involved the relatively low altitude of the aircraft, only 50 to 100 feet, which made them susceptible to ground fire. In addition to napalm, RB-26 crews experimented with incendiary cluster bomb devices and 260 pound fragmentation bombs. Finally, the introduction of the 100 pound white phosphorous bomb proved 'excellent for use in the jungle since it penetrates the canopy before detonation and does not dissipate its effects, as napalm does, on the top layers of foliage'. Aircrews also believed that the white phosphorous bomb had the added advantage of producing 'considerable psychological effects when used at night'.[92]

90 AFHRA, K717.1623, Message from PACAF headquarters to USAF headquarters, dated 1 December 1962. Totals do not include information for the last day of November.
91 AFHRA, K239.0512-415, USAF ORI #415, Anthis.
92 AFHRA, K526-549-2, Draft report entitled 'FARMGATE [sic] TACTICS AND TECHNIQUES', January 1963(?).

## Psychological Operations

The conduct of psychological operations (PSYOP) provided an additional task for some Farm Gate crews in 1962. Special Operations forces enjoyed a long history of conducting psychological operations, but the mission tended to be viewed as a bastard son by conventional forces, a fact highlighted by the Air Force's inactivation of the career field in 1958.[93] Early Farm Gate PSYOP missions centered on using C-47s equipped with loudspeakers and leaflets to broadcast messages and to provide information to persons in regions controlled by the Viet Cong, an area estimated at 40 percent of the South Vietnamese countryside by March 1964.[94]

On early missions between December 1961 and February 1962; however, marginal speaker quality required the pilot of the aircraft to fly at 500 feet and 100 knots, thus making the aircraft extremely vulnerable to anti-aircraft and small arms fire. In fact, a C-47 conducting a leaflet drop on February 11 crashed for unknown reasons leading to the death of the eight Americans and the VNAF observer on-board.[95] As a result of the loss of the aircraft and the difficulty in measuring the effectiveness of the effort, General LeMay argued in March for the return of the mission to the VNAF.[96]

## The Consequences for Failing to Train

The lack of a dedicated and widespread training program for VNAF pilots constituted a fundamental weakness in the air advisory effort and the entire 'training through operations' concept. Assigning VNAF crewmembers to sit in the back seat of a T-28 or to 'observe' operations in the B-26 or C-47 provided little to no real training advantage. Real training involved the assignment of pilots to provide actual flight instruction to VNAF pilots, an initiative that took place only on a very limited scale. Instead, Farm Gate pilots 'demonstrated' the techniques of operational flying and evaluated the state of Vietnamese training and standardization.[97] This approach not only failed to increase capability within the VNAF, but it also promoted a dependency relationship that kept the VNAF on the sidelines as 'second stringers'.

93 Futrell, *Advisory Years*, p. 122.

94 AFHRA, K717.1623, Message signed by Major-General Thomas S. Moorman Jr., Subject: Concept of Employment of Farm Gate, dated 6 December 1961. See also Texas Tech Virtual Archives, item# 024010202, Memorandum from the Secretary of Defense Robert S. McNamara to the President Lyndon B. Johnson, subject: South Vietnam, 16 March 1964, p. 2, http://www.vietnam.ttu.edu/virtualarchive.

95 Futrell, *Advisory Years*, p. 122.

96 AFHRA, K717-1623, Report entitled 'Comments on Notes on Secretary of Defense Meeting', signed by Brigadier-General John B. Henry, Jr., 13 March 1962. See also Futrell, *Advisory Years*, p. 123.

97 Futrell, *Advisory Years*, pp. 127, 131.

The small size of the VNAF pilot base compounded the problem of inadequate training by the end of 1962. One report observed, 'The existing VNAF pilot base is severely taxed now to accomplish the VNAF tasks and is completely inadequate to permit significant VNAF expansion'. The report continued, 'Training programs are in being to broaden the now meager VNAF pilot base, but this program will not produce the assets to significantly increase the VNAF pilot base until late 1964'.[98] One solution to this problem involved Secretary McNamara's order to more than double the number of Vietnamese pilots in stateside training programs from 130 to 300. Although the MAAG retained responsibility for training the Vietnamese in-country, the small military training teams from the USAF and the US Navy proved inadequate to meet the demand for qualified VNAF aircrew.[99] By October 1962, McNamara increasingly sought the creation of a 'wholly adequate Vietnamese Air Force' and he felt that 'Farm Gate ought to train Vietnamese rather than operate'.[100]

## Expanding Farm Gate

At the end of 1962, the US air advisory effort found itself between a rock and a hard place. The requirement for air support within Vietnam continued to increase, however, the number of qualified VNAF pilots and available aircraft proved insufficient to meet these demands. PACAF reported in October 1962 that the operational sortie rate of the VNAF had almost quadrupled from the start of the year, but identified 'the extreme shortage of pilots' as the 'major deterrent' to an expansion of the VNAF.[101] As a result, PACAF recommended that 'USAF effort in SVN be further augmented... to pick up slack during conversion and expansion of pilot base in VNAF'.[102] Based upon the recommendation of the JCS, President Kennedy, with the concurrence of McNamara and the State Department, approved the expansion of Farm Gate in December 1962.[103]

The expansion of Farm Gate demonstrated the growing reliance upon air support in battling the Viet Cong.[104] However, at a more profound level, it represented the failure of the US air advisory to prepare VNAF forces to fight their own war as both Kennedy and McNamara continually advocated. This failure proved all the more damaging in

98 AFHRA, K717.1623, Message from PACAF headquarters to 2nd Air Division, November 22, 1962.
99 Clever, *Support Activities*, pp. 23-31.
100 Futrell, *Advisory Years*, p. 133.
101 AFHRA, K717.1623, Message from PACAF headquarters to Tactical Air Command, 12 October 1962.
102 AFHRA, K717.1623, Message from PACAF headquarters to 2nd Air Division, 22 November 1962.
103 Futrell, *Advisory Years*, p. 134.
104 AFHRA, K717.1623, Message from PACAF headquarters to Tactical Air Command, 12 October 1962.

that many Farm Gate personnel gave their VNAF counterparts good marks for skill and capability when fully trained.[105] In fact, Aderholt described the VNAF as 'great pilots' and he argued that 'It [the war] should have been dealt with as an insurgency, and it should have been the Vietnamese's fight and not ours'.[106]

## The 'Lessons' of Farm Gate

In the final analysis, the US experience with Farm Gate between 1961 and 1963 highlights several important issues concerning advisory efforts in general, and air advisory missions specifically. First, the program demonstrates the need for a variety of skills among advisors including the need for cultural awareness, linguistic fluency, and the requirement for continuity of personnel and close interaction between advisory and host nation personnel. Second, the program reveals the importance of a clear-cut chain of command and an explicit mission statement. Third, the US experience demonstrates the value of less sophisticated technology when training and advising military forces that may lack the technological and physical infrastructure to support state of the art weapons systems or in situations where less technically sophisticated equipment provides a more effective platform for supporting operations in an insurgency environment. Finally, the program underlines the critical part played by airpower in a supporting role during counterinsurgency operations, a case where firepower may prove less important than capability to gain information or move troops and equipment.

The lack of cultural awareness and linguistic abilities constituted a major weakness for effective training and advising by Farm Gate personnel and was symbolic of a larger failure in the entire US effort during the war in Southeast Asia.[107] Waiting for development of English speaking VNAF personnel and the return of VNAF pilots from stateside training programs provided one clear indication of the absence of cultural awareness and language abilities and created a major obstacle to close interaction between the Americans and the Vietnamese. Likewise, a tendency to speak 'derogatorily' of their Vietnamese counterparts and treat them 'like so many undereducated and underprivileged children' further inhibited the growth of close personal relationships.[108] The American attitude could also be particularly insulting to experienced VNAF pilots with extensive combat experience. As King correctly observed, '[W]ho the hell were we to tell them how to run a combat operation when they had people in their organizations who had flown a thousand or two thousand combat sorties within the theater'.[109]

105 AFHRA, K239.0512-240, USAF ORI #240, Anthis.
106 Trest, *Air Commando One*, p. 124.
107 See Robert K. Brigham, *ARVN: Life and Death in the South Vietnamese Army* (Lawrence: University Press of Kansas, 2006).
108 Herrington, *Vietcong*, p. 253.
109 AFHRA, K239.0512-219, USAF ORI #219, King.

A further complicating factor involved the deployment of American personnel for temporary duty assignments ranging from 30 to 179 days, a practice that prevented continuity in both training programs and the development of close personal relationships between the two air forces. As General Anthis remarked:

> Continuity is necessary in working with the South Vietnamese…they work on a friendship or personal basis, in many cases, rather than just the fact that we were there to assist and work with them. What the VNAF people were experiencing was that about the time they got acquainted with the US airman well, learned to respect and trust him, he was gone and the Vietnamese had to start all over again and get reacquainted with a new person.[110]

In addition to problems with developing a close liaison with the Vietnamese, Farm Gate suffered from dissonance concerning its primary mission, as well as a dysfunctional argument over operational command authority. In the case of the former, the initial Farm Gate cadre saw themselves as aerial secret agents and their missions as being closely tied to 'cloak and dagger' operations; a perception reinforced by close contacts with the Central Intelligence Agency in Vietnam, as well as by LeMay's marching orders to King.[111] This perception eventually led to lower morale among Farm Gate pilots and increased frustration as pilots found themselves placed in a training role that significantly differed from their initial expectations.[112] The lack of a clearly understood mission also created confusion throughout the entire chain of command on the exact nature, activities, and objectives of the program. Brigadier-General John W. Roberts, a former wing commander in Southeast Asia, concluded 'There were a lot of people who didn't understand it [the Farm Gate mission]…The people that didn't understand the mission were privy only to the overt part of that mission. The misunderstandings of that role were quite rampant'. He continued, 'I had no problem with what FARMGATE [sic] was supposed to do. It was just a matter of sometimes getting a question answered from higher level. We at PACAF did not have the answers. We knew what the questions were, but we didn't have any answer[s]'.[113] Finally, the tug of war between Farm Gate and the 2nd ADVON concerning command authority exacerbated the confusion and acted as a major 'detriment' to the program.[114]

The USAF air advisory mission also underlines the importance of selecting and employing the appropriate technology when fighting in an insurgency environment. In this case, the use of World War II era propeller driven aircraft proved especially effective due to their ability to operate from austere bases, their relative ease of maintenance,

110 AFHRA, K239.0512-240, USAF ORI #240, Anthis.
111 AFHRA, K239.0512-219, USAF ORI #219, King.
112 Haas, *Apollo's Warriors*, p. 228.
113 AFHRA, K239.0512-405, USAF ORI #405, Brigadier-General John W. Roberts, 2-3 Mar. 1971.
114 AFHRA, K239.0512-219, USAF ORI #219, King.

and their ability to fly low and slow. The belief by some USAF officers that jet aircraft, with their improved speed and range, constituted the most effective weapons systems catalyzed a 'propeller versus jet' debate. For his part, Aderholt warned, 'My God, we are in trouble if we think that jet technology and high performance fighters have made less advanced capabilities obsolete'.[115] Likewise, General Pritchard noted his concern about the USAF obsession with advanced technologies at the expense of more appropriate aircraft for the insurgency environment by remarking, 'I think we're more concerned now about how we retain our 24-wing, 14-carat fighter force, than how we accomplish these other things'.[116]

Finally, the missions conducted by Farm Gate, Ranch Hand, and Mule Train aircrews once again highlight the critical importance of airpower when used in a supporting role, including the transport of troops, equipment, and supplies, or the gathering of intelligence. The ability of C-47s and C-123s to resupply garrisons in isolated and inaccessible areas and to bypass Viet Cong ambushes proved a major contribution of the early US air effort.[117] Likewise, the use of the RB-26 as a photoreconnaissance platform provided major advantages to US and Vietnamese forces in finding and identifying Viet Cong enclaves or troop movements.[118] In fact, the significance of photoreconnaissance in Vietnam clearly demonstrated the great importance of intelligence, surveillance, and reconnaissance assets in counterinsurgency warfare. Although the ability of aircraft to bring firepower to bear should not be underestimated, neither should one neglect the other equally important capabilities provided by airpower in the counterinsurgency arena.

## Conclusion

The experience of Farm Gate and the US air advisory effort between 1961 and 1963 was in fact emblematic of the larger American effort in Vietnam. From its inception the program pursued conflicting aims, the effort to improve the firepower available to ARVN forces and to increase the effectiveness of the VNAF proved at odds with one another. The failure to concentrate on developing a dedicated training program for improving the size and quality of the VNAF led to ever greater reliance on US forces. The traditional American impatience in obtaining results led to a self-fulfilling prophesy in which the 'motivation and leadership' provided by Farm Gate personnel received the credit for the VNAF's 'growing professionalism' while criticisms continued concerning the number of VNAF operational sorties and the professional

115 Trest, *Air Commando One*, p. 12.

116 AFHRA, K239.0512-218, Colonel Robert L. Gleason as quoted in USAF ORI #218, Pritchard. Emphasis in the original.

117 Clever, *Support Activities*, p. 4.

118 AFHRA, K717.1623, Message from PACAF headquarters to Tactical Air Command, 29 October 1962.

competence of the VNAF that 'is still far below that of the USAF'.[119] Ironically, a PACAF report in October 1962 perfectly identified the dilemma faced by US forces: 'This Hq [headquarters] recognizes that FARM GATE must not be permitted to become a crutch to compromise VNAF development, but it is the only air support unit with the capability to increase its performance quickly to meet the expanding requirements'.[120] In concentrating on operations instead of training and by relegating the VNAF literally to the backseat, the Farm Gate program did become, in fact, a crutch—one of the United State Air Force's own making.

In retrospect, one former Farm Gate commander opined, 'We should have had a bona fide Vietnamese pilot and we should have had our butts in the rear seat as soon as he was halfway competent; and had we done this in each of the several squadrons, I think that [the] VNAF would have achieved confidence a hell of a lot faster than they did'.[121] This pilot's hindsight may have been 20/20; however, once relegated to the backseat, it proved difficult for both the VNAF and the USAF to change places.

119 AFHRA, K717.1623, Message from PACAF headquarters to Tactical Air Command, 13 October 1962.

120 AFHRA, K717.1623, Message from PACAF headquarters to Tactical Air Command, 12 October 1962.

121 AFHRA, K239.0512-218, Colonel Robert L. Gleason as quoted in USAF ORI #218, Pritchard.

9

# British Assistance to the Sultan of Oman's Air Force, 1970-1981

*Nikolas Gardner*

## Introduction[1]

Britain's conduct of the Dhofar war has long been regarded as an archetype of a successful counterinsurgency campaign. In 1970, the communist-backed Popular Front for the Liberation of the Occupied Arabian Gulf (PFLOAG) controlled the bulk of Oman's southern Dhofar province. Over the next five years, however, British officers leading Omani regular forces and *firqat* tribal militias decisively defeated the insurgents in what SAS officer Tony Jeapes called 'one of the most successful counter-insurgency campaigns of modern years'.[2] As Geraint Hughes has observed, Dhofar 'is one of the few post-1945 conflicts (alongside Malaya and the Philippines) where Western or pro-Western governments defeated insurgents both militarily and politically'.[3] Recent scholarship has modified the view of Dhofar as a 'model' counterinsurgency. For example, Hughes has pointed out that the remote location and open terrain of the region, the relative stability of the rest of Oman as well as the cultural knowledge of British and Omani forces were significant advantages against a weak adversary with little external support. Such conditions are difficult to replicate

1 The opinions expressed in this article are those of the author and do not reflect the views of the National Defense College, or the United Arab Emirates government.

2 Tony Jeapes, *SAS: Operation Oman* (Nashville, TN: The Battery Press, 1980), p. 11. See also John Akehurst, *We Won a War: The Campaign in Oman, 1965-1975* (London: Michael Russell, 1982), p. xi; Walter C. Ladwig III, 'Supporting Allies in Counterinsurgency: Britain and the Dhofar Rebellion', *Small Wars and Insurgencies,* 19:1 (March 2008), pp. 62-88.

3 Geraint Hughes, 'A "Model Campaign" Reappraised: The Counter-Insurgency War in Dhofar, Oman, 1965-1975', *Journal of Strategic Studies,* 32:2 (April 2009), p. 273.

today.[4] Marc DeVore has documented the extensive support provided to Oman by nearby regimes, with Jordan and Iran contributing advanced weapons and thousands of personnel, who participated in conventional military operations in support of British and Omani forces.[5] Moreover, recent scholarship by James Worrall and Abdel Razzaq Takriti has offered a broader perspective on Britain's role in the Dhofar conflict, examining British diplomatic and economic ties with Oman in addition to military operations.[6]

This growing body of literature, however, focuses almost entirely on the period from 1965 until the suppression of the Dhofar insurgency in late 1975. In addition, studies of British military assistance to Oman place far more emphasis on the role of the army than the other British services. This is understandable given that most scholars have focused on British counterinsurgency methods and the lessons they offer for modern practitioners, but British security assistance efforts in Oman involved all three services and extended well beyond 1975. British assistance was particularly important in the development of the Sultan of Oman's Air Force (SOAF), which grew from a motley collection of small cargo and training aircraft in the late 1960s into a modern force equipped with state-of-the-art fighter aircraft and advanced air defense capabilities a decade later. Loan Service Personnel (LSP) seconded from the Royal Air Force (RAF), along with retired RAF personnel working as contractors played an integral role in operating this equipment and training Omanis to use it during and particularly after the conflict in Dhofar. Drawing on military and diplomatic records held at the British National Archives, this chapter examines British security assistance to the SOAF, focusing on the period from 1970 until 1981. In doing so, it asks two principal questions. First, what was the rationale for British assistance to the SOAF during and after the conflict in Dhofar? Secondly, to what extent did this assistance contribute to the development of a capable, independent Omani air force? It demonstrates that an evolving combination of military, political, and economic factors compelled British military assistance during the early 1970s and prolonged it into the 1980s, despite plans to withdraw British forces as soon as possible after 1975.

4 Ibid., pp. 298-300.

5 Marc DeVore, 'A More Complex and Conventional Victory: Revisiting the Dhofar Counterinsurgency, 1963–1975', *Small Wars and Insurgencies,* 23:1 (2012), pp. 144-173. Other recent studies of the conflict in Dhofar include Robert Johnson, 'Out of Arabia: British Strategy and the Fate of Local Forces in Aden, South Yemen, and Oman, 1967–76', *International History Review*, 39:1 (2017), pp. 143-164; Clive Jones, 'Military Intelligence and the War in Dhofar: An Appraisal', *Small Wars and Insurgencies,* 25:3 (2014), pp. 628-646; Ian Illych Martinez, 'The Battle of Mirbat: Turning Point in the Omani Dhofar Rebellion', *Small Wars and Insurgencies,* 23:3 (2012), pp. 517-526.

6 James Worrall, *Statebuilding and Counterinsurgency in Oman: Political, Military and Diplomatic Relations at the End of Empire* (London: I.B. Tauris, 2014); Abdel Razzaq Takriti, *Monsoon Revolution: Republicans, Sultans, and Empires in Oman, 1965–1976* (Oxford: Oxford University Press, 2013).

## The Sultan of Oman's Air Force and the Conflict in Dhofar, 1970-1975

The Omani Air Force came into existence on 1 March 1959, following an exchange of letters between Sultan Said bin Taimur and the British government the previous year. This agreement was the latest in a series of pacts between Britain and the Omani rulers of the Al Bu Said dynasty extending back to 1798. It provided Sultan Said with considerable British financial aid and military assistance, which proved essential in suppressing an uprising by the Ibadi Imam in the mountainous Jebel Akhdar region. Consisting initially of just two single-engine aircraft used for communication and the transport of casualties, the air force played a limited role in these operations.[7] The 1960s saw the purchase of additional aircraft, including four DeHavilland Beaver single-engine transport planes and its first jets, two Hunting Provost trainers. As the communist-backed insurgency in Dhofar gained strength toward the end of the decade, Said also agreed to the purchase of 24 BAC-167 Strikemaster jet fighters for reconnaissance and close air support.[8]

These procurement efforts, however, did little to quell the Dhofar uprising. By early 1970, the Popular Front for the Liberation of the Arabian Gulf (PFLOAG) controlled two-thirds of the province. As the 1960s progressed, British politicians, diplomats, and military personnel had become increasingly frustrated with Sultan Said, who resisted investing in military equipment as well as infrastructure that might have improved the quality of life of his subjects and diminished support for the insurgents. Their frustration intensified in 1968 after Harold Wilson's Labour government announced that Britain would withdraw from its military bases 'East of Suez' in 1971. Concerned that the rebellion could threaten the stability of the entire Gulf region following Britain's withdrawal, politicians from both the Labour and Conservative parties remained committed to helping suppress the Dhofar insurgents. The Conservatives, however, had fewer reservations about maintaining a military presence in the region and taking active measures to stabilize Oman. Thus, the June 1970 election of a Conservative government under Edward Heath proved a catalyst for decisive action.[9] In July, British officers supported a palace coup by Said's 29 year-old son, Qaboos bin Said Al Said.[10] Educated in England and trained at Sandhurst, Qaboos proved more receptive than his father to British advice. The new sultan initiated a multipronged campaign that included civil development projects,

7 Allen and Rigsbee, *Oman Under Qaboos*, p. 19.

8 Ibid., p. 21; <http://www.mod.gov.om/en-US/RAFO/Pages/about-us.aspx> (accessed 13 March 2017).

9 James Worrall, *Statebuilding and Counterinsurgency in Oman: Political, Military and Diplomatic Relations at the End of Empire* (London and New York: I. B. Tauris, 2014), pp. 69-72.

10 There exist numerous descriptions of the coup, some alleging direct British participation, but the most plausible and well-documented account is found in Worrall, *Statebuilding and Counterinsurgency in Oman*, pp. 72-74.

negotiations with tribal leaders in Dhofar, and a military campaign supported by hundreds of British personnel including an SAS team and senior officers up to the rank of general.

Given Oman's extreme climate, rugged terrain, and primitive transportation infrastructure, aircraft were essential to the successful conduct of military operations on the ground. Sultan Qaboos therefore moved quickly to expand the transport capabilities of the newly renamed Sultan of Oman's Air Force (SOAF), purchasing five Vickers Viscount passenger jets as well as three DeHavilland Caribou and 10 Short Skyvan transport aircraft.[11] The unorthodox Skyvan became the workhorse of the SOAF fleet. In his memoir of the Dhofar war, General John Akehurst, then a brigade commander, described the aircraft as 'an ungainly-looking great box with stubby wings that seemed to defy most of the rules of flight but was nevertheless tough, reliable and versatile'.[12]

The nascent SOAF benefited from the existence of two military airfields at Salalah and on Masirah Island, both maintained by the RAF since the Second World War.[13] Operations in Dhofar, however, took place in remote locations without even rudimentary airstrips. To transport and resupply personnel in rugged terrain, Qaboos purchased eight Agusta-Bell 205 transport helicopters, an Italian-made version of the Bell UH-1 Iroquois, which arrived in Oman in 1972 and 1973. He also purchased four Italian-made Agusta-Bell 206 Jet Ranger helicopters. Still used today by news media in North America for aerial traffic reporting, these smaller helicopters facilitated command and control of forces on the ground.[14] In 1975, the SOAF received an additional windfall in the form of 31 Hawker Hunter ground attack aircraft, a gift from King Hussein of Jordan. The Jordanian Air Force had recently acquired newer F-5 fighters to replace the Hunters, which were in such poor condition that only 16 could be used by the Omanis, and then only after considerable repair work. Nevertheless, they were faster and more heavily armed than the SOAF's Strikemasters, and therefore represented a significant upgrade in strike capability.[15]

Finding personnel to operate and maintain this rapidly expanding fleet of aircraft was a significant and ongoing challenge. In the early 1970s, the vast majority of Omanis lacked basic literacy, let alone the advanced knowledge and skills necessary to operate and maintain modern aircraft. Despite the introduction of an officer training

11 Allen and Rigsbee, *Oman Under Qaboos*, p. 67, <http://www.mod.gov.om/en-US/RAFO/Pages/about-us.aspx> (accessed 13 March 2017); The National Archives, Kew, London, United Kingdom (hereafter TNA), FCO 8/2233, 'Annual Report for 1973, by Defence Attaché Muscat'.

12 Akehurst, *We Won a War*, p. 40.

13 Allen and Rigsbee, *Oman Under Qaboos*, p. 8.

14 Ibid., p. 67.

15 J. E. Peterson, *Oman's Insurgencies: The Sultanate's Struggle for Supremacy* (London: Saki, 2007), pp. 329, 431; Akehurst, *We Won a War*, p. 155; TNA, FCO 8/3336, 'Annual Report for 1978, by Air Attaché, Muscat'.

program, by the end of 1975 the 155-strong officer corps of the SOAF included just 13 Omanis, only one of whom was qualified as a pilot.[16] Regional allies made limited contributions of personnel as well as equipment. For example, Jordanian pilots and technicians accompanied King Hussein's gift of Hawker Hunters in the spring of 1975, but most returned home by the fall. By the end of the year, all of the technicians had departed and only two pilots remained.[17] Iran deployed AB-205 helicopters along with pilots and ground crew to Oman in 1972 and 1973. The Iranians also built a radar facility in Dhofar and stationed eight F-5 fighters there from 1974 until 1977, but British commanders lacked confidence in the skills of Iranian pilots and were therefore reluctant to rely on them for difficult operations such as medical evacuations.[18]

Given the lack of qualified Omani and allied personnel, the SOAF was almost entirely British in its makeup throughout the war in Dhofar. As the British Army officer Ian Gardiner reflected in his memoir of the conflict, the force 'was really the RAF in disguise'.[19] The upper ranks of the officer corps consisted primarily of LSP seconded from the Royal Air Force. These officers took orders from Qaboos, who served as Commander-in-Chief of the Sultan's Armed Forces, but they were required to inform the British Ambassador to Oman before acting on any directive that ran contrary to British interests.[20] Royal Air Force personnel had been seconded to Oman during the 1960s, but the British commitment increased as the SOAF grew following the coup in 1970. While most senior commanders as well as some pilots were LSP, the majority of British officers serving in SOAF were ex-RAF personnel working on contracts with the Sultanate of Oman. At the end of 1973, for example, 28 of a total of 78 officers in the SOAF were LSP, while 47 were contractors. The remaining three were Omanis.[21] Ground crew consisted almost entirely of British contractors working for Airwork Services Limited, a private company that had provided aircraft maintenance and support services to the Omani air force since its establishment in 1959. Despite their civilian status, Airwork contractors worked closely with SOAF personnel. In his annual report for 1972 the British defense attaché commented: 'The technicians, invariably former RAF personnel, are hard and willing workers who have

16 TNA, FCO 8/2475, 'Future British Military Assistance to Oman'; DEFE 11/896, 'Annual Report for 1975, by Air Attaché, Muscat, 1 January 1976', 'Annual Report for 1975, by Defence Attaché, Muscat'.

17 TNA, DEFE 11/896, 'Annual Report for 1975, by Air Attaché Muscat, 1 January 1976'; Middle East Centre Archive, St. Antony's College, Oxford UK (hereafter MECA), Sultan's Armed Forces Association Newsletter, 16 (November 1975).

18 Allen and Rigsbee, *Oman Under* Qaboos, p. 74; Peterson, *Oman's Insurgencies*, pp. 329-331.

19 Ian Gardiner, *In the Service of the Sultan: A First Hand Account of the Dhofar Insurgency* (Barnsley: Pen & Sword Military, 2006), p. 85.

20 TNA, AIR 8/2796, 'Directive to the Commander, Sultan of Oman's Land Forces'.

21 TNA, FCO 8/2233, 'Annual Report for 1973, by Defence Attaché Muscat'.

in the past uncomplainingly shared the discomforts and dangers of life at Salalah with cheerfulness and fortitude'.[22]

This reliance on contractors had both benefits and drawbacks. Because they served the government of Oman or Airwork Services rather than Her Majesty's Government, their actions were not subject to the same limitations as LSP. Significantly, contractors could engage in operations outside of Omani territory which their seconded counterparts could not. This flexibility allowed contract pilots to conduct multiple bombing missions against PFLOAG bases located in the People's Democratic Republic of Yemen in 1972 and especially in the final stages of the Dhofar War in late 1975.[23] On the other hand, British diplomats and military officers serving in Oman observed that the leadership skills and technological savvy of contractors declined over time. Once they retired from active service, the incentive offered by the prospect of promotion disappeared. In addition, retired military personnel were less likely to be familiar with state-of-the-art aircraft and weapons systems, a significant drawback given the SOAF's pace of expansion. Thus, in 1976 a Foreign and Commonwealth Office Report recommended 'the continued feeding in of UK Loan Service Personnel to find the leadership and modern skills sometimes found wanting in British Contract Officers'.[24]

The relative flexibility of contractors could also be drawback. Unlike LSP, contract personnel could leave the SOAF with little notice if they grew weary of service in Oman. Given the spartan conditions in which they served, as well as their isolation from family and friends in the UK, this was an ongoing problem. As the British defense attaché in Muscat complained in late 1973: 'The turnover of European expatriates remains quite high, for many of them one tour of three years is enough for [although] there are financial benefits, the quality of life they lead is barren, lonely for the married man and often uncomfortable'.[25] Working and living conditions in Oman compared unfavorably even with those in neighboring countries. As one report observed: 'A contributory factor to the shortage of contract officers of the right caliber is the unattractive conditions of service compared with the rich Gulf states who offer married accommodation, free family air fares, assistance with boarding school fees and in some cases higher rates of pay'.[26] Contractors with specialized skills were especially likely to be lured away by better employment terms elsewhere. In 1975, the British air attaché observed that 'SOAF have particular difficulty in recruiting helicopter pilots due to the competitive nature of civil opportunities'. Recruiting and training new pilots to replace those who abruptly departed proved difficult and time consuming. According to the defense attaché: 'contract aircrew are hard to replace

22 TNA, FCO 8/2022, 'Annual Report for 1972 by Defence Attaché Muscat'; FCO 8/2233, 'Annual Report for 1973 by Defence Attaché Muscat'.
23 TNA, DEFE 25/375, Major-General K. Perkins, 'Oman 1975: The Year of Decision'.
24 TNA, DEFE 11/901, 'Oman: Annual Review for 1975'.
25 TNA, FCO 8/2233, 'Annual Report for 1973 by Defence Attaché Muscat'.
26 TNA, DEFE 25/375, 'Rundown of Royal Navy LSP in Sultan of Oman's Navy'.

when they leave; a new man takes time to adapt his ability to the singular techniques of flying over this type of terrain, especially when probably in combat for the first time. The longer term problem of how to man the air force when contract personnel leave in sizeable numbers is difficult'.[27]

Thus, while the SOAF played an instrumental role in defeating the rebellion in Dhofar, it is clear that personnel shortages hampered its operations. In his account of British counterinsurgency efforts in Oman, the historian J.E. Peterson describes a shortage of helicopters in 1971 after three of five available Airwork mechanics resigned, and four of eight pilots resigned or were evacuated for medical reasons. Similar shortages of pilots occurred in 1973 and 1974, in the latter case requiring the RAF to supply a squadron of Wessex helicopters to make up the shortfall.[28] Until the war was won, however, the British recognized that there was little they could do to remedy the situation. Given the virtual absence of Omanis with the necessary skills and training, the SOAF was completely reliant on British personnel. But following Britain's ostensible retreat from East of Suez in 1971, politicians were reluctant to commit additional resources to the conflict in Oman. Thus, beyond a cadre of about 30 LSP, the SOAF relied almost entirely on British contractors to conduct operations until the end of the Dhofar war in 1975. As the air attaché in Muscat explained in late 1973: 'There seems no sensible expectation but to see the overwhelming majority of aircrew provided by expatriates as far ahead as one can see, the same can be said of the servicing requirement'.[29]

## Expansion and Omanisation, 1975-1981

Following the Sultan's declaration of victory in Dhofar at the end of 1975, the operational demands on the SOAF diminished significantly. Rather than shrinking, however, its cadre of British personnel grew for two reasons. First, while the British had been heavily involved in the expansion and operations of the air force over the preceding five years, they had not been able to train sufficient numbers of Omanis to manage it even in peacetime. Secondly, and even more significantly, Sultan Qaboos had decided in 1973 to invest in an Integrated Air Defense System (IADS) comprising radar, state-of-the-art fighter aircraft, and anti-aircraft missiles. After extended negotiations with American, French, and British representatives, the Sultan decided to purchase a package that included 12 Anglo-French Jaguar ground attack aircraft and the British-made Rapier anti-aircraft missile system. Signed in mid-1975, the purchase agreement included the provision of additional British technicians and pilots to operate and maintain the sophisticated new equipment, while instructing

27 TNA, FCO 8/2233, 'Annual Report for 1973 by Defence Attaché Muscat'.
28 Peterson, *Oman's Insurgencies*, pp. 270, 314, 334.
29 TNA, FCO 8/2233, 'Annual Report for 1973 by Defence Attaché Muscat'.

Omani personnel how to use it.[30] As a result, the task of training the SOAF expanded significantly in the aftermath of the Dhofar War.

It is tempting to portray the decision to sell the IADS to Qaboos as a British attempt to profit at the expense of an inexperienced ruler who's newly acquired oil wealth outweighed his strategic judgment. In fact, British diplomats and military officers disagreed over the wisdom of the sale and only decided in favor of it after months of internal debate and negotiations with Qaboos himself. This process reveals the mixture of motivations behind British security assistance to Oman as well as the methods employed to provide it, and it is therefore worth examining in some detail.

In 1973, with Omani revenues increasing significantly as a result of rising global oil prices, the Sultan had declared his interest in purchasing an air defense system and requested British advice. In response, a team from the British Ministry of Defence (MOD) conducted a study 'to define an air defence system for Oman'. With an estimated price tag of £70 million, the project was a potential windfall for the British defense industry. Nonetheless, the MOD study concluded that the threat posed to Oman by the air force of the People's Democratic Republic of Yemen – its principal enemy at the time – did not justify the cost of the system.[31] Moreover, the British Army and Royal Air Force expressed concern that the necessity of training Omanis in the operation and maintenance of the system would require the deployment of hundreds of additional British military personnel to Oman. The sale of Rapier missile systems to Oman would also delay the production of similar equipment already ordered by the MOD to fulfill Britain's commitment to NATO.[32] Additional strain on Britain's military resources was a particular concern when a new Labour government took office in March 1974 in the context of inflation, labor unrest, and a significant trade deficit.[33]

Qaboos would not be deterred. When the British Commander of the Sultan's Armed Forces, Major-General Kenneth Perkins, advised him against the purchase, Qaboos directed him 'to get on with it', making clear that he was considering French and American equipment in addition to the British package.[34] The Sultan's willingness to explore other options – particularly a French one – raised British concerns about losing influence in Oman. As a 1974 MOD report speculated: 'An

30 TNA, FCO 8/2233, 'Annual Report for 1973 by Defence Attaché Muscat'; AIR 8/2797, 'Final Report as CSAF from Major-General Perkins'; 'Annex A to DP 15/76 (C) (Preliminary Draft) British Military Assistance to Oman', 2 June 1976.

31 TNA, FCO 8/2234, N.T. Bagnall, 'Provision of Military Equipment to Oman', 7 February 1974.

32 TNA, FCO 8/2235, 'British Military Assistance to Oman', 20 February 1974; 'Proposed Sale of Rapier to Oman'.

33 Worrall, *Statebuilding and Counterinsurgency in Oman*, p. 203.

34 TNA, FCO 8/2234, Hawley to MOD, 4 February 1974; DEFE 11/899, Perkins to Secretary of the Chiefs of Staff Committee, 28 December 1975; FCO 8/2235, R. Anderson, AUS/Sales, 'Rapier for Oman', 16 April 1974.

influx of Frenchmen (or Pakistanis) on the scale that might be required for a French air defense system could reduce British influence in SAF and might in the worst case lead to CSAF's own position being undermined'.[35] This possibility added to existing British fears of losing credibility with Oman and its neighbors. In June 1974, the Minister of State for Foreign and Commonwealth Affairs, David Ennals, contended in a letter to his MOD counterpart, William Rogers, that if Britain failed to offer an IADS to Qaboos, 'the Sultan and his allies, notably Saudi Arabia and Iran, would undoubtedly think that we were holding out on Oman, reviving the suspicions that our interest really lies in prolonging the war'. Conversely, he also suggested that Iran in particular might interpret British reluctance to provide the equipment as a sign that it was preparing to withdraw from Oman, leaving the Shah's regime with full responsibility for the war in Dhofar.[36]

Economic considerations also weighed in favor of the sale. While the primary purpose of Britain's intervention in the Dhofar conflict was to maintain the stability of the Gulf region, the British recognized that Oman and its neighbors constituted a potentially lucrative market for defense sales. In a report written in late 1972, the British defense attaché in Muscat, Colonel C.R. Welch, commented that, 'while in world market terms sales to Oman may be relatively small, SAF is going to expand, the Iranians and Jordanians are here, listening to users' quoted opinions which filter on to other Gulf states and further afield still'. Thus, he continued: 'It is in our interests to redouble our sales efforts despite the small orders, when so many are watching and listening from neighboring countries'.[37] The OPEC oil embargo and the ensuing increase in global oil prices in late 1973 reinforced arguments in favor of arms sales to the Middle East. Even the MOD, which opposed the diversion of British resources away from its NATO commitments, recognized in 1974 that: 'The inevitable increase in the UK balance of payments deficit caused by higher oil prices makes it all the more urgent that exports should be increased and oil producing countries constitute an obvious market. It is therefore, in strictly commercial terms, in our interests to secure as much of the arms business in Oman as is within our capability against increasing activity by the French and possibly the US'.[38] Sultan Qaboos himself added an additional economic incentive, promising to purchase four Strikemasters, as well as three BAC 1-11 passenger jets and a Vickers VC-10 long-range jet, if the British agreed to provide the package of radar, Jaguar aircraft, and Rapier units, with the latter to be delivered by the end of 1975.[39]

35 TNA, FCO 8/2235, 'British Military Assistance to Oman'.
36 TNA, FCO 8/2235, 'Letter from Minister of State (FCO) David Ennals, to Minister of State (Defence), William Rogers, 5 June 1974'.
37 TNA, FCO 8/2022, 'Annual Report for 1972, by Defence Attaché, Muscat'.
38 TNA, FCO 8/2235, 'British Military Assistance to Oman'.
39 TNA, FCO 8/2235, Wright, 'Rapier for Oman', 3 June 1974; Hawley to MOD, 20 April 1974.

While acknowledging the economic benefits of the sale, the MOD expressed concern that it would require the commitment of additional military personnel to Oman. As the 1974 MOD report contended: 'at least in the early stages up to three fifths of the expatriate personnel required to operate and maintain the air defence equipment could only be found by the provision of British LSP and that a minimum of 280 could be required if all the equipment was sold'.[40] BAC assured British military authorities 'categorically', that 'they could provide the Omanis with technical support and training from their own resources'.[41] Despite this assurance, the MOD continued to resist the timeline requested by the Sultan, maintaining that to provide Rapier units to Oman by the end of 1975 would require the diversion of equipment already assigned to British Army units fulfilling the country's commitment to NATO. In fact, the first Rapier units did not arrive in Oman until 1977.[42] Thus, while Britain certainly profited from the decision to sell an IADS package to Oman, this decision was not made lightly. The Labour government that took office in early 1974 was less committed to maintaining a robust military presence in the Gulf than its Conservative predecessor, particularly if doing so would entail additional expenditures. Politicians, diplomats, and defense officials weighed the limited military justification for the system, the extended commitment of personnel necessary to deliver it, and Britain's defense obligations elsewhere against its economic value and the importance of maintaining a strong relationship with Oman and its neighbors. The economic and political arguments for the sale won out only after the Sultan indicated that he would purchase a system despite British advice to the contrary, and BAC agreed to secure contractors to support the project.

As the Dhofar War ended, therefore, the number of British personnel attached to the SOAF increased. The cadre of LSP remained relatively stable throughout the second half of the 1970s, with approximately 30 RAF officers serving in senior command and staff positions, flying aircraft, and training Omani officers. They played a particularly important role in the task of 'Omanisation', training Omani personnel at a series of newly established schools that provided instruction in most of the functions of a modern air force. These schools included a Technical Training Institute, an Aircrew Initial Training School, and a Flight Training School.[43] Prior to attending one of these schools, SOAF officer candidates were sent to the UK, where they completed an officer training course at the RAF Officer Cadet Training Unit. Prospective pilots remained in the UK where they received aviation medicine training as well as initial flight training on piston-engine aircraft before returning to the Flight

40 TNA, FCO 8/2235, 'British Military Assistance to Oman'.
41 TNA, FCO 8/2235, 'Meeting Held with BAC Representatives on Wednesday 24 April 1974 to discuss the Sale of Rapier to Oman'.
42 TNA, AIR 8/2797, 'Report by the Commander Sultan of Oman's Air Force, April-September 1977'.
43 MECA, Sultan's Armed Forces Association Newsletter, 26 (December 1980).

Training School in Oman where they were trained to fly fighter or transport aircraft.[44] Air Commodore Erik Bennett, the British Commander of the SOAF, insisted on LSP rather than contract officers in the training role, partly because LSP usually had more recent experience than retired RAF personnel, but also because of what he viewed as their superior motivation. Bennett described the Flight Training School as 'the cornerstone of the Omanisation policy and its graduates must receive the best training available. This can only be provided by RAF personnel with a career before them; the example which the instructors set is at least as important as the tuition they give'.[45]

While LSP played an important role in training, the expansion of the SOAF at the end of the Dhofar War was almost entirely dependent on contractors. The exact number of British contractors serving in Oman at any given time is difficult to determine given that some were employed directly by SOAF, while others worked for companies like BAC and particularly Airwork. Nevertheless, it is clear that the acquisition of Jordanian Hunter aircraft and the purchase of the IADS in 1975 increased the demand for contractor support. While the task of salvaging the Jordanian aircraft proved demanding, installing a complex air defense system and training Omanis to operate it was an even bigger challenge. Indeed, among British expatriates in Oman, the IADS was jokingly referred to as an acronym for 'it's all double shifts'.[46] Thus, the number of Airwork personnel in Oman almost doubled from 260 in November 1974 to 'nearly 500' one year later.[47] The demand for contractors to serve as ground crew would increase further in March 1977, when the SOAF took over the operation of RAF Salalah.[48] Moreover, even as Omani officers earned their commissions, it is clear that contractors comprised an increasing majority of the growing officer corps of the SOAF. While at the end of 1973, 47 of 73 officers in the force were contractors, two years later they accounted for at least 100 of 155 officers.[49]

This reliance on contractors certainly reduced costs for the British government. While the British expected Oman to cover the salaries, benefits, and even language training of LSP, they were willing to help the Sultan if necessary. In 1973, for example, Britain

44 TNA, FCO 8/3336, 'Annual Report for 1978 by Defence Attaché, Muscat'.
45 TNA, AIR 8/2797, 'Report by the Commander, Sultan of Oman's Air Force, April to September 1977'.
46 MECA, Sultan's Armed Forces Association Newsletter, 26 (December 1980).
47 TNA, DEFE 11/896, 'Annual Report for 1975, by Air Attaché, Muscat, 1 January 1976'.
48 Worrall, *Statebuilding and Counterinsurgency in Oman*, p. 216.
49 TNA, FCO 8/2475, 'Future British Military Assistance to Oman'; DEFE 11/896, 'Annual Report for 1975, by Air Attaché, Muscat, 1 January 1976', 'Annual Report by Defence Attaché, Muscat'. Reports by the British Defence and Air Attachés list 13 Omani SOAF officers and a total of 155 SOAF officers in late 1975. If the number of LSP remained steady at approximately 30 in this period, then it is safe to assume that more than 100 officers' positions were intended to be filled by contractors.

provided £500,000 to reduce the costs of LSP in Oman.[50] The Omani government paid the full costs of deploying loan service personnel to the country for most of the period under examination, but the MOD remained responsible for subsequent medical and pension costs due to casualties incurred in Oman. In contrast, the British government did not provide any financial support to British companies or individuals who did business with the government of Oman. Britain also had limited liability for contractors who became casualties in Oman. This became abundantly clear in June 1978 when five Airwork employees fishing and camping at a beach in Dhofar were killed in an ambush, presumably by remnants of the Dhofari rebel movement.[51] Their surviving spouses were entitled to payments from the Airwork pension plan and a state widow's pension. The contractors were not serving members of the British armed forces, however, and the widows therefore were not deemed eligible for a pension from the Ministry of Defence. An internal memorandum circulated after the incident bluntly stated the government's position on contractors: 'The UK Government has no responsibility whatever for these people beyond the consular care it gives all British subjects overseas'.[52]

As was the case during the Dhofar War, however, heavy reliance on contractors had risks for Britain. Working directly for the SOAF, British companies and individuals had no obligation to report to the UK government or its representatives any orders they received that might run contrary to British interests. This situation had military benefits during the war, when contractor pilots conducted cross-border airstrikes that contributed directly to Britain's goal of defeating the insurgency. But Britain's lack of control over contractors in the SOAF could also endanger British interests. Twice in 1978, Sultan Qaboos ordered the deployment of military forces, including aircraft, as a result of territorial disputes with the neighboring United Arab Emirates. In January, SOAF Jaguars piloted by British contractors made sorties across the border with the emirate of Ras-al-Khaimah. As its Ambassador to Oman James Treadwell commented: 'The Omanis are playing a dangerous game which could quite easily lead to a physical confrontation'.[53]

An even more serious situation arose in October, when Omani intelligence observed a concentration of 'unusually large forces' just across the UAE border near the town of Al-Ain.[54] This was in fact an annual military exercise, but intelligence personnel became 'convinced that the UAE were posed to attack Oman'. As a result, Sultan Qaboos ordered the deployment of military units to the border as well as the arming

50 TNA, FCO 8/2233, Donald Hawley, British Embassy Muscat, to Sir Alec Douglas-Home, 20 January 1974.
51 TNA, FCO 8/3099, D.A. Tatham, Middle East Department, FCO, to MDAC Miers, Tehran, 29 June 1978.
52 TNA, FCO 8/3099, 'British Military Assistance to Oman: Unattributable'.
53 TNA, FCO 8/3110, James Treadwell to FCO and MOD, 25 January 1978; Armitage to FCO, 31 January 1978.
54 TNA, DEFE 70/566, Muscat to MOD (UK), 19 October 1978.

of aircraft in preparation for possible strikes against airfields at Abu Dhabi and Sharjah.[55] The UAE was also a close ally of Britain, and British military personnel were seconded to the armed forces of the emirates. A conflict between the two neighbors would be acutely embarrassing to Britain and potentially disastrous to its position in the Gulf. Fortunately for all, the Commander of the Sultan's army, a British LSP, convinced Qaboos not to initiate military operations. This allowed British diplomats to open channels of communication between the Sultan and Shaikh Zayed of the UAE, defusing the situation. While Qaboos and his advisors later acknowledged that they 'may have acted too hastily', British officials were deeply troubled by their lack of leverage over the Sultan during Oman's recurring border disputes with the UAE. A report prepared prior to the January 1978 incursion into Ras-al-Khaimah acknowledged: 'Although we can only control the use of Loan Service Personnel it is hoped that the Omanis will interpret our wishes more broadly to include the use of British contractors whose involvement could also prove embarrassing. We cannot, however, prevent them from being used in the proposed operation'.[56]

The British also experienced difficulty controlling LSP who served in Oman over an extended period. Although serving officers maintained their commissions in the British armed forces while in Oman, their loyalties could become distorted over time by friendships and financial incentives. This is evident in the case of Erik Bennett, the first Commander of the Sultan's Air Force. Seconded to Oman in 1974, Bennett soon established himself as a competent leader as well as a personal friend of Sultan Qaboos. As one of his counterparts commented in 1976: 'He runs quite a good air force and understands Arabs'.[57] When the Sultan sought to promote Bennett as a reward for his service, however, the RAF would agree only to a local promotion, applicable only in Oman. This created a situation in which it was in Bennett's interest to remain in the country, and therefore to remain in the Sultan's good graces, in order to retain his elevated rank and salary. Over time, suspicions grew about his loyalties. For example, a 1980 report characterized him as 'far too involved in the politics of the place'.[58] These suspicions were not entirely groundless. During the initial stages of the Iran-Iraq War in September 1980, Bennett deliberately withheld from the British Embassy the fact that the Sultan had allowed Iraqi aircraft seeking to avoid Iranian airstrikes to land at a SOAF air base operated by British personnel. While the aircraft soon departed, their presence had the potential to compromise Britain's neutrality in

55 TNA, FCO 8/3336, Annual Report for 1978, by Defence Attaché Muscat.

56 TNA, AIR 8/2797, J.D. Bryars, 'Oman/UAE Border Dispute', 22 December 1977.

57 TNA, DEFE 11/897, K. Perkins to P.M. Stanford, Secretary, Chiefs of Staff Committee, 25 March 1976.

58 TNA, FCO 8/3547, I. T. M. Lucas, 'Air Commodore Bennett: Omani Proposal for Promotion'. See also DEFE 11/897, K. Perkins to P.M. Stanford, Secretary, Chiefs of Staff Committee, 25 March 1976.

the conflict, and consequently the Chief of the British Defence Staff (CDS) initiated a review of the incident.[59]

The British Ministry of Defence directive issued to British loan service officers serving in Oman was ambiguous. It stipulated that, 'If at any time in the execution of your duties you should be faced with a situation where it appears that the employment of British seconded personnel under your command, as directed by the Omani Government, could be against the interests of Her Majesty's Government, cause political repercussions for the United Kingdom, or involve you in a conflict of loyalties, you are to report the situation to HM Ambassador, in advance of taking any action'. But the directive allowed officers some discretion, acknowledging: 'There could... be occasions when the operational circumstances are so pressing that there might be no time to obtain such prior approval.... In emergency you are therefore empowered to authorise the employment of seconded officers on such specific operations, provided you inform HM Ambassador at the earliest opportunity'.[60]

The review by the CDS concluded that this latter clause excused Bennett's conduct. The British Ambassador to Oman in 1980, Ivor Lucas, was less forgiving. Referring to the landing of Iraqi aircraft, he argued that 'the Service Commanders should be told clearly and unequivocally that the spirit of the law requires that they should have reported that particular situation to us'.[61] Nevertheless, Bennett managed to escape censure, remaining in Oman as a loan service officer, and benefiting from continued local promotions. He retired holding the local rank of Air Marshal in 1990, after heading the Omani air force for 16 years, far longer than the usual five-year term of a seconded British service commander.[62] The British might have retained greater control over their personnel in Oman had they removed Bennett earlier, but given his friendship with the Sultan, doing so might have caused more harm than good to British relations with the Sultanate.

The difficulties faced by the British in controlling contractors and even LSP in Oman reinforced the importance of Omanisation. But progress toward the goal of an entirely Omani SOAF failed to meet expectations. A June 1976 report on British military assistance to Oman had confidently predicted withdrawal of all LSP by 1981.[63] Just over a year later, in September 1977, Erik Bennett reported that the number of Omani officers had grown dramatically to 153, from only 13 at the end of the war. Bennett admitted, however, that of this total, '72 are under training of some kind and have yet to enter productive service. Nor can the training of the others

59 TNA, FCO 8/3535, 'Complaint by Commander Sultan of Oman's Air Force'; I.T.M. Lucas to R. E. Palmer, 13 October 1980; R. T. Jackling to H.D.A.C. Mears, 21 October 1980.

60 TNA, AIR 8/2797, 'Directive to the Commander, Sultan of Oman's Land Forces'.

61 TNA, FCO 8/3535, I.T.M. Lucas to R. E. Palmer, 13 October 1980.

62 MECA, Sultan's Armed Forces Association Newsletter, 40 (1990).

63 TNA, AIR 8/2797, Annex A to DP 15/76 (C) (Preliminary Draft), 'British Military Assistance to Oman', 2 June 1976.

be regarded as complete'. Moreover, while these Omani officers were engaged in a range of duties, none were flying aircraft.[64] Indeed, the first Omani pilots did not graduate from the Flight Training School until August 1978, with three qualifying on cargo aircraft while the other two underwent additional training to fly Hunter attack aircraft. Although the school aimed to produce 12 pilots each year, it apparently had difficulty attracting suitable candidates, with only five more graduating in the summer of 1979.[65]

This shortage of capable Omanis hindered the Omanisation of the SOAF officer corps. By the end of January 1980, the force had expanded significantly to a total strength of 2,002, more than five times its size at the end of the Dhofar War. This included 1,562 Omani other ranks, a dramatic increase from less than 200 in late 1975. But the majority of the officer corps remained British, with only 113 Omanis, less than the total reported by Bennett more than two years earlier, alongside 193 British contractors and 29 LSP.[66] Moreover, the vast majority of pilots and unit commanders were British. Senior diplomats and defense officials had long since recognized that the goal of Omanisation of the SOAF by 1981 would not be feasible. Indeed, a 1977 report advised 'flexibility' with respect to the withdrawal of LSP.[67] But as the 1970s drew to a close, the objective seemed no closer. In early 1979, the air attaché in Muscat acknowledged that Omani officers would not take over as squadron commanders until at least 1983. By the end of the year, eight Omani pilots were flying Defender or Skyvan cargo aircraft, while four had qualified to operate Hunter or Strikemaster jets. But most SOAF aircraft, including its newest Jaguar attack aircraft, continued to be operated by British pilots.[68] As the British defense attaché in Muscat observed, the SOAF 'would virtually cease to be effective without British Loan Service Personnel (LSP) and contract officers and NCOs'.[69]

As a result, British officials acknowledged that the Sultan's Armed Forces, and SOAF in particular, would require British assistance throughout the 1980s. As the British Ambassador James Treadwell commented in 1979: 'For some years to come LSP will be needed and for even longer 'Omanisation' will often mean in practice the replacing of a British Loan Service Officer by a British Contract Officer'.[70] But as the SOAF expanded, contract officers became increasingly difficult to attract and retain

64 TNA, AIR 8/2797, 'Report by the Commander Sultan of Oman's Air Force – April to September 1977'.
65 TNA, FCO 8/3336, 'Annual Report for 1978, by Defence Attaché Muscat', See TNA, FCO 3546, 'Annual Report for 1979, by Defence Attaché Muscat', which attributed the lack of Omani officers to 'the lack of education and ability amongst the Omani material available to train'.
66 TNA, FCO 8/3546, 'Official Strength of SAF, 31 January 1980'.
67 TNA, FCO 8/2926, 'Minister of State's Visit to Oman: 26-27 September 1977'.
68 TNA, FCO 8/3546, 'Annual Report for 1978 by Air Attaché Muscat', FCO 8/3336; 'Annual Report for 1979 by Defence Attaché Muscat'.
69 TNA, FCO 8/3546, 'Annual Report for 1979 by Defence Attaché Muscat'.
70 TNA, FCO 8/3336, C.J. Treadwell to Dr. David Owen MP, 25 March 1979.

in sufficient numbers. In 1977 Erik Bennett admitted that the recruitment of contract helicopter pilots had 'all but ceased, mainly because of the high salaries available elsewhere'.[71] In early 1979, the British air attaché complained that 'the expatriate contract officers' rates of pay are now inadequate if SOAF is to be able to recruit (or even to retain) good pilots and officers. A recent pay award was insufficient to raise salaries to a level where the SOAF can compete properly for the rapidly shrinking number of pilots available worldwide'.[72] Until 1975, the prospect of participating in active operations had helped to compensate for the low pay or spartan living conditions, but following the end of the war in Dhofar, it became even more difficult to attract qualified personnel. By the end of 1979, the SOAF faced a shortage of 100 contract officers, nearly 20 percent of the establishment of its officer corps.[73]

In May 1979 the Conservative Party returned to power under Prime Minister Margaret Thatcher. While Thatcher is certainly associated with a more aggressive British foreign policy, her new government was also keen to reduce expenditures. Thus, when representatives of the Sultan enquired into the possibility of Britain subsidizing the cost of LSP, as had been the case under the Heath government in the early 1970s, the Conservative Defence Secretary Francis Pym refused, informing the Omanis that they would have to continue to pay the full costs of seconded personnel. He warned, moreover, that 'this is likely to give rise to further increases in our charges in the future'.[74] While this may have been a means of encouraging the Omanis to reduce their reliance on seconded British personnel, the Thatcher government was no more willing than its predecessors to withdraw its support before the Sultan's armed forces were capable of functioning independently. The ongoing shortage of contract officers in the SOAF, however, forced the British to persevere with the process of training Omanis. This resulted in further postponements of the withdrawal of LSP from the SOAF. At the beginning of 1981, senior British officers in Oman predicted that Omanisation would not be completed until 'about 1989/90'. Recognizing that the SOAF's acquisition of new equipment would require the commitment of additional support, the British worked to discourage additional arms sales to Oman, emphasizing to an American military delegation visiting the country 'the need to restrict the Omanis' desire for excessive military expenditure, and unduly sophisticated military equipment'.[75] Once again, however, the Sultan proved difficult to dissuade, announcing his intention to order the latest British fighter aircraft, the Tornado, during the 1980s. While budgetary constraints eventually forced the SOAF

71 TNA, AIR 8/2797, 'Report by the Commander, Sultan of Oman's Air Force, April to September 1977'; DEFE 11/896, 'Annual Report for 1975, by Air Attaché Muscat, 1 January 1976'.
72 TNA, FCO 8/3336, 'Annual Report for 1978 by Air Attaché Muscat'.
73 TNA, FCO 8/3546, 'Annual Report for 1979 by Defence Attaché Muscat'.
74 TNA, DEFE 11/901, Francis Pym to H.H. Sayyid Fahr bin Taimur al Said, 26 July 1979.
75 TNA, DEFE 11/901, Telegram from MOD UK to British Defence Attaché, Muscat, 7 September 1979.

to choose the more affordable Hawker Hawk, the acquisition of new aircraft would prolong the requirement for British LSP into the 1990s.[76]

## Conclusion

Returning to the questions posed at the outset of this chapter, what factors led Britain to provide assistance to the SOAF during and after the Dhofar conflict, and to what extent did this assistance contribute to the development of an independent Omani air force? Throughout the second half of the twentieth century, British military assistance to Sultan Qaboos and to his father stemmed primarily from a desire to maintain Oman as a friendly, stable ally. The stability of Oman was seen as essential to maintaining British influence in the Gulf more broadly. Thus, RAF personnel provided assistance to Oman's air force from its formation in 1959. By 1970, military necessity dictated the expansion of British assistance. While the numbers of British LSP involved were never large, they were essential to the ability of the SOAF to conduct operations against the Dhofar insurgents. Equally important, if not more so, were the hundreds of contractors who served as officers, pilots, and ground crew. As the 1970s progressed, and Oman's financial situation improved relative to that of Britain, there emerged economic incentives for continued British assistance to the SOAF. Specifically, the sale of an advanced IADS represented badly needed business for British arms manufacturers as well as a way of offsetting Britain's growing balance of payments deficit in the context of rising oil prices. But profit was neither the only, nor even the principal reason for the expansion of British assistance. The British government, and particularly the MoD opposed the sale, and only agreed to support it after the Sultan threatened to purchase French or American equipment. Even after agreeing to support the sale, the MoD fought hard against the diversion of additional RAF personnel and equipment from commitments elsewhere. Ultimately, Britain's decision to sell the IADS and support the consequent expansion of the SOAF resulted primarily from the same desire to maintain good relations with the Sultanate and its neighbors that had prevailed since 1959. In the period under examination, both Labour and Conservative governments shared this desire, and were generally consistent in their level of commitment to Oman.

It is important to evaluate the success of British assistance to the SOAF in light of this overall aim. The British failed to achieve their objective of Omanisation by 1981 or even by the end of the 1980s. Even today, in 2017, there are RAF personnel seconded to Oman. But in addition to training thousands of Omanis to serve in the SOAF, LSP served as a symbol of Britain's commitment to Sultan Qaboos and Oman more generally. As such, they were instrumental in maintaining British relations with Oman, and Britain's reputation with Oman's neighbors. Contractors were a mixed blessing. They may have lacked the skills and reliability of their uniformed

76 TNA, FCO 8/3336, 'Annual Report for 1978 by Air Attaché Muscat'.

British counterparts, and the essential roles they played in the SOAF limited Britain's influence over the Sultan's decisions regarding the use of force. Nonetheless, contractors served in much larger numbers than LSP, and played an essential role in developing the SOAF into a modern air force operating British equipment. In the process, they also helped cement ties between Britain and Oman at a lower cost to the British government than uniformed military personnel. Overall, while the British were not successful in building a fully 'Omanised' SOAF in the period under examination, British assistance to the SOAF certainly influenced the outcome of the conflict in Dhofar, and it helped achieve the strategic goal of maintaining Britain's relationships with its allies in the Gulf. These relationships are proving beneficial as Britain seeks to restore its influence in the region today.

## Select Bibliography


Abel, Jacob. 'Israel's Military Aid to Africa, 1960-1966'. *Journal of Modern African Studies*, 9:2 (August 1971): 165-187.

'Afghan Air Force University: Contract Requirements Were Generally Met, But Instances of Non-Compliance, Poor Workmanship, and Inadequate Maintenance Need to Be Addressed'. Special Inspector General for Afghanistan Reconstruction (SIGAR), SIGAR 16-26 Inspection Report, March 2016, https://www.sigar.mil/pdf/inspections/SIGAR-16-26-IP.pdf.

Allardice, Robert R. and Kyle Head. 'The Coalition Air Force Transition Team: Rebuilding Iraq's Air Force'. *Air and Space Power Journal*, 21:4 (Winter 2007): 1-12.

'Allies May Sell Military Aircraft to Tito to Bolster Yugoslavia against Aggression.' *New York Times*, 7 March 1951.

Aronoff, Josh. '"Get'em in the Air"'. *Vanderbilt Undergraduate Research Journal*, 8 (Spring 2012): 1-8.

Banac, Ivo. *With Stalin Against Tito: Cominformist Splits in Yugoslav Communism*. Ithaca, NY: Cornell University Press, 1988.

Beard, D. 'Should the UK Pursue a Strategy of Increased Involvement in the Training and Mentoring of Foreign Air Power? If So, How Might the UK Approach Be Improved'. Defence Research Paper: Joint Services Command and Staff College, 2012.

Bridgman, Leonard. 'The Story of Vickers'. *Popular Aviation* (June 1939): 40-47, 86.

Brozenick, Norman J. 'Another Way to Fight: Combat Aviation Advisory Operations'. Research Report. Maxwell Air Force Base, AL: Air University, 2002.

Cairny, John T. 'Considerations in Working With Partner Air Forces—Context and Culture'. Strategy Research Project. Carlisle, PA: US Army War College, 2010.

Carr, Brian L. 'Fastmover FID'. MA Thesis: US Naval Postgraduate School, 2005.

Ceh, Nick (ed.). *US Diplomatic Records on Relations with Yugoslavia During the Early Cold War, 1948-1957*. Boulder, CO: East European Monograph Series, 2002.

Christiansen, Betty Barton. *The United States Air Force in Southeast Asia: Military Civic Action*. Washington, DC: Air Force History and Museums Program, 1998, https://media.defense.gov/2010/Dec/21/2001330160/-1/-1/0/AFD-101221-013.pdf.

Clerc, Louis. 'Les relations militaire franco-finlandaises entre 1919 et 1929'. In *Bâtir une Nouvelle Sécurité: La Cooperation Militaire Entre la France et les États d'Europe Centrale et Orientale de 1919 à 1929*. Paris: Centre d'études d'histoire de la défense, 2001, pp. 287-297.

Stephen Clissold (ed.), *Yugoslavia and the Soviet Union, 1939-1973: A Documentary Survey*. London: Oxford University Press, 1948; Reprint 1975.

Cordesman, Anthony H., Adam Mausner, and David Kasten. *Winning in Afghanistan: Creating Effective Afghan Security Forces*. Washington, DC: Center for Strategic and International Studies, May 2009.

Crampton, R.J. *The Balkans Since the Second World War*. New York: Routledge, 2014.

Cully, George D. *Adapt or Die: The United States Air Force's Role in Reconstituting the Iraqi Air Force, 2004-*2007. Maxwell Air Force Base, Alabama: Air University Press, 2017.

Daso, Dik Alan. *US Air Force: A Complete History*. Washington, DC: The Air Force Historical Foundation, 2006.

Deakin, William. *The Embattled Mountain*. New York: Oxford University Press, 1971.

Dimitrjevic, Bojan. 'The Mutual Defense Aid Program in Tito's Yugoslavia, 1951-1958, and Its Technical Impact'. *The Journal of Slavic Military Studies*, 10:2 (1997): 19-33.

Djilas, Milovan. *Conversations with Stalin*. New York: Harcourt, Brace, Jovanovich, 1962.

_____. *Tito: The Story from Inside*. New York: Harcourt, Brace, Jovanovich, 1980.

_____. *Wartime*. Michael Petrovich, trans. New York: Harcourt, Brace, Jovanovich, 1977.

Facon, Patrick. 'La mission militaire aéronautique française en Pologne et la creation de l'aéronautique polonaise dans les années vingt'. In *Bâtir une Nouvelle Sécurité: La Cooperation Militaire Entre la France et les États d'Europe Centrale et Orientale de 1919 à 1929*. Paris: Centre d'études d'histoire de la défense, 2001, pp. 561-579.

Ferris, John. 'A British "Unofficial" Aviation Mission and Japanese Naval Developments, 1919–1929'. *Journal of Strategic Studies*, 5:3 (1982): 416-439.

Finch, Nicole S. and Peter A. Garretson. 'Air Advising: A Critical Component of Joint Engagement'. *Joint Forces Quarterly*, 70 (3rd Quarter 2017): 34-39.

Futrell, Robert. *The Advisory Years to 1965*. Washington, DC: Office of Air Force History, 1981.

Gady, Franz-Stefan. 'Afghan Air Force Receives 4 Light Attack Aircraft'. *The Diplomat*, 24 March 2017, http://thediplomat.com/2017/03/afghan-air-force-receives-4-light-attack-aircraft/.

_____. 'Is North Korea Fighting for Assad in Syria?' *The Diplomat*, 24 March 2016, http://thediplomat.com/2016/03/is-north-korea-fighting-for-assad-in-syria/.

Gardner, Nikolas. 'The Harold Wilson Government, Airwork Services Limited, and the Saudi Arabian Air Defence Scheme, 1965-73'. *Journal of Contemporary History*, 42:2 (2007): 345-363.

Garthoff, Raymond L. *Soviet Military Doctrine*. Glencoe, IL: Free Press, 1953.

Giustozzi, Antonio and Artemy Kalinovsky, with Paul Robinson, Bob Spencer, and Alfia Sorokina. *Missionaries of Modernity: Advisory Missions and the Struggle for Hegemony in Afghanistan and Beyond*. London: Hurst, 2016.

Guelton, Frédéric, 'Typologies des missions militaires française dans l'Est européen'. In *Bâtir une Nouvelle Sécurité: La Cooperation Militaire Entre la France et les États d'Europe Centrale et Orientale de 1919 à 1929*. Paris: Centre d'études d'histoire de la défense, 2001, pp. 51-67.

Guess, George M. *The Politics of United States Foreign Aid*. London: Routledge, 1987.

Guthrie, George M. *Conflicts of Culture and the Military Advisor*. Institute for Defense Analysis, 1966.

How, Julie Lien-ying. 'Introduction: Soviet Advisors with the Kuominchun, 1925-1926: A Documentary Study'. *Chinese Studies in History*, 19:1 (1985): 7-103.

Hoxha, Enver. *The Selected Works of Enver Hoxha*. Vol. 2. Tirana: Nentori, 1982.

Huston, James A. *Outposts and Allies: US Army Logistics in the Cold War, 1945-1953*. Cranbury, NJ: Associated University Presses, 1988.

Kullaa, Rinna. *Non-Alignment and Its Origins in Cold War Europe: Yugoslavia, Finland and the Soviet Challenge*. London: I.B. Tauris, 2011.

Kunick, David D. 'Building Partner Air Power: The Operational Sustainment Imparity'. Joint Maritime Operations Course Paper. Newport, RI: US Naval War College, 2011.

Lamonthe, Dan. 'As US Air War Over Afghanistan Shrinks, A Tug-of-War for Afghan Aircraft'. *The Washington Post*, 5 December 2015.

Lees, Lorraine M. *Keeping Tito Afloat: The United States, Yugoslavia, and the Cold War, 1945-1960*. University Park, PA: The Pennsylvania State University Press, 2010.

Lydon, Mike. '"Right Tech" Solutions for USAF Security Force Assistance'. *Small Wars Journal* (2010), http://smallwarsjournal.com/jrnl/art/right-tech-solutions-for-usaf-security-force-assistance.

Marquis, Jefferson P., Joe Hogler, Jennifer D.P. Moroney, Michael J. Neumann, Christopher Paul, John E. Peters, Gregory F. Treverton, Anny Wong. *Adding Value to Air Force Management Through Building Partnerships Assessment*. Santa Monica, CA: RAND, 2010.

Michulec, Robert. *Ił-2,* Ił-10. Monografie Lotnicze. Gdansk: AJ-Press, 1999.

Moroney, Jennifer D.P., Celeste Ward Gventer, Stephanie Pezard, Laurence Smallman. *Lessons from US Allies in Security Cooperation With Third Countries*. Santa Monica, CA: RAND, 2011.

Moroney, Jennifer D.P., Joe Holger, Jefferson P. Marquis, Christopher Paul, John E. Peters, Beth Grill. *Developing an Assessment Framework for US Air Force Building Partnerships Programs*. Santa Monica, CA: RAND, 2010.

Moroney, Jennifer D.P., Beth Grill, Joe Holger, Lianne Kennedy-Baudali, Christopher Pau. *How Successful Are US Efforts to Build Capacity in Developing Countries? A Framework to Assess the Global Train and Equip '1206' Program*. Santa Monica, CA: RAND, 2011.

Moroney, Jennifer D.P., Joe Holger, Lianne Kennedy-Boudali, Stephanie Pezard. *Integrating the Full Range of Security Cooperation Programs into Air Force Planning*. Santa Monica, CA: RAND, 2010.

Moroney, Jennifer D.P., Joe Holger, with Benjamin Bahney, David R. Howell, Charlotte Lynch, Rebecca Zimmerman. *Building Partner Capacity to Combat Weapons of Mass Destruction*. Santa Monica, CA: RAND, 2009.

Mott, William H., IV. *United States Military Assistance: An Empirical Perspective*. Westport, CT: Greenwood Press, 2002.

Nassaes, Alcofar and Josè Luis. *CTV, Los Legionarios Italiano en la guerra civil espanola, 1936-1939*. Barcelona: Dopesa, 1972.

Newton, Richard D. 'Reinventing the Wheel: Structuring Aerospace Forces for Foreign Internal Defense'. MA Thesis: School of Advanced Military Studies, US Army Command and General Staff College, 1991.

Oliker, Olga. *Building Afghanistan's Security Forces in Wartime: The Soviet Experience*. Santa Monica, CA: RAND, 2011.

Pach, Chester J. *Arming the Free World: The Origins of the United States Military Assistance Program, 1945-1950*. Chapel Hill, NC: The University of North Carolina Press, 1991.

Panecki, Tadeusz. 'La Mission militaire française en Pologne dans les années vingt'. In *Bâtir une Nouvelle Sécurité: La Cooperation Militaire Entre la France et les États d'Europe Centrale et Orientale de 1919 à 1929*. Paris: Centre d'études d'histoire de la défense, 2001, pp. 235-245.

Polak, Christian. 'La mission militaire française de l'aéronautique au Japon (1919-1921)'. *Ebisu—Études japonais*, 51 (2014): 163-183.

Rainero, Romain H. 'Un concurrent pue connu à la suprématie militarie de la France en Pologne: la Mission militaire Italienne à Varsovie (1919-1923)'. In *Bâtir une Nouvelle Sécurité: La Cooperation Militaire Entre la France et les États d'Europe Centrale et Orientale de 1919 à 1929*. Paris: Centre d'études d'histoire de la défense, 2001, pp. 581-595.

Rajak, Svetozar. 'No Bargaining Chips, No Spheres of Interest: The Yugoslav Origins of Cold War Non-Alignment'. *Journal of Cold War Studies*, 16:1 (2014): 146-179.

_____. *Yugoslavia and the Soviet Union in the Early Cold War: Reconciliation, Comradeship, Confrontation, 1953-1957*. New York: Routledge, 2011.

Raymond, Jack. 'US Delivers Jets to the Yugoslavs'. *New York Times*, 11 March 1953.

Roehrkasse, Eric D. 'United States Air Force Military Civic Action in Thailand, 1964-1976: Modernization Theory and US Doctrine'. *Illinois Political Science Review*, 15 (Fall 2015): 68-90.

_____. 'US Air Force Military Civic Action in Thailand, 1964-1976: Modernization, US Foreign Policy, and Military Doctrine'. MA Thesis: Temple University, 2012.

Rolleston, Mort, Ric Trimillos, and Tom Gill. 'Aviation Security Cooperation: Advancing Global Vigilance, Global Reach, and Global Power in a Dynamic World'. *Air & Space Power Journal* (September-October 2014): 92-117.

Roux, Monique. 'Combat Aviation Advisors: Strong, Silent, Professional'. *Shadowspear.com* (19 April 2016), http://www.afsoc.af.mil/News/Article-Display/Article/731538/combat-aviation-advisors-strong-silent-professional/.

Rovighi, Alberto and Filippo Stefani. *La partecipazione italiana alla guerra civile spagnola*. 2 Vols. Rome: Ufficio Storico SME, 1992-1993.

Scott, Paul J. 'Aviation Security Force Assistance: Joint General Purpose Forces as Air Advisors'. MA Thesis: National Defense University, 2013.

Spector, Ronald. *Advice and Support: The Early Years*. Washington, DC: Center of Military History, 1983.

Stoker, Donald (ed.). *Military Advising and Assistance: From Mercenaries to Privatization, 1815-2007*. London: Routledge, 2008.

_____. 'The History and Evolution of Foreign Military Advising and Assistance, 1815-2007'. In Donald Stoker (ed.). *Military Advising and Assistance: From Mercenaries to Privatization, 1815–2007*. London: Routledge, 2008, 1-11.

Sulzberger, C.L. 'US Ready to Sign Tito Arms Accord.' *New York Times*, 11 November 1951.

Suppo, Hugo Rogelio. 'Les enjeux français au Brésil pendant l'entre-deux-guerres: la mission militaire (1919-1940)'. *Guerre mondiales et conflits contemporains*, 3:2015 (2004): 3-24.

Trevithick, Joseph. 'Afghanistan's Terrible, Horrible, No Good Air Force'. *War is Boring*, 17 June 2015, http://warisboring.com/afghanistan-s-terrible-horrible-no-good-air-force/.

Tucker, Aaron and Aimal Pacha Sayedi. 'Advising the Afghan Air Force—Analysis'. *Joint Forces Quarterly* (1st Quarter 2016): 17-24.

Vick, Alan J., Adam Grissom, William Rosenau, Beth Grill, and Karl P. Mueller. *Air Power in the New Counterinsurgency Era: The Strategic Importance of USAF Advisory and Assistance Missions*. Santa Monica, CA: RAND, 2006.

Waligora, David. 'La mission aéronautique française en Russie, 1916-1918'. *Revue Pégase*, 72 (January 1994).

Weber, Nathaniel R. 'The United States Military Advisory Assistance Groups During the Cold War, 1945-1965'. PhD Dissertation: Texas A&M University, 2016.

_____. 'The United States Military Assistance Advisory Group in French Indochina, 1950-1956'. MA Thesis, Texas A&M University, 2010.

Westermann, Edward B. 'Relegated to the Backseat: Farm Gate and the Failure of the US Air Advisory Effort in South Vietnam, 1961-1963'. In Donald Stoker, ed. *Military Advising and Assistance: From Mercenaries to Privatization, 1815–2007*. London: Routledge, 2008, 127-150.

Whittington, Joseph E., Jr. 'Determining Mobility Support Advisory Squadron Effectiveness In Support of Building Partner Capacity'. MA Thesis: Air Force Institute of Technology, June 2012.

White, Nathan A. 'Aviation Foreign Internal Defense (AFID) In Vietnam'. MA Thesis: Air Command and Staff College, April 2009.

Wilbur, C. Martin. 'A Different Kind of Missionary: Soviet Advisors in China in the 1920s'. *Chinese Studies in History*, 21:4 (1988): 3-31.

_____ and Julie Lien-ying How (eds). *Documents on Communism, Nationalism, and Soviet Advisers in China, 1918-1927*. New York: Columbia University Press, 1956.

Zadalis, Timothy M. 'The Air Advisor: The Face of US Air Force Engagement'. *Air & Space Power Journal*, 27:4 (July-August 2013): 4-13.

# Index

## People

**Places**

**Air Bases**



**Schools/Academies/Training Units**



**Military Units & Formations**

**Governments/Political Parties/ Organizations**

**Missions/Programs/Arrangements**

**Conflicts/Battles/Wars**



**Manufacturers/Companies/Organisations**

**Vessels**



**Newspapers/Publications**



**Code Names/Operations**